The Life of Our Language

D0863713

Susan Garzon

R. McKenna Brown

Julia Becker Richards

Wuqu' Ajpub'

THE LIFE OF OUR LANGUAGE

Kaqchikel Maya Maintenance,
Shift, and Revitalization

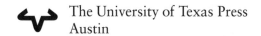 The University of Texas Press
Austin

Requests for permission to reproduce material from this work
should be sent to Permissions, University of Texas Press,
P.O. Box 7819, Austin, TX 78713-7819.

♾ The paper used in this publication meets the minimum
requirements of American National Standard for Information
Sciences—Permanence of Paper for Printed Library Materials,
ANSI Z39.48-1984.

Library of Congress Cataloging-in-Publication Data

The life of our language : Kaqchikel Maya maintenance, shift, and
    revitalization / by Susan Garzon . . . [et al.]. — 1st ed.
        p.   cm.
    Includes bibliographical references and index.
    ISBN 0-292-72813-1 (cloth : alk. paper). — ISBN 0-292-72814-X
    (pbk. : alk. paper)
        1. Cakchikel language—Social aspects.   2. Language mainte-
    nance—Guatemala.   3. Cakchikel Indians—Social conditions.
    I. Garzon, Susan, 1950–
    PM3576.L54   1998
    497'.415—dc21   97-45751

Ri wuj, *Qach'ab'äl,* kichin ri k'ak'a taq ak'wala' ri e petenäq chiqij wakamin

The book *Our Language* is for the future generations of the Pueblo Maya Kaqchikel

CONTENTS

MAPS

FIGURES

TABLES

PREFACE

The four authors of this book got to know each other in Guatemala during the mid- and late 1980s. Brown and I were starting work on our doctoral dissertations, Richards was finishing hers, and Wuqu' Ajpub' was teaching and beginning graduate work. We all grew in knowledge during that time, due in no small part to what we learned from one another as well as from other colleagues, including Narciso Cojtí, Martín Chacach, Guillermina Herrera, Nora England, and Judith Maxwell, who reached across cultural boundaries and set a high standard of collegiality.

This book is greater than the sum of its parts. Although we bring together four distinct personalities and backgrounds as well as two very different cultures, our voices echo each other across the pages. Each author has examined a different aspect in the life of the Kaqchikel language, but all have been touched by common themes, including the richness of Kaqchikel culture and the historical struggle of the Maya people to survive and to live as Mayas within a non-Mayan society. To bring order to our observations, we have confronted the complexity of language use in communities undergoing major economic and social change.

This work reflects recent changes in Mayan studies, in which the Western scholar no longer feels compelled to maintain a posture of complete detachment in order to assure "scientific objectivity." The authors maintain that their scholarship is not compromised by their role as unabashed advocates for Mayan language revival; indeed, it is enriched by their close collaboration with Mayan efforts to strengthen their languages.

ACKNOWLEDGMENTS

We extend our deepest thanks to the Kaqchikel communities where we have lived and worked. We are grateful to the people of San Marcos La Laguna, San Antonio Aguas Calientes, San Juan Comalapa, and the surrounding towns and villages, all of whom made this work possible.

We are also indebted to two institutions central to Mayan studies in Guatemala, whose staffs generously shared their time, expertise, and other resources: the Proyecto Lingüístico Francisco Marroquín (PLFM) and the Centro de Investigaciones Regionales de Mesoamérica (CIRMA). We are also grateful to our colleagues at the Universidad Rafael Landívar for their guidance and support.

In addition, the authors wish to include the following acknowledgments.

Garzon would like to thank her husband, Jan Michael, for his patient support and assistance. She is also grateful to her mother, the late Rosemary Fleming Tharp, for her inspiration and guidance. An initial period of her language study was funded by a Teaching Research Fellowship from the Graduate College of the University of Iowa. Her fieldwork was funded by a Fulbright Grant for Dissertation Research, and work on this book was funded by Dean's Incentive Grants from Oklahoma State University.

Brown would like to thank the Roger Thayer Stone Center for Latin American Studies at Tulane University, Joyce Salisbury at the University of Wisconsin–Green Bay, and his family. His research was funded by grants from the Matilda Geddings Gray, Fulbright, and Shell Foundations.

Richards would like to thank her husband, Michael, for his steadfast support and collaboration, as well as her children, Jane, Vincent, and Celeste. Her graduate study was supported by fellowships from the University of Wisconsin–Madison Graduate School and Alumni Research

Foundation. Her dissertation fieldwork and analysis were funded by the Organization of American States and the American Association of University Women, and work on the preparation of this book was supported through a Fulbright International Exchange of Scholars Award.

Wuqu' Ajpub' includes these acknowledgments:

Quiero agradecer al Corazón del Cielo y Corazón de la Tierra por darme la oportunidad de ser y vivir en el mundo maya. También a las abuelas y abuelos por dejarnos su sabiduría y conocimiento. Finalmente, quiero agradecer a mi querida esposa y a mis dos hijos, la razón de mi existencia, por su ayuda en la conservación de mis ideales, en el capítulo del libro, y en mi trabajo.

(I want to thank the Heart of the Sky and the Heart of the Earth for giving me the opportunity to be and live in the Mayan world. Also the grandmothers and grandfathers for leaving us their wisdom and knowledge. Finally, I want to thank my dear wife and my two sons, the reason for my existence, for their help in the conservation of my ideals, in writing the chapter in this book, and in my work.)

N

MEXICO

BELIZE

ATLANTIC
OCEAN

EL PETÉN

HUEHUETENANGO

ALTA VERAPAZ

IZABAL

EL QUICHÉ

SAN MARCOS

BAJA VERAPAZ

ZACAPA

HONDURAS

TOTONICAPAN

QUEZALTENANGO

SOLOLÁ

CHIMALTENANGO

Tecpán

GUATEMALA

EL PROGRESSO

CHIQUIMULA

Guatemala
⊙ *City*

JALAPA

RETALHULEU

SUCHITEPEQUEZ

Antigua

SACATEPÉQUEZ

San Marcos

JUTIAPA

ESCUINTLA

SANTA ROSA

Comalapa

San Antonio

EL SALVADOR

PACIFIC OCEAN

0   100

Kilometers

Map 1. The Departments and Selected Cities of Guatemala

Map 2. The Mayan Languages of Guatemala

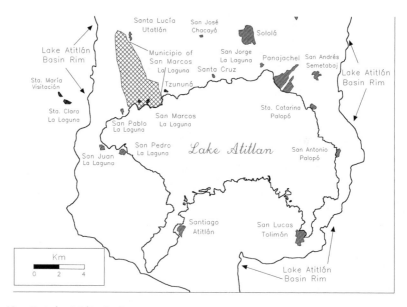

Map 3. Lake Atitlán Basin

1. INTRODUCTION

Susan Garzon

This book is about Kaqchikel Maya, a language spoken in the Central Highlands of Guatemala, and about its prospects for survival. More broadly, it is about the speakers of Kaqchikel, their history of contact with other groups, and the paths they have chosen or been forced to take in their struggle for survival as individuals, families, communities, and a people. Three of the authors draw on ethnographic and sociolinguistic research to describe the shifting balance in the use of Kaqchikel and Spanish in three Mayan communities, examining the way individuals adjust their linguistic behavior to current conditions and the expectation of future changes. The fourth author describes the difficulties Mayas face growing up in a community and a nation divided not only by different languages but also by competing value systems. These accounts of language shift and the conflicts accompanying it are balanced by a description of the steps being taken to maintain and revitalize the Kaqchikel language.

The discussion of linguistic behavior in the Kaqchikel area is framed by two different perspectives. The first is universalist, demonstrating commonalities to be found in the way indigenous peoples of the Americas have responded to recurrent kinds of language contact situations. The second is more particularist, presenting the historical events, trends, and policies that have affected the Kaqchikels and resulted in their linguistic behavior. By shifting the focus from universal patterns to historical circumstances and from the regional level to the community to the individual participant, one can view linguistic behavior in the broadest possible perspective.

Like many other indigenous groups around the world, the Mayas face increasing pressures to discard or modify traditional beliefs and practices, even to the extent of losing their cultures and ethnic identities. Languages are particularly susceptible to loss because speakers often feel compelled to shift to languages which are more useful in the larger society. Among the Mayan languages, Chikomuseltek has already been lost, and others are at risk, as their speakers increasingly shift to Spanish. When a language dies, it takes with it the world view encoded in its vocabulary and semantic categories and expressed through the interaction of grammar and spoken discourse. Centuries-old oral literature also dies or is greatly transformed as the formal and poetic forms of the language fall into disuse and older forms of knowledge are denigrated and forgotten. No dictionary or grammar can possibly store the wealth of information possessed by a body of fluent speakers; nor can a group of recordings preserve the aesthetic potentiality of a living language.

In recent years there has been a worldwide movement among indigenous groups to renew and revitalize their cultures, and this movement has found strong support among Mayas. Historically, Mayas have been one of the most successful groups in the Americas at resisting the intrusions of the dominant society, and today many Mayas recognize the importance of their languages as repositories of cultural knowledge and symbols of ethnic identity. Consequently, groups from all over the area are making efforts to reinforce the status of their languages. An examination of language shift in the Mayan area and the efforts undertaken to contain it should be of interest to speakers of endangered languages and to policymakers working in the field of language maintenance as well as to anyone concerned with the maintenance of diversity in the world's cultures.

This study of language use also provides insights into the structure and dynamics of indigenous communities which have withstood nearly five centuries of domination. Community members now find themselves in the process of redefining themselves as Mayas while at the same time becoming progressively more integrated into the dominant society. The contradictions involved in this transformation are reflected in the choices people make about which languages to learn, use, and pass on to their children. Mayas today operate in a complex social environment in which they must reconcile the competing demands of two often opposing cultural systems. For some bilinguals, knowledge of two languages serves as a tool allowing them to adapt to both systems.

THE KAQCHIKEL LANGUAGE

Kaqchikel is one of thirty Mayan languages spoken in Guatemala, Mexico, Belize, and Honduras. It belongs to the K'iche'an branch of the eastern division of the Mayan family, its closest relations being Tz'utujil, spoken in the area of Lake Atitlán, and K'iche', spoken over a large area extending north and west. The Kaqchikel linguistic region comprises numerous municipalities in the mountainous region of central Guatemala, and Kaqchikel speakers number approximately half a million. This places them among the four largest Mayan language groups of Guatemala: K'iche', Mam, Kaqchikel, and Q'eqchi', in order of number of speakers.

ETHNIC GROUPS IN GUATEMALA

The majority of the Guatemalan population of roughly ten million can be divided into two groups, Indians and Ladinos, with African Americans making up about 4 percent. Together, the Mayas plus a small group of Xincas account for about 53 percent of the population, making Guatemala one of the few nations in the hemisphere with an Indian majority. Ethnic identity is based on both descent and culture. To be recognized as an Indian one must be a descendant of the indigenous population and claim identity as an Indian. To be recognized as a Ladino, one must have inherited or adopted the language and culture of the European colonizers and their descendants. This means that Indians may choose to become Ladinos by rejecting or ignoring their former identity and taking on the outward signs of Euro-American culture, including exclusive use of the Spanish language. It should be noted that although the term "Ladino" is used widely by social scientists and by the indigenous population, those individuals who would be considered Ladino rarely use it to describe themselves, as members of the majority culture of the United States do not customarily refer to themselves as Anglo or Euro-American.

A HISTORICAL OVERVIEW

For many hundreds of years, the Maya people have been one of the major population groups in the Mesoamerican culture area. From their original Highland homeland, the Mayas spread out over a large geographical region. They erected major cities in the Lowland areas of present-day Mexico, Guatemala, Belize, and Honduras, some of which had been abandoned by the time the Europeans arrived. The remains of public architecture, including massive stone pyramids and ball courts as well as monuments inscribed with glyphs, testify to the advanced state of Mayan civilization. Some groups remained in the Highlands, extending their territories and sometimes competing for power. Over the years, the Mayas exchanged goods and cultural practices with other prominent cultures of Mesoamerica, from the Olmecs to the Aztecs, in interactions that were sometimes peaceful and sometimes violent.

The Spanish Conquest of Guatemala had an almost apocalyptic quality, with disease and warfare ravaging the population. However, in contrast to North America, where Europeans pushed Native Americans off their land, often removing their means of subsistence in the process, in Mesoamerica the Spaniards found ways to exploit the Indians, often making use of their skill as farmers. This meant that there was some continuity in daily life and in the traditional social structures and cultural practices underlying it, although in many areas, such as the religious sphere, activities were greatly modified. During the Colonial Period the Kaqchikels, like other Highland groups, endured resettlement and Spanish demands for goods and labor. The national period brought new abuses as Mayan communities lost much of their land base, forcing individuals and sometimes whole families to migrate to coastal plantations to perform seasonal labor.

As in most places in the Americas, the Europeans who invaded and colonized Guatemala maintained a position of dominance. Sure of their own superiority on moral and political grounds, they isolated themselves socially from the people they had conquered. The Mayas, impoverished and cut off from any avenues to power, were subjected to personal and institutionalized discrimination by the Europeans and their descendants. Those individuals who wished to gain access to the rewards of Guatemalan society had to discard their Mayan identity and adopt a Ladino lifestyle.

In the 1960s and 1970s the Mayan population began to take its first steps toward enfranchisement and full participation in Guatemalan society. However, all public life was severely curtailed in the late 1970s and early 1980s when a period of violence erupted, with the military government and its affiliated death squads pitted against rebel groups and their presumed sympathizers. Although all sectors of the population were affected, Mayas bore the brunt of the government's anti-insurgency programs, as community leaders and ordinary civilians were killed or forced to flee. By the mid-1980s the violence had largely subsided in the Kaqchikel area, although fighting continued in other areas and the possibility of further violence loomed over villages and towns. In spite of the obvious dangers of participation in public life, new Maya leaders have emerged, and organizations aimed at promoting Mayan language and culture flourish under a more benign national government. Attitudes prejudicial to Indians have slowly begun to change; but after centuries of oppression Mayas still face obstacles to full participation in Guatemalan society.

TRADITIONAL KAQCHIKEL CULTURE AND ENVIRONMENT

The Kaqchikel area is lovely to behold, with gently curving mountainsides beneath clear blue Highland skies. Gracefully contoured volcanic cones add to the beauty, particularly at Lake Atitlán, where they ring the smooth, crystalline waters. However, they are also reminders of the geological volatility of the area. There have been recurrent earthquakes in the region throughout the historical period; the latest occurred in 1976, when most towns in the Kaqchikel area were damaged and a few were leveled, including San Juan Comalapa, one of the communities discussed in this volume.

Corn has been the principal grain underlying Mesoamerican culture since the advent of large-scale agriculture, and it is a central symbol of Mayan religion as well as the basis of the Mayan diet, along with beans and squash. Traditional Mayas continue to cultivate corn in winding rows that cross the mountainsides and stretch across the valleys below. Men and women share the workload; the men are responsible for cultivating crops, while the women process them. This division of labor results in an interdependence between husband and wife which fosters marital stability.

Women often spend part of their day weaving on backstrap looms. The intricately brocaded blouses they design and weave are mainly worn by women of the household, although they may be sold. Each town is known for the unique colors and designs of the women's clothing, though in recent years women have begun to borrow styles from other communities to supplement their own. Children learn to work alongside their parents from an early age: girls make their first crude attempts at tortillas and small weavings and boys accompany their fathers to the fields.

INCREASING INTEGRATION WITH THE NATIONAL SOCIETY

In recent times economic pressures caused in part by a growing population have forced Mayas to search for new ways to enter the cash economy. In some cases, Mayas have sought new markets for traditional products, such as textiles. In other cases, they have gained supplementary skills or migrated to larger urban areas to find work. Guatemala City, with a population of about one million, is a common destination, since it is only a few hours by bus from some Kaqchikel communities. Educational opportunities have expanded in Indian communities, particularly the larger ones, allowing students to acquire primary and sometimes secondary schooling without leaving their hometowns. Major towns also have bus service connecting them to the capital and other cities. The language and culture of the dominant society have entered homes through radios, which offer programming exclusively in Spanish. More affluent families also have television, which broadcasts Latin American shows and North American shows dubbed in Spanish.

Under these changing conditions, individuals must balance their need and desire to participate in Ladino society with their wish to maintain traditional Mayan culture. One of the areas of contention is language use. Parents must decide whether they will continue to speak Kaqchikel among themselves and pass it on to their children. Their children, growing up in an increasingly Spanish-speaking environment, must decide whether they will try to achieve and maintain full mastery of Kaqchikel or drop the language in favor of Spanish.

OVERVIEW OF THE CHAPTERS

Chapter 2 begins by surveying the types of language contact relations that have prevailed in the Americas. I examine the conditions fostering different levels of multilingualism with varying degrees of stability. Although most data come from the Western Hemisphere, occasional examples are included from outside the region. This discussion provides a framework for understanding the different types of contact relations that have evolved in the Kaqchikel area during its history. The section dealing with language shift looks at both causal factors and characteristics of the process.

In Chapter 3 Brown presents a history of the Kaqchikel Maya area, examining the influence of historical trends and events on language use. In his discussion of pre-Conquest Guatemala, Brown focuses on contacts between the Kaqchikels and other groups, looking at the probable extent of outside influence on language use among both commoners and the elite in Kaqchikel society. For the post-Conquest period, he discusses the often contradictory language policies in effect during the Colonial Period and places language policy within the context of the ruling power's efforts to control Mayan land and labor.

Case studies are presented in Chapters 4 through 6. The first is a study of a small town at the stage of incipient bilingualism: San Marcos La Laguna, situated on the banks of Lake Atitlán. Richards describes the chronic difficulties and periodic disasters Marqueños have faced over the last four hundred years and recounts their successive attempts to create a viable space for themselves in an often inhospitable environment. As townspeople begin to add Spanish to their speech repertoire, this change can be seen as one in a long series of adjustments aimed at achieving economic stability for individuals and the community at large. Richards's discussion of language use includes an analysis of the way Marqueños perceive language variation in the region and a look at traditional Kaqchikel ways of speaking. She also examines the increasing use of Spanish within the community and the role of schooling in language spread.

The following two case studies deal with communities at intermediate to late stages of shift. Brown's study of San Antonio Aguas Calientes, presented in Chapter 5, actually deals with four communities in the Quinizilapa Valley: San Antonio, two villages, and an adjacent town, which are experiencing different levels and rates of language shift. San Antonio has been closely associated with Spanish society since colonial times, and Brown examines the strategies employed by Mayas to survive in the shadow of Ladino society. In his analysis of language shift, Brown utilizes survey data to identify correlations between language use and factors such as educational level and economic activity. He focuses on the crucial role of adults in the "shift generation"—Kaqchikel-speaking parents who switched to the use of Spanish with their children.

Chapter 6 is a case study of San Juan Comalapa, a large Mayan community. Many young adults in the town are children of the shift generation, and I report on a small but increasing group of these young adults—individuals with a secondary education. I analyze their employment and residence histories to determine the likelihood of their maintaining strong ties with their community and continuing to use Kaqchikel. I also focus on the language histories of young women in the group, assessing the extent of language shift in the community by examining the ability of those who were raised in Spanish to acquire Kaqchikel later.

In Chapter 7 Brown describes the development of the language revitalization movement in Guatemala, focusing on four areas important to revitalization: the use of Mayan languages within homes, literacy programs in these languages, the role of bilingual education, and the resurgence of Mayan religion. In his discussion of literacy, Brown reports on an informal literacy program in Comalapa and the unique ways it has benefited those involved. He also highlights the special contributions of Kaqchikel speakers to the revitalization movement. Finally, Brown discusses the role played by Maya scholars in framing provisions of the Guatemalan Peace Accords dealing with the status of the Maya people.

Wuqu' Ajpub' (Arnulfo Simón) provides a Mayan perspective on language change in Chapter 8, describing the varying language contact situations he has experienced as a Maya growing up in Comalapa and advancing through the Guatemalan educational system. He depicts in concrete terms the conflict and pain experienced by an individual coming to maturity in a society that systematically denigrates his language and culture. As a Maya educator, he challenges policymakers to create the necessary conditions for developing a truly multicultural nation.

In the concluding chapter I suggest that modern language relations between Kaqchikel communities and outside groups differ qualitatively from earlier types of language relations, in which an accommodation was made to other languages without placing Kaqchikel at serious risk. I discuss the course of shift from Kaqchikel to Spanish in San Marcos, San Antonio, and Comalapa, focusing on the replacement of Kaqchikel by Spanish in Mayan homes and public contexts and looking at the role this shift has played in an ongoing transformation of attitudes and values within the community, especially among young people. The chapter concludes by presenting a possible scenario in which Kaqchikels and other Mayas take active steps to maintain their languages for themselves and their descendants.

2. INDIGENOUS GROUPS AND THEIR LANGUAGE CONTACT RELATIONS

Susan Garzon

LANGUAGE CONTACT IN THE MAYAN AREA

The common predecessor of the modern Mayan languages was spoken about 4,200 years ago, probably in the region of the Cuchumatán Mountains of Guatemala (Campbell and Kaufman 1990: 55). Since then, speakers of Mayan languages have spread into Highland and Lowland areas of Mexico and Central America. They have come into direct or indirect contact with a number of other language groups, including the Olmecs and Izapans, early groups who probably spoke Mixe-Zoquean languages and who contributed loanwords to the Mayas as well as influencing their writing system (Campbell and Kaufman 1990: 54–55). Mayas also encountered groups from Central Highland Mexico, including people from Teotihuacán, the Toltecs, and finally the Aztecs (Mexicas). The European Conquest brought Mayas into a lasting contact with Spanish speakers, and in more recent times they have interacted with speakers of American English, English Creole (in Belize), and a number of European languages.

The quality of these relationships has varied, resulting in different levels of bilingualism and varying degrees of stability for the languages in contact. In some cases, few people at the local level learned the outside language, with only the elite or certain cultural brokers becoming bilingual. In other cases, one of the languages eventually replaced the other among a group of speakers. When we consider the relationships that have developed between speakers of Mayan languages and the other groups with which they have come in contact, it is clear that each situation is distinct in some ways, due to different historical circumstances surrounding the contact period. Nevertheless, certain types of language relations are recurrent. These recurrent patterns are found not only in the Mayan world; they have occurred among indigenous people in many parts of the world at different times in their histories.

OVERVIEW OF THE CHAPTER

Indigenous communities in the Americas can be placed on a continuum reflecting their relations with other language groups. At one end communities have virtually no bilingual speakers, while at the other end widespread multilingualism is the norm. Where a community falls on the continuum depends on a number of factors. First is the nature and extent of contact between language groups: how close they are in geographic and cultural terms and the importance of trade, intermarriage, and other contact. Another important factor is the distribution of power and status among the groups; groups of comparable status are more likely to develop stable multilingualism than groups in which one party dominates. The likelihood of multilingualism is also enhanced when language boundaries coincide with other significant boundaries, such as those delimiting ethnic or exogamous groups, particularly when languages become recognized symbols of these groups. Also relevant is speakers' willingness to learn second or auxiliary languages, a characteristic that relates to their community's openness to cultural borrowing.

This chapter provides a framework for analyzing the wide range of language contact relations found among indigenous peoples, focusing on patterns that have recurred among groups in the Americas, whether in contact with other indigenous groups or with Euro-Americans. Groups are classified according to their level of multilingualism—low, moderate, or high—and which sectors of the population are multilingual—all, the dominant group, or the subordinate group. The section on widespread bilingualism includes a discussion of the connection between language maintenance and maintenance of ethnic identity, followed by a section examining the types of linguistic codes adopted in contact situations. A major portion of the chapter is devoted to language shift situations. Factors leading to the initial and later stages of shift are identified, as are characteristics of the process itself. The changing relationship between gender and language use is also discussed in the context of shifting communities.

LEVELS OF MULTILINGUALISM

Our knowledge about the extent of multilingualism in a group depends on the quality of the source material. To determine current usage patterns, researchers can examine the problem directly, producing verifiable data. Examining language use patterns in the past is more difficult; scholars must rely on less direct and consequently less reliable means of data collection. Nevertheless, researchers have succeeded in gathering enough information about Native American groups prior to and during the early period of European expansion to form some general ideas about the extent of multilingualism in different areas. The following discussion draws on research covering both current language use and language use in earlier centuries.

Low Levels of Multilingualism

A number of indigenous North American groups have experienced little or no bilingualism, including several tribes of the plains and prairies and some eastern groups. This situation is most likely to occur when political organization is at the village or tribal level and communities have little friendly contact with language groups outside their area (Sherzer 1973: 787).

Limited multilingualism may also occur when communities are linked by a colonial or imperial superstructure. In this case, the economies of the invaders and the indigenous population are intertwined, although there may be little day-to-day contact between them. The dominant group does not interfere in local affairs any more than is necessary to exact tribute or taxes and to retain some measure of local control. Otherwise, the local community handles its own affairs. Typically, the local indigenous community consists largely of monolingual speakers of the subordinate language. There may be a few members of the dominant group who reside or work in the community, such as government agents, missionaries or other religious leaders, and individuals involved in trade and commerce. These people often find it advantageous to learn the local language to some extent. Bilinguals thus come to function as brokers between the two groups. For the most part, though, community members have little direct exposure to speakers of the dominant language.

Even if members of the two interlinked language groups are in close proximity, social barriers may prevent close interaction. Under these circumstances, the two groups will maintain separate social systems, each with its own internal mechanisms for acquiring prestige. Social segregation is enforced primarily by the dominant group, which is loath to share its resources and privileges. However, the indigenous community may also erect barriers if its integrity is endangered by the dominant group.

Throughout history we find numerous examples of communities in which conquest results in separate speech communities with bilingualism restricted to brokers. Following the Conquest of the Americas, the relationship between Europeans and the indigenous population often led to a low level of bilingualism. The Spaniards who controlled large areas of America were concerned with ethnic and religious purity after their long conflict with the Moorish population in Spain. This ideology, together with the Europeans' desire to manipulate and exploit the Indians, led to contact of a restricted nature between Spaniards and Indians. Until the latter half of this century the inhabitants of many Highland Mayan communities were largely monolingual in the Mayan language. The few Spanish-speaking Ladinos (non-Indians) who moved into the towns and performed administrative functions or opened small businesses learned enough of the Mayan language to function within a primarily Kaqchikel-speaking milieu. However, other Ladinos were rarely bilingual. In recent years the Mayan population has become increasingly bilingual, and resident Ladinos are less likely to learn Mayan, although reportedly there are still towns in more remote areas where the earlier pattern persists.

Separate speech communities may have been common in colonial Peru as well. There Indian communities made use of bilingual brokers to defend themselves in the legal arena. Early brokers were Indian nobility trained in Spanish literacy by the Jesuits. This training was unpopular with Spanish-speaking clergy and laypeople, however, who criticized the Jesuits for enabling the Indians to lodge formal complaints against them (Mannheim 1991: 76). To some extent the Spanish religious orders were maintaining a pattern begun under the Inkas, who had controlled a large area inhabited by groups speaking various indigenous languages. The Inkas communicated with local administrators by use of a lingua franca—Southern Peruvian Quechua. However, ordinary people, particularly those living in more remote areas, probably had little use for the imperial language. The need for bilingual brokers has not diminished in modern times. Bruce Mannheim (1991: 76) reports that modern Quechua communities still make certain that some of their members can speak for them in legal situations.

The Spaniards have also segregated minority groups within their own national boundaries. Susan Flinspach (1989: 22) reports that Spanish and Basque speakers in Spain maintained separate speech communities, linked only by a few bilingual members, until the early 1900s.

Moderate Levels of Multilingualism

When groups in contact enjoy comparable status and engage in regular travel or trade as well as occasional intermarriage, a higher incidence of bilingualism can be expected.

Evidence of substantial bilingualism among Apachean and Pueblo groups in the Southwest extends back at least to the late sixteenth century. Paul Kroskrity (1993: 63–64) identifies conditions favoring the development of Apache-Pueblo bilingualism, including the existence of stable trade networks, the Apaches' tradition of establishing winter settlements outside pueblos, and the existence of military alliances between the two groups. In the more recent past, knowledge of multiple Indian languages probably declined among Pueblo groups, although many Southwest groups acquired Spanish and English as the need arose, and the Arizona Tewas have continued a tradition of bilingualism in Tewa and Hopi (Kroskrity 1993: 218–219).

A moderate level of multilingualism was also found in the southern Mexican town of Mazapa de Madero earlier in the twentieth century. Most inhabitants spoke Teko, a Mayan language related to Mam. At that time, as now, contact was frequent between the inhabitants of Mazapa and those of nearby Motozintla, where Mochó, another Mayan language, was spoken. Reportedly, communication between Teko speakers and Mochó speakers was not difficult, since there were bilinguals in each group. Mazapans also intermarried with other language groups, bringing home Mam- and Spanish-speaking spouses. Pressure could be brought to bear on an in-marrying spouse to learn the local language; a Spanish-speaking wife who married into a Teko-speaking family in 1915 reported that her sisters-in-law taught her Teko so that she would be able to defend herself against the joking and teasing that she could expect as an outsider (Garzon 1985).

Increased bilingualism may also result from political alliances such as those formed among tribes in the southeastern United States. Both intertribal marriages and native institutions such as the *fani mingo* (the adoption by a tribe of an advocate within a neighboring tribe) probably created the conditions for limited bilingualism among tribes in the Choctaw-Chickasaw region in the early eighteenth century (Galloway 1995: 322).

Widespread Multilingualism

There does not appear to be any single type of contact situation that always results in widespread multilingualism, although multilingual communities often share certain characteristics. Not surprisingly, bilingualism may be prevalent in border areas between language groups. In the Great Basin, although bilingualism was somewhat limited, extensive intermarriage between the Shoshonis and their immediate neighbors resulted in bilingual border populations (Miller 1978: 612–613).

In general, a high incidence of multilingualism has been associated with small groups living in an area of linguistic diversity and experiencing close contact and intermarriage.

Prior to this century indigenous groups in California enjoyed a high level of multilingualism. The area had high population density and was characterized by stable villages with well-marked societal boundaries and a profusion of languages representing diverse language families. Reportedly, multilingualism was valued, and many individuals spoke three or more languages (Miller 1978: 611–612).

Widespread multilingualism is also found among indigenous groups in the Vaupés region of the northwest Amazon (Jackson 1989; Sorensen 1967), although in this area the population density is relatively low in contrast to California. Multilingualism is particularly strong in the Vaupés region due to a rule of exogamy that requires men to seek wives from language groups other than their own. As they grow up, children are exposed not only to the local language but also to the language of their mothers' villages and to languages spoken by other inhabitants of the longhouses where they live. In addition, people travel frequently, particularly young men looking for wives. In addition to the languages of the longhouse, most individuals learn Tukano, the lingua franca of the region. Arthur Sorensen (1967) points out that it is taken for granted in this area that people will learn a number of languages over their lifetimes and use them under appropriate circumstances.

Among autonomous groups, distinctions between languages may be maximized even when there is a great deal of interaction. This is most likely when groups identify their language as a symbol of group identity. Instead of merging features of neighboring languages through borrowing or shifting from one language to another, distinct languages are maintained. In this way, the Arizona Tewas have maintained their own language in spite of strong cultural influence from the neighboring Hopis (Kroskrity 1982). This phenomenon can also be clearly seen among language groups in the highlands of Papua New Guinea. The presence of hundreds of small local languages in the region today can be attributed in part to the role that languages traditionally played in marking group boundaries. Although groups were linked by trade, marriage, migration, and warfare, communities made a conscious effort to maintain the distinctiveness of their speech, thus promoting the maintenance of distinctive languages (Kulick 1992: 1–3).

When one language is dominant in a region due to the political or social ascendancy of its speakers, bilingualism may lead to language shift, resulting eventually in a population monolingual in the dominant language. (The process of language shift is treated in a later section of this chapter.) However, shift does not always occur. In the Vaupés region individuals continue to acquire languages of comparable status to their own even when a dominant language is part of the linguistic environment; Sorensen (1967) found that many people learned Spanish or Portuguese, although neither language was in a position to displace any of the local languages.

Widespread Bilingualism among the Dominant Group

In some cases, members of a colonizing group find themselves interacting with the local population on an intimate basis and end up adopting the local language as one of their mother tongues, alongside their own ethnic language. This is particularly likely to occur when the colonizers are a small group or relatively isolated from their home country and when the language of the subordinate group is spoken uniformly throughout the region and therefore represents an effective medium of communication over a large area.

Colonial Yucatán and modern Paraguay constitute examples of regions with widespread bilingualism among the dominant group. At the time of the Conquest, both areas lacked the resources sought by Spaniards, so they did not become major colonial centers. In the Yucatán, according to Nancy Farriss (1984), Yukatek Maya was the native language of a large Indian population spread out over the peninsula. In addition, it became the first language of Spaniards born in the Yucatán and of mestizos, a racially mixed population. During colonial times upper-class Yucatecans of Spanish descent spent their infancy and early childhood in the care of Maya women. These Spanish Creoles often chose to speak Yukatek among themselves and apparently in some cases never achieved full mastery of Spanish. Yukatek served as a viable means of communication throughout the region, since it was widely spoken and had relatively little regional variation. In fact, until the late eighteenth century, each Mayan community continued to have a group of inhabitants who were literate in Yukatek. Even some mestizos, who might be expected to identify with their European ancestors, were literate not in Spanish, but in the Mayan language (Farriss 1984: 110–112).

Paraguay provides another example of a bilingual dominant group.

Guaraní, the indigenous language, is spoken by the great majority of the population, according to Joan Rubin (1985). Its strongest base is in rural areas, but even in Asunción, the capital, the majority of the people, including many of the elite, are bilingual in Guaraní and Spanish. A knowledge of Guaraní is strongly associated with identity as a Paraguayan, even among the upper classes.

Paraguay's history offers further insights into the widespread use of an indigenous language among the dominant group. During colonial times the area attracted few European women, and many Spanish men took one or more Indian wives, thus creating affinal and kin ties with the Guaranís. These ties remained strong for the Spaniards' mestizo descendants (Service 1971) and probably contributed to the spread and maintenance of Guaraní among the upper classes. Guaraní's physical extension has probably also been a factor in its maintenance; a relatively uniform variety of the language is spoken over a large geographical area. Partly because of this, Paraguayan leaders were able to utilize the language as a symbol of national unity during two major wars (Rubin 1985).

Political expediency also contributed to the use of Quechua among the landed class in Peru, in this case during the Colonial Period. In the area around Cuzco, landowning descendants of the Spaniards used their knowledge of Quechua as a tool in establishing their political legitimacy in opposition to colonial administrators. The Spanish Creoles claimed descent from the Inka nobility, revising history to suit their needs and adopting bilingualism as a symbol of their roots (Mannheim 1991: 71–74).

The emergence of bilingual elites is not restricted to the Americas. Historically, a number of dominant groups in Europe also learned the language of the conquered. In some cases there was a complete shift to the subordinate language. The Vikings, who conquered large areas of Western Europe during the Middle Ages, shifted from their own language to the local language within a relatively short time; they became French speakers in Normandy and English speakers in England. The French-speaking Normans later invaded England, where they eventually learned English and lost their use of French.

Languages which today are in a seemingly unassailable position have not always been so. For example, although English, with all its institutional support, has replaced some of the Celtic languages in recent times, it was in a much weaker position in the fourteenth century. At that time there was concern that the Anglo-Norman nobility living in Ireland would shift to the use of Irish. In response, the Statutes of Kilkenny of 1366 declared that Englishmen who spoke Irish might forfeit their lands (Grillo 1989: 84).

Widespread Bilingualism among a Subordinate Group

When a subordinate group has frequent contact with a dominant or prestigious group, it is common for members of the subordinate group to become bilingual, while members of the dominant group remain monolingual. Although bilingualism may be maintained for years, it is often the case that within a few generations members of the subordinate group stop using their own language and shift entirely to the dominant language. This is especially likely if the community is integrated into a strong state-level society, a common situation for immigrant groups. However, even in a society with a nationalistic ideology, some groups are able to maintain the viability of their languages; their members gain mastery of the dominant language but continue to use their traditional language on a regular basis. There are a number of interrelated factors that tend to strengthen the position of the subordinate language in a community.

1. The community is able to maintain some degree of independence and autonomy, so that the basic integrity of the group and its ability to survive are not seriously threatened. When this is not the case—for example, when individuals must leave their community and accept integration into the larger society in order to support themselves—language shift is probably inevitable.

2. There is a cultural emphasis on interdependence and ties within the group, with a high value consciously placed on group maintenance. In some cases, barriers exist to restrict the integration of outsiders and the loss of group members.

   In North America a number of religiously based immigrant groups have succeeded in maintaining separate speech communities. This is particularly noteworthy in view of the strong pressures to assimilate experienced by immigrant groups in the United States. Members of these groups, notably the Old Order Mennonites, Old Order Amish, Hutterites, and Orthodox Hassidim, learn their respective languages in the home and acquire enough of the dominant language to allow them to interact adequately with members of the dominant society.

The extent of bilingualism found in these communities might indicate an imminent merging of the dominant and subordinate speech communities. However, the communities' near self-sufficiency and insular attitude suggest that they are not socially integrated into the larger society in a meaningful way, and in most cases language loyalty goes hand in hand with other culturally conservative attitudes. In spite of this linguistic conservatism, shift is possible among these religious groups, as in the case of an Old Order Mennonite group in Virginia whose members now speak only English (Huffines 1980: 48).

In the Highland Mayan area of Chiapas communities such as Zinacantán and Chamula have maintained cargo systems (civil-religious hierarchies) promoting strong ties and reinforcing the traditional reward system within the community. At the same time, the intrusion of outsiders has been limited.

3. The subordinate language enjoys prestige outside the region and often has an established literary tradition. Migration of language groups within India has led to a number of cases of apparently stable bilingualism. Marathi speakers whose forefathers migrated to Gujarat many generations ago continue to speak Marathi at home, although they switch to Gujarat with neighbors and in the workplace. A similar situation exists among Bengalis in Delhi and Malyalam speakers in Madhya Pradesh (Srivastava 1989: 12–13). Not all migrant groups follow this pattern, but those who do are likely to have a mother tongue which is the dominant language in some other area of India and which has what may be considered "a great tradition" (Srivastava 1989: 14). The importance of a body of literature, particularly sacred literature, can also be seen in the maintenance of Hebrew as a written language over many years.

4. The dominant group is willing to tolerate or even foster cultural diversity. This is what R. A. Schermerhorn (1978) refers to as a centrifugal orientation. Switzerland and Singapore are examples of nations which have accommodated different language groups comfortably and in which many citizens are multilingual.

5. Language communities practice social compartmentalization. Certain contexts are reserved for the expression of indigenous culture, including use of the ethnic language. Without the ability to maintain separate language functions for each code, the tendency would be for one language gradually to take over the functions of the weaker lan-

guages, resulting in language shift (see Fishman 1989: 183–184 for a discussion of social compartmentalization in diglossic societies). Less need for compartmentalization may exist when groups share comparable status. The people of the Vaupés region of the Amazon have norms relating to the use of different codes (Jackson 1989) but do not seem to require a strict division of labor for the languages involved.

6. Community members derive meaning and satisfaction from participation in the group and its traditions. This condition relates to all the previous ones. In some cases, individuals may identify with their own group because the dominant group does not have much to offer them. Minority groups may find that barriers restrict their access to full participation in the dominant society at all but the lowest or most superficial levels, or they may find aspects of the dominant culture objectionable. Even if full participation is feasible, ethnic groups may offer their own emotional and material rewards for continued allegiance. When language use is consciously tied to full participation in the life of the ethnic group, it is most likely to be maintained.

ETHNIC IDENTITY AND LANGUAGE MAINTENANCE

Inhabitants of most multilingual areas can have few doubts about the existence of a connection between language and ethnic identity. Joshua Fishman suggests that ethnicity is an integral part of the daily life of a people, and as such it is naturally linked with language:

> [Ethnicity] is language-related to a very high and natural degree, both overtly (imbedded as it is in verbal culture and implying as it does structurally dependent intuitions) and covertly (the supreme symbol system quintessentially symbolizes its users and distinguishes between them and others). Indeed this is so to such a degree that language and ethnic authenticity may come to be viewed as highly interdependent. (Fishman 1989: 217)

Language is often important in maintaining a sense of solidarity within an ethnic group. However, it also serves to maintain boundaries between groups. In this case, it is not essential for the groups to be separated by the use of entirely different languages. What seems important is that each group identify a type of speech behavior as its own. In that way, an opposition is maintained even if the actual medium used is similar (Spicer 1971: 799).

The content of a group's culture may shift without affecting ethnic boundaries. This principle is exemplified by changes in the language usage of the Gaelic-speaking fisherfolk studied by Nancy Dorian (1981). At a time when other Gaelic speakers, such as the crofters, were first acquiring English, the fisherfolk were differentiated from the rest by remaining largely monolingual in Gaelic. As a consequence, fewer English words entered the Gaelic of the fisherfolk, and their language was considered purer. As the fisherfolk began to learn English, the focus shifted to their use of English, which was considered less perfect than that of other Gaelic-English bilinguals. Finally, as other formerly Gaelic-speaking groups entirely lost their use of Gaelic, the fisherfolk were marked by still being bilingual, although their English might be indistinguishable from that of other groups in the region (Dorian 1981: 59–60).

Use of a minority language may continue to play a significant role in community interaction, even when many speakers lack fluency. This is true of some of the towns of the Malinche Volcano in Mexico, where the Mexicano language signals group membership. However, proficiency is not necessarily required. Individuals must know enough Mexicano "to defend themselves." For instance, Mexicano is used in obscene challenges which are used to test outsiders or strangers. In order to meet the challenge, the individual must give an appropriate response in Mexicano (Hill and Hill 1986: 116–117). The use of Mexicano is also prescribed when people get together to drink *pulque*, a traditional alcoholic beverage. Even individuals with little knowledge of Mexicano will use the correct phrase in that language to ask for a refill (Hill and Hill 1986: 115–116).

The data on Native American communities suggest that the relationship between language and ethnic identity can be complex, due to overlapping identities among inhabitants of multiethnic communities. Jane Hill and Kenneth Hill describe the contradictions that exist in Mexicano society, where individuals "are at once rural cultivators and urban factory workers, speakers of an indigenous language and speakers of Spanish, deeply loyal to their communities, but equally deeply patriotic citizens of the Mexican state" (Hill and Hill 1986: 43–44). These observations echo Paul Kroskrity's (1993: 222) finding that Arizona Tewa speakers have a repertoire of identities and can alternate among them. This may be a common adaptive strategy for individuals who regularly cross cultural boundaries and one that allows them to maintain a psychological space for multiple languages.

In recent times a large number of ethnic groups worldwide have begun movements aimed at cultural preservation and promotion. Language takes on an additional importance when an ethnic group, striving to achieve a sense of collective identity, claims the local language as a central symbol. For example, many of the new generation of Maya leaders in education and philosophy have a profound sense of the importance of Mayan languages, recognizing their symbolic, communicative, and affective importance (England 1988). However, even when a group maintains a strong sense of ethnic identity and identifies language as a central symbol of that identity, the language may still be endangered. A group may fail to transmit their language to the next generation for practical reasons, yet continue to appreciate it even after it is no longer used as a primary medium of communication. In fact, its symbolic value may be enhanced (Edwards 1985: 71).

Over the years, there have been numerous reports of language groups continuing to lose their language even though ethnic consciousness and pride were on the rise. For example, Wick Miller (1971) reported that a number of Shoshoni families in the community he studied took pride in being Indian; however, these were often the families who used English most. The Irish language was largely lost in Ireland in the late nineteenth century at a time when people were experiencing an intense sense of Irish identity (Spicer 1971: 798), and in more recent years even those individuals with strong emotional attachments to Irish have not always spoken the language or actively promoted it (Edwards 1985: 51).

Even the leaders of an ethnic group may fail to actively promote use of the language. According to Wolfgang Dressler (1982: 330), a number of Breton nationalists paid only lip service to the maintenance of Breton. Instead, they chose to identify more strongly with other values.

Likewise, leaders of Native American groups, faced with a rapidly declining group of speakers, sometimes choose to channel limited resources into areas with a better chance of success than language revitalization. Nevertheless, dedicated groups have formed within many tribes, and they are designing and carrying out innovative programs in language renewal. The need for multiple approaches arises from the wide range of situations in which North American language groups find themselves. At one end of the range are those few languages with thousands of speakers, including children, while at the other end of the range are many languages with a few elderly speakers. In addition, in some cases speakers live in one central area, while in many others they are spread out geographically.

Although a comprehensive examination of existing language renewal programs is beyond the scope of this book, North American groups are taking some of the following approaches:

1. Immersion preschools (originally used in teaching Maori to children in New Zealand, these schools were successfully introduced in Hawaii and are now spreading to other Native American groups)

2. Bilingual education programs, whose goals include indigenous language maintenance

3. Master-apprentice programs pairing up fluent speakers and younger adult learners

4. Community-based classes for adults and children and associated activities such as immersion weekends

5. University and tribal college programs in Native American language and culture, sometimes set up in conjunction with tribal groups, as well as individual classes in indigenous languages.

Descriptions and summaries of various programs in Native American language revitalization in North America can be found in a number of sources (including Cantoni 1996; Hinton 1994; *Human Organization* 1988; *Language* 1992; Reyhner and Tennant 1995; Sims 1996).

LINGUISTIC CODES USED IN CONTACT SITUATIONS

When language groups come into contact, their choice of code is part of their overall interactional pattern. William Leap (1993: 149–150) points out that Native American groups in North America traditionally adopted one of three strategies in dealing with speakers of other indigenous languages. When languages were closely related, speakers might all use their own language, making allowances for differences in their interlocutors' linguistic systems. This pattern was followed by speakers of Northern Ute and Chemehuevi, Isleta and Taos, and Chickasaw and Choctaw. When speakers of two unrelated languages came into contact, one or the other language might be used. Leap (1993: 149–150) explains that the rules of accommodation differed. Among Eastern Pueblo groups hosts used their guests' language, while among Northwest Coast groups guests or their designated speakers used their hosts' language. In some cases, speakers might follow the first strategy, all speaking their own language. Allan Taylor quotes the observations of a nineteenth-century traveler concerning bilingual speakers of Yurok and Karok:

"two of them will sit and patter gossip for hours, each speaking in his own tongue. A white man listening may understand one, but never a word of the other" (Stephen Powers, cited in Taylor 1981: 175).

Lingua Franca

A third strategy adopted by Native American groups has been the use of a lingua franca. These are particularly useful when various language groups come into contact for the purposes of trade or some other joint effort. Often the lingua franca is the native language of one of the groups. Taylor (1981: 177–179) mentions a number of North American languages which have historically fulfilled this function, including the Muskogee language, utilized by the tribes in the southeastern United States belonging to the Creek Confederacy; Ojibwa, spoken in the Great Lakes region; Peoria, used along the Mississippi River between the Ohio and Arkansas Rivers; Cree, used in the Hudson Bay area; and other languages, among them Teton Sioux, Comanche, Navajo, and Hupa.

Following the European invasion, European languages were sometimes used as lingua francas. To some extent, this reflects the intensity of European contact and the unwillingness of Europeans to learn Indian languages. However, under the circumstances, Native Americans sometimes may have found it to their benefit to adopt a European language as a lingua franca, thus limiting the Europeans' access to the indigenous language and culture.

Pidgin

Pidgins and trade jargons have also sometimes emerged to meet the need for a common means of communication. Pidginized forms of Native American languages probably predate the Conquest, although a lack of historical records makes accurate identification and dating difficult. Examples of pidgins include Mobilian, a pidginized form of Choctaw-Chickasaw, spoken widely among the tribes of the southeastern United States beginning in the late seventeenth century; pidginized Delaware, spoken in parts of New Jersey, Delaware, New York, and Pennsylvania in the seventeenth century; and Chinook Jargon, spoken along the Northwest Coast until recent times (Taylor 1981: 184–186). De Reuse (1994: 319–320) provides insight into the process by which a trade jargon developed in the nineteenth century between Swedish explorers and Chukchi speakers in the Bering Sea area. According to one of the explorers, the Chukchi used their own language with members of the expedition, but instead of correcting the Europeans' errors they courteously adopted the modified forms. In time a jargon resulted, characterized by a limited vocabulary, including some Swedish words, and a simplified grammar. In some cases, pidgins may have enjoyed a function beyond that of simply facilitating communication. Sarah Grey Thomason and Terrence Kaufman (1988: 175) suggest that speakers of both Mobilian and Pidginized Delaware used these pidginized languages with Europeans in part to prevent them from learning the Indian languages in their full forms.

Although pidgins have developed into creoles in some parts of the world, I am unaware of any confirmed cases of indigenous groups of the Americas becoming creole speakers. One possible candidate, Michif, is best analyzed as a dialect of Cree, having a combination of Cree verb morphology and French nominal system (Thomason and Kaufman 1988: 105). Michif may be considered a "mixed language," a somewhat loose term which typically includes those linguistic codes containing the grammatical system of one language and the lexicon of another (Bakker and Mous 1994: 4–5). Other languages of the Americas in this category include Callahuaya, Media Lengua, and Island Carib (Bakker and Mous 1994).

In addition to the lingua francas already discussed, a number of tribes used Plains Sign Language, a medium of communication probably predating European contact (Taylor 1981; Wurtzburg and Campbell 1995). During the nineteenth century, four nomadic tribes were especially proficient in the language: the Kiowas, Comanches, Cheyennes, and Arapahos. The first two tribes formed an alliance, as did the latter two, and knowledge of Sign Language may have facilitated communication between the allies (Taylor 1981: 188).

Spread of Local Languages

Although many empires have introduced their own language into conquered areas, in some cases they have promoted the use of a local language as a lingua franca. Typically, this has occurred in areas where a large number of languages were spoken natively. The pre-Conquest Inkas are an example. During their expansion, they promoted first Jaqi, the ancestor of present-day Aymara and a widely known trade language, then Quechua, the language of a powerful group with a well-developed naval trading industry. At the time of the Spanish Conquest, court officials in Cuzco were trilingual, speaking Puqina, the language of the royal family, as well as Jaqi and Quechua (Hardman 1985).

Interestingly, the Spaniards continued the spread of Quechua after they conquered the Inkas. This was due in part to the policies of the Catholic religious orders in the Andean region. Shirley Brice Heath and Richard Laprade (1982) explain that many clergy wished to make Catholicism more meaningful by introducing it via a language which people already understood. To that end, both Quechua and Aymara were adopted by members of religious orders, as tools in carrying out religious education. The spread of Quechua was aided by Indian chieftains who had previously been local administrators under the Inka Empire and who therefore knew Quechua as well as Spanish officials who learned Quechua in order to carry out their duties (Heath and Laprade 1982).

In North America fur traders associated with the Hudson's Bay Company contributed to the spread of Ojibwa, a Native American language, as a lingua franca. Local officials of the Hudson's Bay Company often had Ojibwa-speaking wives, and many of the company's employees spoke the language natively (Taylor 1981: 178).

LANGUAGE SHIFT AMONG THE SUBORDINATE GROUP

Language contact sometimes results in shift; the community gives up its indigenous language in favor of the language of the dominant group. If the displaced language has no remaining speakers, the shift may be said to have resulted in the death of the language.

Language death is not a new phenomenon. Indo-European languages such as Hittite and Gothic died out during historic times, and certainly many American Indian languages died out during the period of European conquest and colonization. Following European contact, language death was sometimes swift, as population loss and social upheaval devastated indigenous communities. Martha Hardman de Bautista (1985: 190–191) suggests that in the Andean region many local languages died out with all their speakers in the years following the Spanish Conquest. When a language community is very small, a local disaster may wipe out the entire group along with its language; this occurred on St. Lawrence Island, Alaska, in 1878–1879, when a famine decimated a large village and resulted in the death of the local language (de Reuse 1994: 297).

Though rapid language death is still possible among small, isolated groups, the greatest threat to indigenous languages today is displacement by languages of the dominant societies that encompass them. Dominant and subordinate speech communities can coexist within a society for hundreds of years, each maintaining its own social structures, even though the local community is tied to the dominant society by demands for labor and tribute or the necessity of acquiring outside commodities. However, the linguistic equilibrium may be quickly altered when the relationship of the groups changes significantly and a language which once had a stable pool of speakers begins to lose ground to a societally dominant language. Worldwide, many indigenous speech communities are undergoing shift to a dominant language; Harald Haarmann (1986: 57) has identified 200 speech communities in Europe alone that are at various stages of incorporation into the dominant society.

When a community shifts to the language of the dominant group, there are usually a number of forces at work. The causes are often rooted in economic and political conditions common to a large number of ethnic communities worldwide. However, the actual combination of factors varies. R. D. Grillo (1989: 61) found a number of interrelated causes for the decline of Celtic languages in the British Isles during the nineteenth century, including industrialization, urbanization, agricultural change, education, and the rise of centralized state institutions involved in economic and social management and welfare.

Economic Factors

Changes in language use often are associated with economic change. This is not surprising since language has a strong instrumental value. New economic opportunities arising from greater interaction with the dominant society are often tied to the ability to speak the dominant language. Consequently, speakers of subordinate languages may see learning a dominant language to be in their best interest. If the most important economic and social rewards become associated exclusively with the dominant society, individuals may no longer perceive a need to actively affirm membership in the local community, and symbols of ethnic and community membership, such as use of a local language, may become obsolete. In this case, language shift occurs. In other cases, parents may shift to the use of the dominant language with their children for purely practical reasons even though they continue to identify strongly with their community or ethnic group.

Industrialization and Urbanization

Industrialization is one of the factors frequently associated with language shift, particularly among European groups. Fishman (1972: 148) describes a common scenario: the means of production are controlled by one speech community while the productive labor is supplied by members of another. Although both groups may maintain their respective languages for a time, eventually the group providing labor feels compelled to adopt the language of the elite. Fishman points out that the workers often learn the dominant language long before they learn the sociocultural patterns of the dominant group or gain access to its privileges.

The effect of industrialization can be viewed in Susan Gal's (1979) study of Oberwart, a bilingual town in Austria. The peasant community is traditionally Hungarian-speaking, but many children of farmers have chosen to live in town and work in the local industry. As a result, they now identify themselves as workers and speak German. Although the shift to German is progressing throughout the population, the trend is especially strong among young women, many of whom wish to escape the hardships of farm life.

Industrialization does not always entail language shift, however. Michael Hechter (1975) examined language shift in Wales as it related to the development of the coal mining industry there. He found that although the Welsh language declined during the late nineteenth and early twentieth centuries, this was due to the effects of heavy English migration into the area, and not to industrialization per se. Hechter suggests that during the period prior to 1921 the Welsh workers probably had little need for English. This is because they were most likely confined to the least-skilled occupational levels, where bilingual supervisors could serve as language brokers, and because their political affiliations were restricted to regional associations. Industrialization did begin to show a negative effect on the Welsh language in the 1920s, but this was in conjunction with the advent of a universal education act which made English the only permissible medium of education as well as the incursion of English institutions, including industrial trade unions.

Urbanization often plays a role in language shift, sometimes combined with industrialization. John Fought (1985: 29) notes that cities like Mexico City are able to weaken indigenous cultures by sending the national culture outward through a communicative network and at the same time drawing rural people into the city. This pattern is particularly strong in the Third World, where large metropolitan areas are often sur-rounded by impoverished rural areas.

While economic pressures often influence people to learn a job-select language, at the same time there may be countervailing economic forces that impede loss of the subordinate language. In the Malinche Volcano region of Mexico many rural townspeople leave their communities for extended periods to work in nearby factories where Spanish is spoken. However, they often rely on their home communities as a source of aid in difficult times or as a place to retire. Therefore, they must be able to count on community ties. A knowledge of Mexicano is helpful in reestablishing themselves locally (Hill and Hill 1986).

Problems of Subsistence in the Community

While individuals are often drawn to the rewards of the larger society, pressures to shift may also result from economic conditions within the community. Traditionally, the economy of Mazapa de Madero, a small Teko-speaking town in Chiapas, Mexico, has been based on peasant agriculture, with corn as the main crop. However, due to population growth, the land base is no longer sufficient to support all of the popu-lation. Although some young people choose to remain in the town, mi-grating seasonally to work on plantations, hiring themselves out as farm labor, or taking jobs such as tailors, taxi drivers, or laundry women, many young people leave Mazapa to study and find employment in ur-ban areas throughout Mexico. In a mid-1980s survey, Teko speakers were questioned about migration experiences among their offspring, most of whom are adults. Out of 139 sons and daughters, over one-third had migrated from Mazapa, and many had found spouses outside the community. Language usage reflects this orientation toward the larger society. Only 6 out of the 139 individuals continue to speak Teko; the rest are monolingual in Spanish. In this formerly Mayan town adapta-tion to changing economic conditions has included the loss of the in-digenous language (Garzon 1985).

As a community loses its traditional subsistence base, young people have fewer opportunities to learn the traditional culture and the lan-guage associated with it. This has been the case for the Arizona Tewas.

When subsistence agriculture played a major role in the economy of the reservation, the practical activities of planting, cultivating, and herding constituted an obligatory part of one's informal education, an education which entailed significant intergenerational interaction with kinsmen and community members. Today subsistence patterns have yielded to a cash economy in which the economic security of a household depends heavily on the wage work or salaried employment of at least one of its members. Yet for young people, the slim economic base of the reservation provides few opportunities and acts as a "push-factor" (W. Hodge . . .), a force which encourages abandonment of the reservation in either a physical sense (actual urban migration) or a psychological one (adoption of a nontraditional, "urban" orientation). (Kroskrity 1982: 58)

Demographic Changes

The primary function of a language is to facilitate communication. As language shift progresses, the pool of monolingual speakers of the indigenous language diminishes, and its primary function ceases to exist. The situation is particularly critical if there are only a small number of communities where the language is spoken or if ties between the communities are weak. Part of the problem lies in the necessity for individuals to marry outside of the language group. The couple are likely to raise their children in the language they share, which is often the dominant one.

Migration of outsiders into the area may also cause pressure on local languages. When Ladinos (non-Indians) began to settle in Mayan towns along the Mexican-Guatemalan border in the last century, the social structure of these towns was permanently altered. The influx of Spanish speakers undoubtedly contributed to the townspeople's shift to Spanish, one part of a larger process of assimilation to the norms of rural Mexican culture (Garzon 1985). In Europe industrialization has often brought outsiders into minority language areas, as in the case of Catalonia (Woolard 1985) and Brittany (Timm 1980), thus weakening the hegemony or even viability of local languages. Similarly, immigrants to Francophone Canada may choose to learn English as a second language rather than French, thereby increasing the ratio of English to French speakers in an area.

Nationalistic Pressures

Political ideologies affect people's choices about the use of a language. In some cases the dominant group may be openly hostile to an ethnic group and its culture and wish for its assimilation or, in an extreme case, annihilation. The use of a minority language can be severely curtailed, although under pressure the minority group may harden its resolve to defend its culture and seek covert forms of self-expression.

El Salvador in the 1930s represents an extreme case of repression. In 1932 the government killed some 25,000 people perceived to be Indians, in the belief that an earlier uprising had been caused by "Communist-inspired Indians." The oppression did not end there. Three years later there were still demands in the media for the total extermination of Indians. As a result, many individuals stopped speaking indigenous languages, to avoid identification as Indians. The long-term linguistic consequences were the abandonment and extinction of Lenca and Cacopera and a severe decline in speakers of Pipil (Campbell and Muntzel 1989: 183).

In Spain, under Francisco Franco's regime, minority languages were specifically targeted. The use of Basque was effectively prohibited in the public areas of rural Spanish towns and villages for at least fifteen years, with the result that today there are virtually no monolingual Basque speakers under the age of fifty (Flinspach 1989: 22). Similarly, Franco's government identified the Catalán language as a tool and symbol of Catalán resistance, a notion not without some truth (Woolard 1985: 94). Use of the language was severely repressed, and the government attempted to discredit it by labeling it a dialect or "patois" (Woolard 1985).

Educational Policies

When a multiethnic nation adopts a strong nationalistic orientation, one of its most effective instruments for carrying out its policies is the school system. The dominant language becomes the school language, and minority children must learn in a language which is not their mother tongue. While use of the dominant language is stressed, the minority language becomes devalued. Since many nations have gone through a period of intense nationalism, members of most minority groups can remember a time when children were ridiculed and punished for using their native language in school, and indeed this kind of practice persists in some areas.

In Chiapas, Mexico, during the 1920s and 1930s, rural teachers with a nationalistic sense of mission sometimes told parents that it was detrimental to the children to speak anything other than Spanish with them.

According to parents in Mazapa de Madero, this was a major reason why they chose not to teach their children Teko (Garzon 1985). This practice continues in some areas. Hill and Hill (1986: 113) describe a graduation ceremony they attended in a Mexicano-speaking town in which the school director, the son of Mexicano speakers, urged parents to speak to their children in Spanish.

In the United States, during the late nineteenth and early twentieth centuries, many Native American children were sent to distant boarding schools. Children were often punished for using their home languages during their long residence at school; as a result, many young people returned to their communities with greatly diminished use of their native languages.

Even when educational policies are less severe, the exclusion of minority languages from the schools affects the way community members view them. Dorian sums up the overt and subtle influence of schooling which fails to recognize the child's home language:

> The schools in East Sutherland can be seen to have played a negative role with regard to Gaelic on three levels: they excluded it as a medium of communication; they excluded it from the curriculum for the most part; and in taking both these actions they transmitted to the community at large a low assessment of the value and utility of the Gaelic language. (Dorian 1981: 84)

Formal schooling can have another deleterious effect on language maintenance, although an indirect one. It cuts down on time spent in intergenerational activities and promotes peer group solidarity instead. Among the Arizona Tewas, most young people attend urban-based schools for the duration of their secondary education. There they are removed from the influence of their Tewa-speaking elders and are brought into contact with young people from other southwestern tribes. Since English is the language of instruction and the only language shared by the students, it is not surprising that young people become dominant in English (Kroskrity 1982: 57–58).

While educational policies can have a profound negative impact on language maintenance, they are not successful in all situations. Often it is a combination of educational policies and supportive attitudes on the part of parents and the community that brings about change in language use. When the educational system is viewed as irrelevant or harmful by community members, and there is no consistent effort by the government to enforce educational policies, promotion of the dominant language may be ineffective. Charles Wagley (1949) presents an example of a partially thwarted effort to teach Spanish to children in a town in the northwestern Highlands of Guatemala earlier in this century:

> The teachers were in agreement that the girls generally learned more Spanish than the boys, but that they completely forgot it soon after their school years were over. This is the bane of life to all three teachers. They pointed out certain women who had been prize students, who had actually learned to read and write Spanish, and who three or four years later could not or would not understand a single word of Spanish. (Wagley 1949: 31)

This situation does not appear to have changed greatly in recent years, although John Watanabe reports that today some Chimaltecos value education as a means of better defending themselves against Ladino manipulation (1992: 236) and some families try to provide an education for those sons who will not inherit land (1992: 150).

Nationalistic educational policies may have unforeseen results, not all of which are detrimental to indigenous languages. Even when an educational system has an assimilationist ideology, the system may inadvertently create the conditions for the emergence of a group of indigenous professionals, some of whom do not support a shift to the dominant language. Linda King (1994) reports that in Mexico bilingual schoolteachers and ethnolinguists have emerged as the most articulate of the indigenous participants in the debate over indigenous education and language policy.

> From the mid-1970's on, a new Indian consciousness began to express itself throughout Latin America; it was primarily the voice of Indians who had been schooled in national education systems and subsequently employed by the state either as community development workers or as schoolteachers. They were looking not only for a new Indian identity but also for the chance to put pressure on those in positions of power in the government to influence the future of Indian policy. (King 1994: 68)

One Indian organization, ANPIBAC (National Alliance of Professional Bilingual Indians), has promoted the development of standard alphabets for Indian languages and a bilingual education system extending from primary school to higher education (King 1994: 70–71).

Reevaluation of a Language's Prestige

A dominant language is often considered to have higher prestige than an indigenous language, and this is commonly cited as a factor contributing to shift (Fasold 1984: 217). Of course, prestige is an elusive variable to work with. As long as the dominant culture remains the "outside" culture, and the local community is able to maintain its traditional system of rewards and punishments, community members may see their local culture as more valuable. However, as the communities become increasingly integrated into the national society, their members start to accept its values and begin to accord greater prestige to its language. It is at this early stage of social change that the ideological foundations of language shift may develop. Susan Gal (1979) points out that the impetus for shift from Hungarian to German among people in Oberwart, Austria, originated with a change in their understanding of the symbolic value of the two languages. "Specifically, language shift began when German gained prestige because choice of it, as opposed to Hungarian, came to symbolize the speaker's claim to worker rather than peasant status" (Gal 1979: 17).

In the Papua New Guinea community studied by Don Kulick (1992: 258), it is the villagers' changing interpretation of the world that has opened the way for adoption of Tok Pisin and loss of the local language, Taiap. Tok Pisin and now English have gained prestige as new goals and values have emerged. Kulick emphasizes that language shift has begun in the absence of macrosociological forces such as industrialization or proletarianization, although these forces may become associated with language shift within a few decades.

When minority languages become associated with rural poverty, they are especially prone to low prestige. Many indigenous languages of the Americas fall into this category, since the dominant societies have steadily pushed native people off their land, leaving them without adequate means of subsistence.

In many cases the language of the dominant group has many speakers worldwide, is standardized, and has a substantial body of literature. These and other characteristics may lend the dominant language an aura of authenticity and prestige which the local language lacks. As speakers of the subordinate language begin to interact more with members of the dominant culture, they sometimes feel ashamed of their lack of knowledge of the dominant language. They are acutely aware of their inability to defend their interests adequately, and they may feel socially inferior because of it. These feelings can hasten the progress of shift to the dominant language.

THE PROCESS OF LANGUAGE SHIFT
Changes in Social Networks

As communities undergo the kinds of economic and social changes that accompany greater integration into national societies, community members may alter their patterns of interaction, resulting in a transformation of social networks. Changes in these networks may lead individuals to acquire additional languages and allow other languages to fall into disuse. The existence of strong or weak social networks in a community has also been used to explain resistance or receptivity to language shift.

In a study on language use in the Gail Valley of Austria, John Gumperz (1976) linked continued use of Slovenian with the maintenance of in-group social networks. He found that although many communities in the region had ceased to use Slovenian, shifting entirely to German, people in the Gail Valley had maintained their bilingualism. Gumperz attributed the continuing viability of the Slovenian language to the endurance of a social system in which ties based on kinship, occupation, friendship, and religion often overlapped. In addition, community members seemed to have maintained psychological barriers against outsiders. The situation in the Gail Valley is changing, as residents find increased economic opportunity outside the valley and as outsiders move into the area. Not surprisingly, the result is a shift to monolingualism in German for many individuals (Gumperz, reported by Milroy 1987: 169–170).

Within a multilingual community, an individual's choice of codes is often influenced by social network. In Oberwart, a bilingual Austrian town, Gal (1979) found that individuals with predominantly peasant networks tend to speak Hungarian, the traditional language of the community, while those with predominantly worker networks tend to speak German, the language of the larger Austrian society. Kroskrity points out that people's language use depends not simply on their social networks but more specifically on their reference groups ("that group to which a person psychologically orients himself and whose perspective he imaginatively adopts in order to generate meaningful behavior" [Kroskrity 1993: 137]). Individuals may have considerable contact with dominant-language speakers, for example, in the workplace. However, if their primary reference group consists of traditional speakers of the subordinate language, their speech will probably resemble that of the latter group. Conversely, individuals whose reference group consists of shifting individuals are likely to shift as well. According to Kroskrity (1993: 103), many Arizona Tewa young people no longer identify mainly with their extended kin; instead, they identify with others in their age group—a group that is shifting to a predominant use of English.

Social network theory has some limitations for explaining language shift in its later stages, when a whole generation of speakers may choose to speak the dominant language with their children, not because their networks are substantially different from those of their parents, but because change within the community or the expectation of such change has caused modifications in norms of language use. In some cases the parents elect to teach their children the dominant language even though they themselves maintain traditional social networks.

Shrinking Domains of Use

Sociolinguists have long been concerned with the differing functions of languages in multilingual communities. A common way to address the question is to look at the types of domains corresponding to different languages in contact situations.

As language shift progresses, its course can often be described by tracing the gradual spread of the dominant language across domains which were previously reserved for the minority language. Often the dominant language begins by replacing the minority language in more public domains such as the school and the municipal government. In the last stages, the dominant language replaces the local language in its final refuge, the home. When this process is complete, the minority language may cease to exist.

However, other patterns do occur. In one variation, the Latinate pattern (Hill 1983: 260), the language is preserved in its elevated forms even after speakers no longer use it in the home. Only the formal registers of the language are preserved, and they are used for restricted ceremonial purposes. Hopi and Yaqui may survive in this form (Hill 1983: 260), as may other American Indian languages, such as Gros Ventre (Taylor 1989: 171), Chiapanec, and Southeastern Tzeltal (Campbell and Muntzel 1989: 185–186).

Changing Norms of Accommodation

As norms for appropriate use of a language change, the rules that regulate linguistic accommodation are also likely to alter. In Oberwart Gal (1979) found that some bilingual residents in their sixties and seventies continue an old pattern of speaking Hungarian with each other even if there are monolingual German speakers around. However, younger people recognize a different norm, one requiring bilinguals to switch to German if there are any monolingual German speakers around.

Catalán speakers have an accommodation norm which takes a somewhat different form. Since at least the time of the Franco regime, most Catalán speakers have recognized a rule requiring them to use Castilian when addressing anyone who is not clearly a native Catalán. This rule is fairly rigid and precludes the use of Catalán even with people who understand and have some proficiency in it. Thus, the use of Catalán functions as a strong marker of in-group identity. However, the continuing viability of Catalán is threatened in part by large-scale immigration of Castilian-speaking laborers. Without the existing norm, outsiders might learn Catalán and add to the pool of speakers, particularly since the two languages are genetically related and reportedly many non-Cataláns already have passive competence (Woolard 1989).

Factors in the Final Stages of Shift

Language shift often progresses in an orderly fashion, with the dominant language replacing the local one in ever more domains. In its final stages, the shift is likely to be abrupt and rapid. This occurs when a generation of parents fails to transmit their mother tongue to their children and when children reject the indigenous language.

Intergenerational Break

When the shift begins in earnest, one or two generations may be pivotal. According to Leonard Bloomfield (1933: 463), "In the situation of conquest the process of extinction may be long delayed; then, at some point, there may come a generation which does not use the lower language in adult life and transmits only the upper language to its children." This intergenerational break seems to be part of the process referred to as "tip" (Dorian 1981: 51).

This kind of shift presupposes a bilingual generation with mastery of both the dominant and subordinate languages. The existence of societies with stable multilingualism demonstrates that societal bilingualism is not a sufficient condition for shift; but if a large proportion of a community is bilingual, the community is at greater risk of losing its native language.

Parents often have very practical reasons for shifting to the dominant language with their children. As communities and ethnic enclaves lose their former isolation and relative self-sufficiency, parents want their children to have the skills necessary to survive and advance in the larger world. For example, even in traditional Irish-speaking areas of Ireland parents may teach their children English to prepare them for eventual emigration (Grillo 1989: 62).

Although peasant communities and other traditional groups often appear conservative and resistant to change, the shift by parents to the dominant language may be an anticipatory change. Parents recognize that if their families are to survive and prosper the children must be prepared for a world different from the one in which they themselves were raised. The shift to an outside language may reflect a change in values that is still underway. Reporting on a village in Papua New Guinea, Kulick (1992) notes the anticipatory nature of the villagers' shift to Tok Pisin, responding as it does to changes in their world view rather than to immediate economic, political, and social forces.

In some cases parents may prohibit the use of the subordinate language in an effort to prevent their children from speaking the dominant language with an "accent." It is commonly believed that if a child learns a subordinate language first that language will necessarily cause linguistic interference in the dominant language. Uriel Weinreich suggests that the desire for unaccented speech may arise from societal pressures:

> The usefulness of a language in social advance usually has a highly significant corollary: the importance of knowing that language well. In a situation of this type, there may even be a premium set on the concealment of the fact that a language was secondarily acquired. The effort exerted to overcome all traces of interference is therefore particularly strong. . . . (Weinreich 1968: 78)

Individuals may react strongly to these pressures. Research on Pennsylvania German populations suggests that while Old Order groups continue to transmit German to their children less conservative groups do not. One of the reasons for the latter groups' reluctance is their aversion to accented English, which marks a person as rural and unsophisticated.

In contrast, members of an indigenous group may choose to maintain a variety of the dominant language marked by transfer from their ancestral language. William Leap (1993) points out that among North American tribes Indian English may serve various functions, including that of ethnicity marker.

At Isleta Pueblo a continuum of speech styles exists which includes different varieties of Isletan English. Pueblo members are strongly discouraged from using standard "metropolitan" English when they discuss matters of personal concern among themselves. As Leap explains, "English discourse *within* pueblo settings needs to follow pueblo-based rules of speaking, not conform to expectations established within the non-Indian world" (1993: 197; Leap's emphasis).

A similar situation exists among the Mohave Tribe of western Arizona. Susan Penfield-Jasper (1982) reports that among the Mohave, Indian English has become the dominant code, and it functions as a marker of tribal identity, just as the ancestral language once did. Those young Mohaves who use a more standard variety of English in the home can expect teasing, and in the high school non-Mohaves who want to join Mohave peer groups learn aspects of the Mohave English dialect.

The Indigenous Language as a Second Language

A decision on the part of parents not to speak a subordinate native language with their children may be the immediate cause of the demise of a language. However, this is not always the case. Children may still learn the language even if they do not learn it directly from their parents.

An early study by Viola Waterhouse (1949) indicates that speakers of Chontal Hokan learned Spanish as a first language but acquired Chontal as they became adults. Children were exposed to Chontal by hearing adults speak it with each other. As they matured, young people recognized Chontal as the adult language of the town and made a conscious effort to learn it. As individuals became engaged in adult activities, they had opportunities to improve their skills. For example, one man gained in proficiency when he served as town policeman for a year.

At Isleta Pueblo a similar situation exists; many children learn English as a first language, then acquire mastery of Isletan Tiwa as they take on the responsibilities and enjoy the cultural rewards of adult life. In fact, acquisition of Isletan Tiwa is mandatory for tribal members who wish to establish permanent residence in the community and become active participants in pueblo life (Leap 1993: 178–181).

Studies carried out among Mexicano (Nahuatl) speakers in Mexico indicate that Mexicano may also be learned as a second language. It was not uncommon for individuals in these Mexicano-speaking towns to learn Spanish from their parents and then learn Mexicano as young adults. Hill and Hill (1986) found this to be the case in a number of communities. In fact, they believe that in one town all the men under forty whom they interviewed had learned Mexicano as a second language. Some evidence exists that this pattern can be sustained over multiple generations; a seventy-two-year-old Mexicano speaker from another town claimed he had learned Mexicano as an adult although he had grown up in that town (Hill and Hill 1986: 121–122).

Similarly, in a community studied by Judith Friedlander (1975: 84–85) many parents chose to speak Spanish with their children in compliance with teachers' wishes. Nevertheless, the children still learned Mexicano, apparently through indirect exposure in the home and additional exposure in other settings.

The evidence from these studies indicates that, in a town where the subordinate language is still widely used, a child who has been brought up in the dominant language may still learn the local language outside and sometimes inside the home. This is especially likely if the indigenous language is associated with the assumption of adult status in the community.

Even when a generation of speakers has largely shifted to exclusive use of the dominant language, some individuals may choose to speak the indigenous language. The most complete description of this phenomenon comes from Dorian's (1981: 106–109) study of Gaelic speakers in Scotland. There she discovered a group of English-dominant adults who continue to use Gaelic even though they never acquired full mastery of the language. Since most individuals choose to shift entirely to the dominant language when they lack fluency in the subordinate language, Dorian was interested in why these individuals were different. Some were simply the youngest siblings in a home which progressively became more English-speaking as the older siblings went to school and came home speaking English. However, in other cases the individuals had consciously chosen to learn Gaelic. Often they had formed a close relationship with a Gaelic-speaking relative, frequently a grandparent. Another experience which sometimes led to a desire to use Gaelic was migration from the area, either temporary or permanent. Members of the East Sutherland communities who went to live in other cities seem to have cultivated a sense of solidarity and pride in their homeland by

speaking Gaelic among themselves. Dorian also attributes this willingness to maintain Gaelic to personality factors, notably an inquisitive and
gregarious disposition. It should be pointed out that these people are not
fluent, and their speech deviates noticeably from that of fluent speakers
(Dorian 1981).

The role of grandparents in passing on an indigenous language is also
noted by Kroskrity (1993: 102) for the Arizona Tewas. Children often
spend considerable time with grandparents while they are growing up,
so they learn Tewa even if their parents rarely use it.

Attitudes of Young People

Children may reject the use of the subordinate language even though
their parents are willing to continue speaking it. Norms of accommodation may change within the family as well. In Arizona Tewa families
many young people respond in English even when their parents address
them in Tewa or Hopi (Kroskrity 1993: 41). The same phenomenon
occurs in shifting communities in Europe. In the Hebrides parents who
speak to their children in Gaelic may be answered in English (Williamson and Van Eerde 1980: 76). Among a group of Albanian Greeks shifting from Arvanitika to Greek, many children pressure their parents not
to speak Arvanitika, especially in public. The children have had some
success in changing their parents' speech habits (Trudgill and Tzavaras
1977: 181).

Norman Denison (1977) describes the stage at which a community is
likely to undergo a tip to the dominant language, emphasizing the crucial nature of the parents' shift with their children but also noting the
importance of their children's attitude toward the subordinate language:

> . . . there comes a point when multilingual parents no longer consider
> it necessary or worthwhile for the future of their children to com-
> municate with them in a low-prestige language variety, and when
> children are no longer motivated to acquire active competence in
> a language which is lacking in positive connotations such as youth,
> modernity, technical skills, material success, education. (Denison
> 1977: 21)

Language and Gender

The literature on language shift has revealed a relatively consistent pattern in language use by men and women at different stages in the shift.

In the early stages, men often take the lead in learning the dominant language and becoming bilingual, while the women continue to be largely monolingual in the minority language. Later, when the shift is nearing completion, it is often the men who continue to use the minority language after the women have stopped speaking it. This switch in roles is demonstrated by Gal's (1984) study of Oberwart and by Marjut Aikio's (1992) study of Sámi reindeer herders in Finland.

In Oberwart the oldest women of the community limit their conversation almost entirely to Hungarian; Gal attributes their limited use of German to conditions before World War II, when women were restricted in their range of social contacts and thus had little exposure to German. In contrast, young women today show a clear preference for the use of German, a choice which is consistent with their desire for an urban life rather than life as a peasant wife. Young men use Hungarian more often than their female counterparts, and this is consistent with their desire to continue farming (Gal 1984).

Aikio (1992) found a similar situation among reindeer herders in Finland. While men were becoming bilingual early in the shift, many women chose to use only Sámi, possibly as a sign of their rejection of Finnish peasant culture, in which women led more restricted lives. Nevertheless, language shift progressed, and today women are largely monolingual in Finnish, while men continue to use Sámi as part of traditional rituals held in the forests.

A similar pattern can also be found in cases of dialect shift, as shown by Patricia Nichols's (1983) study of the inhabitants of African-American communities in South Carolina. There older women tend to be conservative in their use of creolized varieties of English, while young women use more standard English than their male peers. Nichols attributes this pattern to different employment opportunities for men and women, resulting in different social networks and varying need for standard English. The divergence in use patterns begins around the age of ten, when girls become more restricted in their social activities and are expected to behave like young ladies.

While a switched role for men and women seems to be common to a number of language communities undergoing shift, this does not appear to be a universal pattern. According to Bea Medicine (1987: 163), it was women who often acted as cultural brokers during early interactions between the Sioux Indians and Euro-Americans, presumably with the result that women were among the first to become bilingual. In modern times, Sioux women continue to perfect their linguistic abilities in both Lakota and English (Medicine 1987: 164).

CONCLUSIONS

Indigenous groups in the Americas have experienced language relations of various kinds. When groups of comparable status come into contact, trade and intermarriage may result in moderate or high levels of bilingualism lasting over generations. Lingua francas, whether full languages or simplified forms, often facilitate communication between groups. If one of the groups attains ascendancy, groups in close contact may shift to its language.

When one language group extends its power or influence over another, the type of language relations that results depends in part on the extent of contact between the dominant and the indigenous population. Imperial groups often have limited goals, restricted to drawing off local resources in the form of tribute or taxes. Consequently, interaction between the groups may be minimal and can be carried out by a small group of bilingual brokers using one of the groups' languages or some third language. If there is a local elite class with ties to the foreign power through marriage or exchange of resources, that group will probably be bilingual. This is a common pattern for empires with far-flung territories.

When the conquering group colonizes the area, there are different possible linguistic outcomes. If the colonizers are few in number, have weak ties to their own land, and are surrounded by speakers of a single indigenous language, they may end up learning the local language, and in the course of time they may stop passing on their own language to later generations. In contrast, if the colonizers constitute a larger, more cohesive group, the outcome of contact may be a society divided ethnically and linguistically, with brokers facilitating political administration and the exchange of goods and services. Segregation of the two groups may have both positive and negative results. While the subordinate group is denied access to the power and resources of the larger society, it may be able to maintain a large part of its traditional culture.

When the dominant group's presence is more intrusive, the local population is likely to shift to the dominant language. This is often the case when indigenous towns border metropolitan areas. However, even when a community is tied into the larger society and many individuals learn the dominant language, shift may not be inevitable. A community may maintain a high level of bilingualism over a number of generations without endangering the indigenous language. The probability of this occurring depends on a number of factors, such as the economic viability of the community, group cohesiveness, conscious identification of the language with ethnic identity, and the attitude of the larger society toward indigenous cultures within its boundaries.

In many multiethnic nations language shift has occurred on a large scale in recent times. In rural areas land shortages and rising population make traditional communities less self-sufficient at a time when national institutions are entering the towns, altering long-standing patterns of social organization and alignment. In some cases, national governments carry out policies that undermine the viability of ethnic communities and threaten the continuation of traditional culture. These policies often include the prohibition or neglect of the indigenous language in educational settings. Parents switch to the dominant language with their children, acknowledging the power and prestige of the dominant language and anticipating their children's need to get along in school and the larger society. By so doing, families enhance their chances of survival. However, this change contributes to the further infiltration of outside values into indigenous homes, including values that denigrate local culture.

As the bilingual population increases, the communicative function of the indigenous language is weakened. Young people have less exposure to the language and may not make the effort or have the opportunity to master it. As the indigenous language becomes less necessary for communication, however, it may take on renewed importance as a symbol of ethnicity.

Maintenance of indigenous languages is possible in societies tolerant of ethnic diversity, where minority languages enjoy prestige commensurate with languages of wider currency. It is sad to say that since the Conquest few if any indigenous languages in the Western Hemisphere have been accorded the prestige due them as repositories of great cultural wealth. However, programs aimed at cultural renewal and revitalization of languages together with a growing consciousness of the value of indigenous cultures could change this situation, particularly if nationalistic forces can be redirected to encourage the development of all sectors of society.

3. A BRIEF CULTURAL HISTORY OF THE GUATEMALAN HIGHLANDS

R. McKenna Brown

INDIAN CULTURE AS PRE-CONQUEST RELIC

Language and ethnicity are closely linked in the Mayan world. Both are constantly evolving, in part due to contact with external influences. This chapter explores some of the forces that over time have shaped the life of the Kaqchikel language today.

The task of defining "Indianness" is central to the question of Mayan ethnic identity today in Guatemala. Any institutional effort to effect cultural change must reflect some stance on what is held to constitute Mayan culture. For example, Maya activists unanimously advocate the promotion of Mayan culture, yet do not share a complete consensus on exactly what that culture is. History becomes important because one widely held view, implicit in early scholarship and influential today among Mayas and non-Mayas alike, considers "true" Indian culture to be only those features surviving from the pre-Conquest period. In this light, the centuries of exposure to European and African culture are seen as "contamination" and the incorporation of non-Mayan elements is seen as a weakening or polluting of Mayan culture.

This view of contemporary Mayan culture as a pre-Conquest relic contains several dangerous implications. One is that the survival of "true" Indian culture hinges on the impossible historical task of recuperating what has been, to a large degree, irretrievably lost. Another implication is that to become "authentic" the Mayas today must reject most of what has been going on in the world for the past five hundred years as though they had no valid stake to claim in it. Hence, the Mayas are essentially barred from successful participation in the contemporary world or risk being branded sellouts, traitors, or *desculturados* (separated from their culture).

Recent anthropological definitions of Mayan culture are not limited to its prehispanic component (Fischer 1996; Hawkins 1984; Otzoy

1988; Smith and Boyer 1987; Warren 1978). Mayan culture (and, by extension, most postcolonial "traditional" culture) is now seen not as a historical relic, nor as a product of European origin imposed upon the Indian, but as a synthesis of native and imported elements developed within the constraints imposed by a marginalized status within the national and world economies.

The stipulation that only Mayan culture of pre-Conquest origin is genuine does not fit well in a historical analysis of the Highlands, and it is especially difficult to apply in the case of the Kaqchikels. First, the notion of some early pristine Mayan culture is largely illusory. Before the Conquest, the Highland Mayas had withstood sustained and intense contact with other cultures for centuries. Second, for the Kaqchikels in particular, the period immediately before, during, and after the Conquest brought acute social, cultural, and demographic upheaval, leaving little of the previous lifeway wholly intact. And, finally, the process of erecting a Spanish colonial society upon the smoking waste of the invasion using Indian labor profoundly touched and reshaped virtually every aspect of the Mayan community which serves as the bastion of Mayan culture. Today many of the features of Mayan community life considered most traditional date from this period, products of the struggle to remain ethnically intact against the pressures of the colonial system.

Thus, history reveals many supposedly "authentic" Mayan customs to be of Spanish origin or the product of colonial history. The effect is dispiriting and perturbing for many Maya activists, who seek to boost cultural self-esteem in the face of a common belief that a culture formed under oppression is somehow of less worth than the dominant culture. Consequently, the search for aspects of Mayan culture to promote as objects of ethnic pride becomes fueled in part by a craving to establish a concrete link with the prehispanic past (Fischer 1996). And for the modern Mayas, the most conspicuous link to the past that is indisputably non-Spanish is found in the Mayan languages. These languages offer a uniquely authentic cultural possession for their speakers, perhaps more than other surviving aspects of prehispanic life, such as *milpa* agriculture, which are shared throughout Mesoamerica. As a banner of ethnic pride, the Mayan languages are appropriate because throughout the centuries of foreign incursions and upheaval in the Guatemalan Highlands they have remained largely intact.

The Mayan cultures and languages did not develop in isolation. Historically, they participate in the Mesoamerican cultural and linguistic area that encompasses much of central and southern Mexico and the Yucatán. The region has hosted such an intense and constant contact among successive and contemporaneous civilizations through trade, migration, and warfare that many cultural and linguistic features have come to be shared among genetically separate groups. Anthropologists have long recognized traits that are widely distributed throughout Mesoamerica among both Mayan and non-Mayan cultures (Kirchoff 1952; Kroeber 1939). These traits include maize agriculture, differentiated male and female costume, market-centered economy, and a shared calendar used for divination (Tax 1953).

Mesoamerica is also recognized as a linguistic area (also called diffusion area or *Sprachbund*) marked by structural similarities across unrelated language group boundaries. Some thirty linguistic features are shared among Mesoamerican languages (Campbell 1977). Terrence Kaufman (1973: 461) attributes the high degree of shared linguistic features to centuries of intense contact that spread them along with aspects of material culture and social organization.

Cultural Intrusions

The assumption that the Spaniards encountered culturally pristine societies in their Conquest of Guatemala is contradicted by the fact that the Highland Mayan cultures had been profoundly touched by repeated invasions from Mexico for at least a thousand years before the Spaniards' arrival. Increasing population and land pressures in central Mexico, as well as the search for cacao and labor, motivated these invasions, at least in part (MacLeod 1973). As Christopher Lutz (1976: 50) observes, the populations of Highland Guatemala had been "Mexicanized and Toltecized before they were ever Hispanized."

These cultural intrusions did not affect the Highland population uniformly. Their impact varied by social class and geographic area. Foreign influence would take hold most strongly among the urban elites at the top of the social pyramid, while the rural peasantry at the base would be least affected. This pattern of response to foreign influence, also found outside Guatemala, continues to modern times. Jorge Suárez (1982) attributes it to the Mesoamerican tradition in which states were loose aggregates of fairly autonomous communities of different ethnic groups who coexisted with little intermingling.

Referring specifically to Highland Guatemala, Lutz (1976) concurs that those Indians most influenced by the Mexican invasions were the urban elites—those same classes that would be first absorbed into the Spanish colonial society, the first to reside and work in Spanish towns and to live in Spanish households. The pattern in which members of a separate speech community serve as brokers with a dominant group is found throughout the history of Mayan communities.

The Mexican incursions followed the geographically easiest trails—coastal plains and riverbeds that for centuries served as trade routes. Groups living in the less accessible areas, such as Highland Chiapas, the Verapaz region, and the Cuchumatán Mountains, were much less affected than those of the Central Highlands, including the K'iche's, the Tz'utujils, and the Kaqchikels.

The material and ceremonial aspects of Mayan culture were most affected by the repeated invasions, while the linguistic behavior of the underclasses remained relatively untouched (Suárez 1982). Hence, amidst the constant intercultural contact fostered throughout Mesoamerica's history of trade, migrations, and warfare, a large proportion of the lower strata apparently carried on in linguistic isolation. This hypothesis is supported by the linguistic fragmentation found in present-day Mesoamerica (Suárez 1982).

The first arrivals were of the Teotihuacán civilization of central Mexico. Their arrival dates from the Early Classic Period (A.D. 300–700) and resulted in the building of temple mounds arranged around ceremonial plazas and ball courts. Archaeological remains from this period show unprotected settlement patterns around ceremonial centers in open valleys near running water (Lutz 1976), giving the impression that the Early Classic Period was relatively peaceful. The center of Teotihuacán influence, Kaminaljuyú, lies in present day Kaqchikel territory. The linguistic impact of these early invaders was not so lasting as their material contributions. Though they may have been Otomí speakers, no evidence of Otomí loanwords in Mayan languages has yet been established (Kaufman 1976: 115).

A series of military invasions occurred during the Late Classic Period (A.D. 700–1000) bringing the Pipil-Nicaros, Nahuatl speakers from the Gulf coast of Mexico, who caused extensive population displacement. Archaeological evidence from this period shows settlement patterns changing radically from open valleys to protected hillsides, reflecting a growing militarization of the area. It appears that the Pipils controlled vast areas of the region by the end of the Late Classic Period (Lutz 1976). There is little evidence of linguistic influence in the Mayan languages from this period, however (Campbell 1977).

The next invasions were either by Nahuat or Nahuatl speakers of Toltec ancestry from the Tabasco-Veracruz region of Mexico, who entered the Guatemalan Highlands some ten generations prior to the Spanish Conquest (about A.D. 1250) and came to control large sections of the

Central Highlands (Fox 1978). The Late Postclassic Period begins as new political systems emerge under this Toltec influence, evidenced in K'iche'an architecture (Smith 1955) and in many features of the conquest system brought from Mexico, including tribute, warfare as a means of social mobility, and government offices related directly to conquest (Fox 1978).

The Toltecs were to have a profound effect on their new subjects, who would in turn absorb their new rulers. Though the Toltecs brought many architectural, administrative, and religious practices, they became speakers of the local Mayan languages (Lutz 1976). These invaders—mostly warrior males—became priests and rulers of many Highland groups or chiefdoms, such as the K'iche's and the Kaqchikels. The *Popol Vuh* mentions them as founding fathers of the K'iche' kingdom, who arrived under divine commission from the Toltec god Nakxit. Toltec influences suggested by the Nahuatl loanwords in the K'iche'an languages from this period involve religious and military terms (Campbell 1977). They took Maya women as wives, and it would seem that their original language was lost in the subsequent generations. The *Popol Vuh* alludes to their linguistic assimilation: "Alas! We left our language behind. How did we do it? We're lost! Where were we deceived? We had only one language when we came to Tulan, and we had only one place of emergence and origin. We haven't done well" (D. Tedlock 1985: 173).

However, the degree of linguistic assimilation of the Toltec elites is not completely clear. For example, there is no documentary evidence that the conquistador Pedro de Alvarado and his Nahuatl-speaking Mexican allies had any trouble communicating with the Guatemalan leaders during the conquest (Miles 1965). The Toltecs' original language may have survived as the code of trade, diplomacy, or other functions.

Thus, on the eve of the Conquest, the populations of Highland Guatemala had experienced repeated incursions from Mexico. The waves of invaders had radically affected settlement patterns, architectural styles, and religious practices. Their influence would be most strongly felt among the urban elites and least among the rural masses. The most evident Mayan cultural trait to remain strongly intact would be the Mayan languages.

THE KAQCHIKELS IN THE CONQUEST

Due to their central location, the Kaqchikels have over time withstood perhaps more intense and turbulent exposure to foreign incursions than most other Highland Maya groups. The period of history surrounding the Spanish Conquest of Guatemala was especially tumultuous for the Kaqchikels, who played a central role in a scenario of rapidly shifting alliances, bloody warfare, massive population displacements, and devastating plagues.

By 1250 A.D. the Highland Mayas were organized into five kingdoms: the K'iche', Poqomam, Tz'utujil, Mam, and Kaqchikel. The strongest were the K'iche's, who embarked on a rapid military expansion, bringing many of their neighbors under their control. At its zenith, around A.D. 1450, the K'iche' state included approximately 1,000,000 inhabitants (Carmack 1968). The Kaqchikels at this time were divided into four main lineages: the Xahils, Zotzils, Tukuches, and Akahals. The first three branches, the western Kaqchikels, were close allies of the K'iche's and served as their military arm (Richards and Richards 1988). Their capital was near Chichicastenango. The Akahals, centered around Chimaltenango to the east, were continually battling the K'iche's and their western cousins.

By around 1470 the K'iche' kingdom had grown administratively cumbersome and suffered periodic revolts by its subject peoples. The western Kaqchikels broke their alliance and moved their capital from Chichicastenango to Iximche', near present-day Tecpán, where they embarked on their own campaign of military expansion. They remained at constant war with the K'iche's and also fought with their neighbors to the southwest, the Tz'utujils. Eventually the Tecpán Kaqchikels briefly came to rule over the Akahals; by the time of the Spanish invasion, they controlled over forty towns and their power seemed to be on the rise (Fox 1978).

On the eve of the Conquest, Moctezuma sent word from Mexico to the Guatemalans to desist from their warfare and to join in the fight against the encroaching Spaniards (MacLeod 1973). It appears that they either ignored or rejected his plea. However, the Kaqchikels did send emissaries to Hernán Cortés to enlist his help against the K'iche's, Tz'utujils, and Pipils of the Pacific piedmont. The Spaniards were happy to oblige.

In 1524, shortly after the fall of Moctezuma in Mexico, one of Cortés's generals, Pedro de Alvarado, embarked on the Conquest of Guatemala. He and his men were accompanied by Tlaxcalan soldiers from Mexico who had aided the Spaniards in the overthrow of the Aztecs. Two other powerful allies against the Guatemalans were their own political turmoil and the ravages of European diseases (MacLeod 1973; Richards and Richards 1988). Alvarado and his armies were preceded by European germs causing epidemics of smallpox, pneumonic plague, and typhus, against which the Indians had no immunities. *The Annals of the Kaqchikels* (1953) recount in graphic language how victims of all ages were laid waste by horrible epidemics. Present-day epidemiological calculations estimate that one-third of the Highland population died from these epidemics and that the survivors were severely weakened for at least another year.

Alvarado entered Guatemala along the Pacific coast from Mexico. The first obstacles to his progress were the K'iche's and the Tz'utujils, who fought him fiercely. But the Kaqchikels had sent troops and supplies to help the Spaniards defeat these enemies as well as for subsequent campaigns against the Pipils (Lutz 1994). With the help of his Kaqchikel allies, Alvarado was victorious. He then settled his troops at Iximche', restocking provisions from the Kaqchikel larder while planning the next expedition to be launched against the Pipils of the Pacific piedmont. Returning from the Pipil campaign, Alvarado demanded such onerous tribute duties from the Kaqchikels that they revolted against their new allies and guests. The Kaqchikels then abandoned their capital and took up arms in protracted resistance.

Months of bloody warfare ensued. A temporary peace was achieved when the Kaqchikels surrendered in 1530. Yet persistent abuses by the Spaniards caused the *cacique* Kaji' Imox (Sinakán) to pick up arms again and lead a five-year revolt until he was caught and hanged by Alvarado in 1540. Thousands of Kaqchikels were enslaved and resettled. Many were pressed into shipbuilding. Alvarado sold two thousand Kaqchikels in Peru (Polo Sifontes 1977).

During the early stages of the Guatemalan Conquest, the Spanish capital was little more than a military camp, moving frequently with the fortunes of the campaigns. At the time of the Kaqchikel rebellion, a more permanent site was selected on the slopes of the Agua Volcano, at the eastern edge of Kaqchikel territory where the city of Santiago de Almolonga was founded in 1527. During its brief life, this capital probably contained some one hundred and fifty Spanish households as well as an Indian *barrio* populated by Mexican allies and their families. In 1541 the city was destroyed by a mudslide, and a new capital was built three miles to the north, in the valley of Panchoy. This city was called Santiago de los Caballeros de Guatemala.

Though close to many Kaqchikel communities, the area immediately surrounding the new capital seems to have been sparsely populated. Lands in nearby valleys were ceded to Spaniards for agricultural and/or cattle production to provide for the new city's sustenance. Many of these plots, called *milpas,* were settled with a labor force of enslaved Indians and evolved into communities that still exist today. The ethnic and linguistic backgrounds of the Indians resettled in these *milpas* tended to be quite heterogeneous. For example, the Spanish gathered speakers of at least five different languages to found the present-day Kaqchikel town of San Antonio Aguas Calientes (Lutz 1994). The lack of a shared ethnic identity may account for the fact that most of these communities today have become Ladinoized. However, in the communities of the Quinizilapa Valley, despite the ethnic mixture of their original settlers, a strong Kaqchikel identity emerged that still exists today.

Kaqchikel towns quickly became pulled into the economic orbit of the new colonial economy. Typically, a community would be assigned a particular supply "task" for the Spanish capital. For example, San Antonio Aguas Calientes was to supply grass for horses, as evidenced in a petition to the Crown in 1672 in which the inhabitants of San Antonio ask that their tribute demands be lessened:

> El común de San Antonio Aguas Calientes del valle de Guatemala pide perdón de tributos rezagados. Como es notorio, nosotros tenemos por oficio el dar sacate en esta ciudad en que nos ocupamos todo el año con que no tenemos lugar de poder sembrar a que se llega el que no tenemos tierras en que hacerlo y para pagar el tributo de maiz nos obliga a yrlo a buscar a otros pueblos a mucho costo en cuya atención a Vuestra Alteza pedimos y suplicamos sea muy servido. (Año 1672, A3.16 40 663 2809)

> The community of San Antonio Aguas Calientes in the valley of Guatemala requests to be excused from tributes levied. As is well known, we have as our task giving hay to this city, which keeps us busy all year long so we don't have anywhere to plant [corn] to the point that we have no lands on which to do so, and in order to pay the corn tribute, we have to go look for corn in other communities at a very high cost and we request and plead for your attention to this.

The residents of San Juan Comalapa were ordered to produce specified quantities of cocoa, salt, hens, reed mats, honey, and chili pepper, in addition to providing agricultural labor and other services (Francisco Del Paso, cited in Mejía 1985: 11–12).

Heavy labor demands were made to supply food for mining enterprises, further conquests, and other lucrative ventures. The new capital city required foodstuffs as well. Many Kaqchikel communities were enlisted in the provision of goods and services to the metropolis, and their new role significantly transformed their structure.

THE COLONIAL PERIOD

The Conquest of Mexico was accomplished with relative speed and ease compared to the Conquest of Guatemala. The implementation of an orderly colonial system was stalled for many years by events outside Guatemala and by the nature of the Conquest's leader, Pedro de Alvarado, whose first concern was his own enrichment. Rather than perform the sedentary tasks of administering a new government, Alvarado campaigned relentlessly, voyaging to Spain, the Spice Islands, and Peru to cement his personal fortune. The trauma of the Conquest and early Colonial Period critically weakened Mayan social and political organization. The face of the Mayan world was radically recast, and all previous customs had to accommodate a new order that ultimately served a distant foreign master (MacLeod 1973).

The Spanish Conquest of Guatemala in some ways echoed the Mexican intrusions of previous centuries but in other ways signaled a radical transformation. The preceding invaders eventually settled and became absorbed by their hosts, and the influence of their distant metropolis receded. In contrast, the Spaniards were not absorbed by the Indian society; rather, they built a separate world on top of it that consumed the human and material surpluses from below. And despite the periodic contractions of Spanish authority that characterized the following centuries, the control of Guatemalan resources remained firmly in non-Indian hands. The ensuing decades would disrupt most aspects of Indian life: community location and composition, social and political organization, genetic constitution, labor cycles and economic activity, belief systems and ceremonial life.

During the Colonial Period, the Indian community was caught between two competing forces: the labor needs of Creole enterprise and an alliance of Crown and Church craving subjects and souls.[1] In accommodating these forces and trying to remain intact, the new Mayan community was formed.

Local Spaniards sought fortune in a growing and increasingly capricious world commodities market in which control over a plentiful and cheap labor supply was their chief asset. Yet rapid declines in the Indian population inspired the development of successive labor systems. The colonial economy saw in the Indians an ideal work force able to travel great distances quickly on short notice to perform any task without complaint; needing minimal maintenance, able to subsist on small plots of the poorest soils while reserving the best yields for Spanish consumption; and content to relinquish their own family and community life for the betterment of the invaders. Thus, the Indian was pressed into the service of feeding and supplying an economic machine geared toward the production of wealth to earn the newcomers goods and influence.

The alliance of Church and Crown sought in the Indians an expansion of royal and Christian domain. The Crown sought ideal subjects to replicate Spanish life in the New World: Spanish in outlook and speech, populating Spanish-modeled towns, and increasing the number of the earth's souls entrusted to royal stewardship by gladly exchanging the fruits of their toil for the rewards of enlightened Christian rule. The Church, additionally, sought an inner transformation of the Indians: that they abandon their world view and its rituals intimately tied to the yearly agricultural cycle and accept the Christian deity and honor Him and His agents in their daily living.

The Reducciones

When the Spaniards first arrived in Guatemala, they reported that the Indians were settled in cities, just one of their many failures to understand the Indian world. The Mayas preferred a dispersed settlement pattern gravitating around a ceremonial and military center visited for periodic trading or ceremonial use or in times of crisis. It was likely just such a response to crisis that the Spaniards observed and interpreted as normal behavior.

Spanish attempts to organize and control the Indian populations for labor recruitment and religious conversion were frustrated by these dispersed settlement patterns as well as aggravated by tremendous population declines. Hence the Crown attempted to round up the Indians and settle them in nucleated towns, called *reducciones,* built on a Spanish model. The royal desire to "civilize" the new subjects coincided with the Creole need for more effective access to tribute and labor sources and the clerical goals of more efficient conversion. The justification of the system is evident in a letter from the bishop of neighboring Honduras, written in 1584 to the Crown, requesting permission to gather together the Indians of his territory:

> Que el obispo de Honduras había informado que los indios de su diócesis necesitaban de doctrina pero que no se les podía atender por la gran diversidad de lenguas, por vivir derramados en los montes, o

en pueblos pequeños y distantes, hecho que no permitía a los minis-
tros doctrinarios atenderlos constantemente y que por la pobreza de
los aborígenes no podía ser sostenido el cura y para salvar todo lo
anterior, era necesario reducir varios pueblos pequeños en nucleos
mayores, proyecto que ya existía y por esta razón se ordena al presidente, Garcia Valverde, que ponga en vigor las leyes que ordenan la
reducción y concentración de los indios para su doctrina. (AGCA
A1.29 1513 639 1584)

The bishop of Honduras had reported that the Indians of his diocese
needed doctrine but that he could not serve them due to the great
diversity of languages, because they lived spread out in the hills,
or in small and far away-hamlets, which did not allow the ministers
to serve them constantly, and that due to their poverty the aborigines could not support a priest and to solve all the forementioned
it would be necessary to reduce several small towns into larger nu-
clei, a project which already existed, and for that reason the president, García Valverde, is ordered to put in force the laws ordering
the reduction and concentration of the Indians for their religious
instruction.

The cultural effect of the *reducción* was doubtless one of simplifi-
cation, as fragments of linguistically and ethnically distinct groups were
forged into a single new community under Spanish supervision. The dispersed patterns favored by the Indians actually retarded the spread of
communicable diseases, and these newly formed towns suffered from
recurrent epidemics. Referring to population losses alone, Murdo
MacLeod (1973) posits a cultural or structural "amalgamation" in Indian communities. He cites communities reporting numerous clans in
1520 reduced to two or three by a later date.

However, resistance to cultural fusion existed. George Lovell (1985)
reports cases in the Cuchumatán region of pre-Conquest ethnic affiliations persisting in *barrio* formations, recognized as tax-paying entities
one hundred years later. Lovell also states that many Indians left the
reducciones to settle in small outlying communities, returning to pre-
Conquest patterns.

Though life in a *reducción* may have increased the Mayas' exposure to the Spanish language, it may not have markedly increased their
need to use it. During this period, the Crown's policy was to restrict access to Indian communities to missionary clergy trained in the native
language.

Colonial Language Policies

During the Colonial Period, the Crown's goal to fashion the denizens of its new territories into proper imperial subjects held constant. However, royal strategy on how best to "Castilianize" the Indians vacillated considerably, particularly with regard to Crown policy on the Indian languages. Specifically, whether Indians were to be taught the Castilian tongue or receive religious instruction in their own languages became an issue producing a long series of alternating tactics and contradictory decrees.

New World language policies revolved around the question of Indian participation in the Spaniards' world. The Crown wished to forge a direct bond between Indian and court through a common language—its own. Others preferred a more circuitous link. The Creole role as broker in the regulation of Indian labor and tribute was justified and enhanced by the presence of language barriers. The Church, seeking above all native conversion, quickly deduced that the indigenous languages would prove the most expedient medium for its purposes. The missionary orders constantly pressed their case before the Crown, seeking royal endorsement and funding for Indian language education. At times, Crown policy reflected the missions' interests in Indian languages; otherwise, policy promoted the use of a single imperial language.

Spanish instruction for the Indian population generally found little support in the New World. Indians who indeed learned Spanish did not tend to teach other Indians. Bilingualism endowed them with a lucrative status as interpreters which they were loath to share or endanger. The land-holding *encomenderos,* commissioned by the Law of Burgos with the education of their charges, were reluctant to finance such instruction. The New Laws of 1542 transferred this duty to the missionary orders who worked most closely with Indian communities. But many of these friars had received linguistic training in Spain that specifically equipped them for the task of studying and describing the new languages they encountered. These friars produced grammars and dictionaries for the languages they studied, as well as religious works. They also found that the Indians accepted conversion much more readily in their own languages than in Spanish.

The Crown's attempts to impose its will in the face of intractable resistance were diverse. A series of contradictory edicts issued from Spain from 1550 to 1778 evidenced the Crown's indecision. In 1550 King Carlos V asked the missionary orders to make the teaching of Spanish to the

Indians a priority, since, ostensibly, the mysteries of the faith could only be taught in that language. Pronouncements were directed at specific orders and regions. The Augustinian and Franciscan orders working in Guatemala, for example, received orders to teach Spanish to the Indians in the city of Santiago (AGCA A1.23 191 1511 139 1550), and Franciscans received orders to teach Spanish to the Indians under their charge in Nicaragua (AGCA A1.23 191 1511 140 1550).

The missionaries did not comply, in part because Spanish language instruction would have slowed their own agenda of evangelization and also because of logistical obstacles. There were simply not enough Spanish teachers for the job, and most Indian communities were far too poor to pay for such services. Decades later the Crown issued another decree whose phrasing reflected a clearer recognition of local realities: local administrators were to establish Spanish classes without causing inconvenience or expense to the Indians and only for those Indians who voluntarily requested them (AGCA A1.23 1514 68 1605).

In the case of Mexico, the need for a unifying language was admirably filled by Nahuatl, the tongue of the Aztec empire. Recognizing its utility both as a tool of conversion and as a lingua franca for New Spain, the friars took up Nahuatl enthusiastically, using it as a language of mission operation for many different Indian groups. Charles V's successor, his son Philip III, responding to proposals from friars, pronounced Nahuatl the official language for the Indians of New Spain in 1570.

New Spain also saw efforts by friars of the Franciscan and Dominican orders to teach Indian students to read and write Latin, in order to enhance their grasp of Christian doctrine and enable them to help translate works of Latin into Nahuatl. Several schools or *colegios* were established with royal support, most notably Santa Cruz de Tlatelolco, founded near Mexico City in 1536. But the Indian students were too successful, at times surpassing Iberian clergy at Latin and forgetting their subservient status. Complaints arose that the schools were producing proud Indians. Shirley Brice Heath (1972: 30) cites from the *Códice Franciscano* a critic who warned that "the Indians who know Latin recognize by their saying of the masses and sacred rites which priests are idiots." The Crown withdrew support, and these *colegios* ceased to function by the end of the sixteenth century.

Attempts to install Nahuatl as an Indian lingua franca, or to instruct young Indians in Latin, are not documented in Guatemala at this period. However, throughout the late sixteenth and early seventeenth century

Guatemala received a series of imperial rulings stipulating that missionaries know the Indian languages of their flocks. At least eight edicts were sent as general policy reminders between 1575 and 1629.[2]

Apparently, these edicts were to be taken in earnest. Between 1609 and 1636 the Crown made repeated inquiries about clergy who were not knowledgeable in the languages of their parishes. For example, the Crown wanted to know why a friar named Diego de Canave had been at his post in Trujillo for three years and still had not learned the local language (AGCA A1.23 1515 75 1620).

Fifty years later Crown policy reverted to its previous stance supporting Spanish instruction of Indians. In 1686 King Charles II mandated that all officials of both Church and Crown comply immediately with all Spanish promotion laws. Subsequent edicts in the 1690s called for schools to be established in "todas las ciudades, villas, pueblos, y lugares donde vivieren aborígenes" (all the cities, villas, towns, and places where aborigines live; AGCA A1.23 1523 36 1691) to teach the Indians the Castilian tongue.

Colonial Racial and Ethnic Policies

During the initial phases of the Spanish Conquest and colonization of the New World, race became the prime determinant of social status. The forceful collision of the European, Amerindian, and African races simplified previous in-group stratifications. In the New World all Spaniards became conquerors, all Indians the conquered, and all Africans the enslaved. But the racial underpinning of the colonial social order gradually weakened as miscegenation and cultural change produced a much more complex system.

Spaniard mixed with Indian to produce a burgeoning class of mestizos. Spaniards and Africans together produced mulattos, and the progeny of Indian and African were called *zambos*. In time, the racially mixed populations rivaled the numbers of their original components. As individual genetic features became more generally distributed, cultural and linguistic traits became the more salient markings of social status, particularly in the case of Highland Guatemala. Central American tribute documents from the eighteenth century reveal the porous nature of the ethnic boundary between Indian and mestizo. In 1798 the government attempted to reexamine the system in which self-identification might determine exempt status in a series of decrees to "establish who were truly Indians from the so-called 'Ladinos' upon changing their dress and as such asked to be exonerated of paying tribute" (AGCA A3.16 4795 241 1798).

The Spaniards recognized ethnic and language differences among the Indians, especially as they applied to alliances and conquest warfare, and they manipulated these divisions in creating a new society. Of particular interest in Guatemala was the special status given to Mexican Indians, mostly Nahuatl-speaking, who accompanied the Spanish invasion. The Mexicans were allotted certain towns and *barrios* as their own and made exempt from certain taxes in reward for their services. In 1770 the residents of a town neighboring the capital requested tribute reclassification because they were descendants of "tlascaltecas y mexicanos" (AGCA A3.2 B165 708 1770).

Though some tribute requirements were exclusively levied on Indians, the offspring of an Indian with a non-Indian was exempted, as well as Indians involved in certain marriage arrangements with non-Indians. In 1793 the president of Costa Rica, Bernardo Troncoso, advocated prohibiting Indians from marrying mestizas because the first thing they did in these cases was request exoneration from tribute (AGCA A3.1 4284 528 94 1793). By the end of the eighteenth century petitions for tax-exempt status from Guatemalan Indians document the institutional means and incentives to escape Indian identity. Several documents of this period contain petitions from taxpayers throughout Guatemala asking to be reclassified as Ladinos.[3]

The Colonial Period witnessed many pressures on the Mayas to Ladinoize, a process providing an escape route for the discontented in Indian communities and those on the economic or social fringe. Indian identity was intimately tied to the community of origin and residence, and the response to relocation of an individual outside this community was almost always to Ladinoize.

THE MODERN PERIOD

By the dawn of the eighteenth century, as the balance of European powers shifted, the might of Spain was eclipsed by the expanding influence of England and France. In 1700 the Spanish Crown passed from the Hapsburgs to the Bourbons, precipitating a century of reforms attempting to introduce the principles of the Enlightenment into colonial government. These reforms would affect the Mayas in several ways.

The intent of the Bourbon reforms was to make colonial administration more efficient and productive. The traditional alliance of landholders, Crown, and Church was to make room for emerging merchant and entrepreneurial classes. Efforts to curb the power and influence of the clergy limited monastery construction and the collection of Church taxes, especially in Indian parishes. Commercial reforms attempted to stimulate the economy. Export taxes were reduced, encouraging planters to experiment with new crops. Education reforms called for universal education, and the establishment of rural schools eventually became part of the modern political agenda.

The Bourbon reforms did not meet universal acceptance; as a result, Central American politics became increasingly polarized. Forces sympathetic to Crown and Church coalesced under the Conservative banner, while those favoring Creole enfranchisement, republicanism, free trade, and commercial development formed the ranks of the Liberals. The conflict climaxed in the War of Independence in the early nineteenth century, and bloody clashes between the two factions characterize much of modern Central American political history. Shortly after Independence the Liberals came to power, led by Mariano Gálvez, whose modernization plan included a national head tax, the encouragement of foreign investment to finance the construction of roads and port facilities, and anticlerical measures. Response to the Liberal program was popular revolt, culminating in a Conservative uprising that brought Rafael Carrera to power. Carrera's strategy was to dismantle the Gálvez reforms and to reinstate the power of the Church and other hispanic institutions. By the latter third of the nineteenth century the Liberals were once again in power, under Rufino Barrios, who was more successful at implementing the changes begun under Gálvez. The legacy of the Barrios administration has been a national economy ever more geared to and dependent upon agricultural exports and a migratory labor force from the Highlands.

The Liberal strategy for progress relied on foreign capital earned through commodity exports, and the Barrios administration coincided with the rise of coffee production. Guatemala's chief assets were certain geographical advantages of soil and climate and an abundant labor supply. But the Indian population, who traditionally had shown little enthusiasm for mercantile projects involving Spaniards, were more inclined to labor in their own fields than in those of entrepreneurs. The Mayas and their tenacious hold to community were perceived as an obstacle to progress.

Barrios aimed to liberate the Mayas from the confines of their communal lives, increasing their contact with the "civilizing" influence of the Ladino population. In general, his efforts to stimulate export production were detrimental to Mayan communities. Ladinos were encouraged to settle in Indian towns, often monopolizing new commercial activities. Communal lands were usurped and sold at low cost to commercial planters. Forced labor, vagrancy laws, and debt peonage were used to induce the Indians to provide labor on the plantations (Woodward 1985), resulting in the seasonal migrations to the Pacific coast that continue to the present day and have been so movingly described by Rigoberta Menchú (Burgos Debray 1992) and Gaspar Pedro González (1995).

Barrios also renewed attacks on the power of the Church, to the point of exiling many bishops. The cutback in the numbers of clergy left many rural communities without a priest and diminished the influence of the Church in many Mayan communities. The ensuing years have witnessed growing assaults on the Indian community that formed during the Colonial Period and served as a bastion of Mayan culture and language. The introduction of vaccines and antibiotics through national health programs resulted in population growth, escalating demand for a dwindling land supply. Growing numbers of Mayas are obliged to seek their livelihood outside their natal community in a Spanish-speaking world.

The introduction of regular bus transportation, mass media, and public schools has brought the outside world to the Mayan community and, with it, increased need for the Spanish language. Whether the resulting expansion of bilingualism will threaten the survival of the Mayan languages remains to be seen.

NOTES

1. The term "Creole" is generally understood as the offspring of Spanish parents born on American soil. Colonial policy restricted Creoles from holding important political and religious posts reserved for peninsulars, those born in Spain.

2. "Que los seculares nombrados para el servicio de doctrinas deben conocer la lengua indígena de tal lugar a donde se les destine" (May 3, 1575, A1.23 1512 479 1575). "Se ordena al presidente de Oidores se tenga especial cuidado en el cumplimiento de las leyes que disponían que para la nominación y servicio en curatos de pueblos de indios, el clérigo debería tener conocimiento de la lengua indígena predominante de la región" (June 25, 1605, A1.23 1514 68 1605).

3. "Instancia de San Andrés Juárez indio del pueblo de Stgo. Atitlán, sobre que sus hijos no deberían pagar tributo por haber sido abbidos [*sic*] con mujer ladina" (AGCA A3.16 4741 239 21 1790). "El apoderado de Franciso Hernández, indio oficial de zapatería, vecino del Barrio de los Horteleros de Santo Domingo Ciudad de Guatemala, casado con Magdalena Girón, mestiza, hija de Lope Girón de Alvarado, pide que éstos no paguen tributos por ser de clase mestiza. Corre agregada la información de legitimidad de Magdalena Girón de Alvarado" (AGCA Tributos A3.16 2803 521 40 1621).

4. CASE STUDY ONE
San Marcos La Laguna

Julia Becker Richards

THE COMMUNITY
Introduction

San Marcos La Laguna, located in the Department of Sololá on the northwestern shore of Lake Atitlán, is one of the smallest *municipios* (municipalities) in the country. With a population of approximately 1,500 and occupying a land area of twelve square kilometers, it is a land-scarce community, particularly considering that less than half the land is cultivable.

From a linguistic standpoint, San Marcos is situated at the border of three Mayan language areas: Kaqchikel, K'iche', and Tz'utujil. The southern boundary of the community is defined by Lake Atitlán itself. To the north lies the *municipio* of Santa Lucía Utatlán, a community of K'iche' speakers. To the west San Marcos borders the Tz'utujil-speaking *municipio* of San Pablo La Laguna, and to the east it borders the Kaqchikel-speaking community of Tzununá, a village or township belonging to the town of Santa Cruz La Laguna. As in most of the towns located on the shores of Lake Atitlán, the population in San Marcos is nucleated within a single administrative community. The town itself, however, is divided into three distinct residential neighborhoods or *barrios* on the slopes of two hilly ridges that form the wall of the San Marcos arroyo canyon.

For much of its history San Marcos has been relatively inaccessible, mainly due to its location on the northwestern shore of Lake Atitlán, an area with limited commercial contact with larger regional market centers. In addition, high promontories separate San Marcos from its neighboring communities, further inhibiting communication with nearby lake and Highland communities.

There are three ways to approach the town of San Marcos La Laguna—by water, by a steep footpath that extends from the northern crater rim of the Lake Atitlán Basin to the town located on the shore one thousand meters below, or by a dirt road along the shoreline of Lake Atitlán, which links the town to neighboring San Pablo to the west and Tzununá to the east.

Until 1978 all access to San Marcos was restricted to travel on footpath or by canoe (see Richards and Richards 1975). In the mid-1960s a launch service began on Lake Atitlán, crossing the lake from Panajachel three times per week. It did not dock at San Marcos but rather at neighboring San Pablo and San Pedro La Laguna. In 1974–1975, the time of my first fieldwork in San Marcos, one had to leave San Marcos at 3:00 A.M. to undertake a cautious hike in the stygian predawn in order to catch the boat in San Pablo at 4:00 A.M. Produce for market had to be carried out on men's backs with the aid of a tumpline or, in the case of women, in large baskets carefully balanced on top of their heads.

The first launch service directly linking San Marcos to other communities was initiated in 1978. This came about when a private German foundation donated a forty-passenger motorized launch to the San Marcos Consumer Cooperative. Mismanagement on the part of the cooperative, however, as well as exorbitant costs needed to maintain the precision motor, ended the service. In the same year a private launch company in Panajachel began providing San Marcos with twice per day service. For several years these transportation facilities had little economic impact on the town. No more than a handful of people from San Marcos traveled across the lake to Panajachel by motorized launch because of the costly fare. Some people—mostly women—used the launch service to journey to San Pedro, but for the most part villagers continued to walk or travel by canoe. Most of the launches that today ply the Panajachel–San Pedro La Laguna route that includes San Marcos belong to two entrepreneurial families from San Pedro. With over six stops scheduled per day at each of the towns on the route, Marqueños almost exclusively use the commercial launch service to move about within the region, in spite of the considerable cost. Over the years the large wooden canoes that could transport fifteen or twenty people and their cargo— once a common sight over all of Lake Atitlán—have been replaced by steel-hulled motorized launches.

The footpath that ascends the arroyo canyon of San Marcos and links the town with the K'iche'-speaking community of Santa Lucía Utatlán has fallen into disuse in recent years, and what was once a magnificent foot causeway is now overgrown with vegetation and practically impassable. In 1974–1975 and even in 1979–1981 (my second fieldwork period in San Marcos) at least a dozen Marqueño families made the four-hour trek up the steep mountain path to the Santa Lucía market two times per week to sell fruit; in addition to these regular vendors, many other Marqueños traveled along the path on a less regular basis to attend the Thursday or Sunday markets or transact other business.

In years past many Marqueños also regularly traveled to the Santa Clara La Laguna market held on Saturdays. Today, however, only one family relies on this market. With the introduction of motorized transportation, the market centers frequented by Marqueños have shifted away from the K'iche' Highlands to the Tz'utujil community of San Pedro La Laguna (which began an ad hoc market in the early 1980s) and the Kaqchikel community of Panajachel (a bus runs from here to the market center of Sololá).

Although Marqueños regularly journey to larger market centers to sell their fruit, transactions of lesser magnitude occur within the immediate context of the western shore communities. Until the early 1980s there was a footpath that linked San Marcos to neighboring towns. In 1982 a dirt road was completed. At the time this was seen as certain to bring about a major transformation of the community—a prospect feared by many Marqueños and welcomed by others. In actuality it has had little significant impact on the community, largely because rains cause deep ruts to develop, rendering passage difficult. At best there are one or two trucks per week that pass through town. The road is mostly used today by the San Pedro schoolteachers who work in San Marcos and travel each day to and from the community on motorcycles.

The History of San Marcos La Laguna

The people of San Marcos refer to their community as *qa siwan tinamit,* 'our community in the ravines.' This depiction is not only a geographical fact—San Marcos is a rather isolated town set on steep mountain slopes—but also connotes a metaphorical dimension wherein poverty and a cataclysmic social history place the town and its people on the very margin of survival.

To be sure, the history of San Marcos is one of serial catastrophe; plagues, mudslides, and land boundary disputes have forced the inhabitants to relocate their settlement several times. The original Marqueño homeland was in the present-day location of Paquip, approximately ten kilometers south of San Lucas Tolimán, in the upper piedmont region. According to historical reconstructions of the prehispanic Quichean kingdoms (see Carmack 1968; Orellana 1984), Paquip probably lay on the Tz'utujil-Kaqchikel Lowland frontier, alternately subject to Tz'utu-jil or Kaqchikel rule as land was gained or lost in internecine conflicts.

According to San Marcos oral history, the inhabitants of Paquip were plagued by attacks of mountain lions (although McBryde [1945: 120], in his history of the lake region, says that they were plagued by attacks of vampire bats). Following the imposition of Spanish colonial order, the inhabitants ostensibly defied the mandates of an early Spanish priest to convert to Christianity. For their recalcitrance, they suffered divine punishment and were forced by menacing lions to abandon their home-lands. After their exodus from Paquip, probably around 1580, the in-habitants settled on the lakeshore near present-day Cerro de Oro. The owner of the land, a resident of Santiago Atitlán, evicted them from this location, and the Marqueños were forced to take refuge across the lake at the base of a steep arroyo valley at a site called Payan Chicol (today Jaibalito). This land was under the jurisdiction of Santiago Atitlán; therefore, after the town was founded as San Marcos Paquip in 1584, it fell under the administrative control of the *corregimiento* of Atitlán. Gerardo Aguirre (1972: 109) writes that later a number of Kaqchikel-speaking inhabitants of Sololá moved into the Payan Chicol valley and "together they intermingled and formed a town." By 1707 the name of the town had changed to San Marcos La Laguna (Aguirre 1972: 110).

After a series of floods, mudslides, and other natural disasters (not to mention extensive litigation with Santa Cruz La Laguna and Tzununá over ownership of the land), the Marqueños fled Payan Chicol to a nearby valley. In September 1721, after a massive mudslide virtually destroyed the community once again, the Marqueños moved to another arroyo valley about three miles west of Jaibalito.

In 1724 Marqueños petitioned the royal *audiencia* and were granted the right to relocate in their present-day site. This land, like the Payan Chicol site, belonged to a Maya from Santiago Atitlán whose descen-dants were living in San Pablo. Although the land was officially surveyed and the town was legally founded in 1726, extensive litigation ensued. Disputes between San Marcos and San Pablo over municipal boundaries continue to this day.

The people of San Marcos were not spared additional hardships and disaster. In 1846 a September tropical storm caused a torrent of water and mud to cascade down the arroyo, and the town was completely de-stroyed. After rebuilding the town, the inhabitants were victimized once again, in 1881, by yet another flood. This deluge ravaged the commu-nity, leading the inhabitants to rebuild it on the two mountainous flanks about two hundred feet above the level of the lake. In 1949 the church, the school, and the municipal building, the only community structures remaining in the valley floor, were destroyed by yet another flood and subsequently were moved and rebuilt.

Physical Characteristics of the Town

When one arrives at the San Marcos dock by boat today, several newly incorporated features of the community immediately stand out. The shore of the San Marcos bay (where bulls were pastured in 1975 and onions were grown in 1980) has recently been parceled into several lots where "chalets" have been built. Some of these are weekend retreats belonging to Guatemala City families; others belong to permanent residents, mostly Europeans, who have bought land in San Marcos with the expectation of living alternative lifestyles.

Another major change in the physical landscape of San Marcos is the presence of an exceptionally large municipal building prominently situated on the hill above the dock. This three-story structure was completed in 1988 with funds allocated to the local government from what was known as the "eight percent" fund. Since the 1985 Constitution of Guatemala mandated that eight percent of the national budget be apportioned directly to the country's municipal governments, significant infrastructural developments have altered the appearance of many communities like San Marcos. In San Marcos the eight percent funds have been used to construct a public meeting building and amphitheatre, an extension to the primary school, and a small parklike area lined with commercial stands. The funds have also been used to replace the steep winding dirt paths circulating through the town with several cement streets.

The town of San Marcos is tightly clustered within three *barrios*. Chwinimab'aj is located on the eastern saddleback ridge of the *municipio;* it is the largest of the *barrios* and includes half of the San Marcos population. On the western saddleback ridge lies the second largest barrio, Xelema', with one-third of the population. Pacheb'en, located on the eastern terrace above the alluvial valley and below the municipal building, is the smallest of the San Marcos residential clusters, accounting for about 15 percent of the population.

In 1980 over half of the households lived in single-room dwellings; now the majority maintain at least one additional room, usually a separate structure, where cooking and eating take place. Some families have an additional room that they use as a formal living space, housing a radio or television (twenty homes now have televisions), an altar, framed photos of family members, and other belongings. The traditional type of house construction, consisting of simple cornstalk cane walls or cornstalk cane frames plastered over with mud in wattle-and-daub fashion (which in 1980 accounted for 91 percent of the house dwellings), has in many cases been replaced by adobe wall constructions. Type of house construction is an indicator of wealth in the community, with wealthier families using more elaborate lime stucco wattle-and-daub or adobe constructions. With few exceptions, laminated sheet metal now caps the household structures, replacing the straw roofing once characteristic of Lake Atitlán dwellings.

Religion

There are four churches in San Marcos. The Catholic church is located in the valley between the two sides of town. San Marcos is predominantly (approximately 75 percent) Catholic. Unlike some Highland Mayan communities, where conversion to Protestantism has approached 50 percent or more (see Stoll 1990), San Marcos has not experienced widespread conversion. However, the town has seen a gradual shift to Protestantism, from approximately 7 percent of the families in 1974 (Kagan et al. 1979: 7) to 10 percent in 1981 and to 25 percent in 1995.

In the last forty years a deep rift has grown between the "modern" Catholics or followers of Catholic Action (a movement brought to the community from San Pedro in 1949) and the traditional Catholics, whose religious rituals center around the activities of the *cofradía*, the traditional hierarchical religious institution dedicated to the maintenance of saints and the observance of religious ritual (cf. Orellana 1975; Warren 1978). The majority of the followers of Catholic Action live in the Chwinimab'aj and Pacheb'en neighborhoods, which are generally acknowledged to be more "progressive" than Xelema', the neighborhood where the *cofradía* is located.

The Protestants in San Marcos belong to three different churches: the Assembly of God, the Prince of Peace, and the Pilgrim Church. Protestantism came to San Marcos in the 1950s from San Pedro La Laguna; but unlike San Pedro, where Protestants are from some of the community's more wealthy and influential families (Paul 1968), in San Marcos Protestants have tended to be among the most economically and socially marginal families. In the past five years or so that characterization h:

changed somewhat, however, with more prominent disaffected Catholics converting to Protestantism.

Within the past few years there has been an accelerated conversion to Protestantism, due ostensibly to a focal event. In 1994 the old Catholic church in San Marcos was demolished to make way for the construction of a modern one. The mayor of San Marcos, a key figure promoting the construction of a new church, promised to have the municipal government pay the bulk of the expenses (apparently he was not too clear about the separation of church and state). The old church was demolished and construction began on the new one; however, funding for the construction ran out, leaving only half-constructed walls as testimony to this monument of false promise. Now, with the Catholic community divided over the wisdom of having embarked upon the project in the first place and being, moreover, without a church structure in which to celebrate the Mass, more and more of the community's families are fleeing the factionalism within the Catholic church and are entering the Protestant churches. One of the key persons who recently switched affiliation is the mayor himself.

Agriculture and Occupation in San Marcos La Laguna

Land in San Marcos is held in communal usufruct. San Marcos is one of the few Indian municipalities of Guatemala whose community land title remained unaffected by the reforms of the Barrios administration enacted before the turn of the century. This means that, in theory, individual or household land rights are granted by the municipal governing body on a temporary basis and then renegotiated in order for land to change hands among community members.

In actuality, however, a good portion of the community's land is locked in de facto family ownership. This valuable family-locked land includes property located close to the town center as well as fertile, silt-laden lakeshore land that extends approximately 100 meters from the shoreline into the alluvial valley.

In years past, intensive cash cropping of onions, coffee, oranges, avocados, and *jocotes* (*Spondias purpurrea*) took place in the lakeshore alluvial valley. Further up the San Marcos arroyo the land is strewn with large boulders—testimony to the community's many floods and mudslides—and there some fruit trees are planted amid sporadically occurring corn and beans or *milpa* plots. The area near the lakeshore has experienced the most dramatic changes over the nearly twenty-five years of my acquaintance with San Marcos. In 1974–1975 the area nearest the lake was used almost exclusively to pasture bulls. The bulls did not belong to Marqueños, but to townspeople from neighboring communities who would place their male calves in the charge of Marqueños for about one year. The Marqueños were paid the dollar equivalent of about ten cents per day to care for and feed each calf. In the period 1979–1981 far fewer cattle were pastured on the lakeshore in order to use the land for growing onions. Onion cultivation had become a major cash crop in all the towns on the western end of the lake. The more cash-rich Pedranos, Juaneros, and Pauleños used gasoline-powered water pumps to irrigate their crops, while Marqueños carried buckets of water from the lake to splash-irrigate the onion gardens.

By the early 1990s the lakeshore land had fallen almost entirely into the hands of outsiders, mostly foreigners who gradually moved to San Marcos through an association with a private voluntary organization, Live Better, that receives donations from Europe. This organization began operating in San Marcos in 1989 as an early childhood intervention effort, providing nutritional supplements and preschool training to San Marcos children under six years of age. Today an estimated fifteen families—friends, relatives, and associates of the project—live in the lakeshore region, constituting what the Marqueños refer to as the *barrio de gringos* (neighborhood of foreigners). Now, as the Live Better development project is coming to a close and no longer providing employment for widows, preschool training for children, or the many other services it once provided, there is an ironic twist. In the perception of Marqueños, this organization that entered the community to assist in its development ultimately dispossessed many townspeople of their land.

Because of the communal nature of land tenure in San Marcos, it is uncertain what the future holds for land sold to foreigners and Guatemalan nationals. A similar situation exists in the case of agricultural land sold to Maya entrepreneurs from neighboring communities such as San Pedro Laguna or Santiago Atitlán. Unlike other lake communities, where land ownership is predominantly in private hands, in San Marcos land theoretically cannot legally be sold but only leased for a period of twenty-five years.

Prior to the late 1980s the fruit and coffee trees growing in the community belonged to Marqueños. This is not to imply, however, that Marqueños were in complete control of their production resources. The almost perpetual debt cycle into which most families were bound kept them at a disadvantage in the market economy. Although Marqueño families owned the fruit trees, they often sold the production rights to the trees to brokers from San Pablo and San Pedro well in advance of the harvest period. These brokers generally disbursed their advances at critical times in the yearly cycle, when food and money in San Marcos were scarce. With the high morbidity rates that existed in San Marcos, villagers frequently sold tree rights when they needed to buy medicine for a family member. Because Marqueños generally had to sell rights to their trees far in advance of the marketing season, they were at a considerable disadvantage in obtaining a fair price for their produce. At harvest times, the brokers would come into San Marcos with laborers from their own towns to pick the avocados or oranges from trees whose rights had been sold to them in advance.

During the early 1980s the cycle of economic insolvency for many Marqueño households was so great that certain poorer households had to sell tree rights at paltry prices, in order to pay off other outstanding debts. In 1981 no individual Marqueño had ever negotiated a bank loan. Because of lack of access to institutional credit facilities, they had to resort to borrowing from loansharks at rates that were sometimes ten times greater than commercial bank rates. The same outside fruit brokers would often fill in as moneylenders and charge interest rates as high as 10 percent per month. This practice of selling picking rights only contributed to the Marqueños' continued impoverishment and subordinated regional economic status.

In 1987 a major land sale occurred in San Marcos due to the corruption of local authorities, especially the mayor of San Marcos himself. Several hundred *cuerdas* of land were sold to Pauleños and Pedranos, who quickly put the land into coffee production. Much of this land included the fertile valley land cultivated in fruit trees and coffee located behind the lakeshore properties. Not only are the Marqueños at a disadvantaged position now in having sold the picking rights to most of their trees, but they have lost the land as well. During my visits to the town, the lamented topic of Marqueños' having lost land to outside Mayas, Ladinos, and foreigners was brought up repeatedly.

In my early periods of fieldwork in San Marcos, about half the families of the community engaged in seasonal migratory labor. Today hardly anyone in the community migrates to the Pacific coastal plain to work as a laborer on a cotton plantation or to the higher-elevation Pacific piedmont region to work on a coffee plantation.

In San Marcos the migratory wage labor market traditionally functioned as an important means of generating cash for the household unit.

In a retrospective migration survey that covered the years 1977–1980, most (70 percent) of the 104 households experiencing a migratory episode had only one member migrating, but in the remaining 30 percent there were two, three, four, or even five household members who migrated (M. Richards 1987: 346). Migrants tended to be predominantly male, but an appreciable number (22 percent) were females. The average age of the female migrants (seventeen) was younger than that of male migrants (twenty-three). Most migrants engaged in only one migratory episode during the season, but there were some individuals who migrated in serial fashion, going for two- or four-week stints, returning to San Marcos to rest, and then embarking upon a new migratory venture. Marqueños primarily migrated to work on cotton plantations (70 percent of migratory episodes) and coffee plantations (27 percent of migratory episodes). In 3 percent of the migratory episodes Marqueños went to other types of plantations (sugarcane, citronella, cattle ranches). Whereas men tended to migrate to cotton plantations, women generally migrated to coffee plantations.

Through migration, many Marqueños gained enhanced exposure to the Spanish-speaking Ladino world. From the moment Marqueños boarded the trucks in San Pedro or Santiago and journeyed to the coast to the time they returned to their home community, they temporarily joined the ranks of a rural proletariat labor population. As migrants, Marqueños became integrated into the commercial plantation system and came into contact with Ladinos and Indians from other places.

Marqueños typically became employed on a plantation through an organized labor recruitment process. Highland labor contractors with connections to the management of specific plantations advanced sums of cash to potential workers, usually during the town festival or at critical times of food shortage. Marqueños thus were bound into a debt labor system from which it was very difficult to escape, especially since debt cycles were often multiple—Marqueños had to pay off some debts by incurring others.

A decline in cotton production in Guatemala curtailed the participation of migrant labor; although coffee continues to rely heavily on migrant labor, few Marqueños today migrate to coffee plantations. This is due to alternative income-earning strategies available, mostly in the form of small crafts sold to tourists or more commonly to brokers involved in the artisanry export market. One of the principal products Marqueños manufacture today are small rice-filled crocheted balls. On a good day a Marqueño can make a dozen of these, which can be sold for about a twenty-five *quetzal* profit (roughly five dollars). Another primary source of cash for Marqueños is working as agricultural day laborers in the neighboring communities of San Pablo, San Juan, and San Pedro.

From 1975 until about 1988 between twenty and forty Marqueño women were able to generate cash through weaving. An American adventurer who rode his bicycle down from Illinois and eventually came to live in San Marcos in 1975 set up a weaving business wherein he designed the fabrics and commissioned women to weave for him. This enterprise had a marked effect on the local economy, especially because it afforded the women involved a viable source of cash income. The American eventually married a Marqueña and in 1981 moved out of San Marcos and took up residence in Panajachel; although he is still in the weaving business, over the years he has gradually reduced his purchase volume from San Marcos to the point that today his business involves only one or two Marqueñas. Most commercial weaving done by Marqueñas today involves weaving and embroidering *huipiles* for sale to other Marqueñas who do not possess those skills or have insufficient time to weave or adorn their own clothes.

The mainstay of the Marqueño economy is still maize and bean agriculture. I have chosen to discuss some of the alternative modes of income generation first because that is where the greatest changes have come about over the years. Traditional agriculture is extremely important within the culture, functioning as a subsistence activity for Marqueños. However, San Marcos is land scarce, and, more importantly, good cultivable land is in short supply. The best agricultural land is close to the town and the lakeshore, precisely the land that has been sold to outsiders.

The main *milpa* fields are located on the slopes of the mountains above the town. However, there is a diminishing return on cultivating land that is increasingly distant from the town (some plots being located as far as a three-hour walk away): only for a limited number of families—those endowed with sufficient teenage or adult male laborers—is it worthwhile to work the distant parcels of cultivable land. Most of the San Marcos lands that lie beyond a one-hour walking distance fall within a jurisdiction of communal usufruct; although theoretically anyone can petition land for a subsistence parcel, the family's demographic profile can mitigate against being granted that land. For example, a male head of household from a newly formed family with two children under five years of age would not be granted a parcel of land lying three hours away from the community because he simply would lack the time to secure production adequately; distant lands tend to be allocated to households with several teenage sons.

The household's demographic structure essentially dictates its economic production. However, even the older, larger, and wealthier households in San Marcos have a limited economy of scale. In 1980, for example, the average-sized household had planted less than half a hectare in a *milpa*. Corn and beans produced from the *milpa* are rarely sold, and production never satisfies consumption needs. Slightly over half the households in the 1979–1980 agricultural cycle could produce enough corn to sustain them for two months of the year; for the remaining ten months they had to buy corn at the market price. Only 35 percent of households could produce enough corn to last them more than six months (M. Richards 1987).

Economically speaking, San Marcos operates on a very thin margin of survivability. When one factors in the high incidence of infectious disease that affects the population and the cost of cure, that very thin margin is made even thinner. During the two periods in which I undertook intensive fieldwork in the village, it became clear that Marqueños had little choice but to resort to practices such as seasonal wage labor migration in order to cover basic survival needs or to pay off multiple creditors. The overlaid cycles of debt to which many Marqueños had become bound forced them to scramble to earn cash or to negotiate yet another debt. Most Marqueños had resorted to practicing a kind of "fugitive" behavior with regard to their economic strategy. Today, although migratory labor is no longer a principal feature of Marqueño life, the need to generate money to buy the day's food or the medicines needed for a sick household member or to pay off a debt being demanded by a creditor keeps the majority of Marqueños in a state of constant economic uncertainty. The lack of a projective economic venture places them at a continual disadvantage in terms of the price of goods, land, and labor and subjects them to a perpetual cycle of exploitation.

Schooling in San Marcos

The first opportunity available to San Marcos residents to receive formal schooling occurred at the end of the eighteenth century. In response to a communiqué from King Carlos III urging the creation of public primary schools, the mayor of Sololá authorized the establishment of a regional school in San Pedro La Laguna in 1779. This school was to serve children from the western Lake Atitlán communities of San Marcos, San

Pablo, San Juan, and San Pedro. According to early parish records, only a handful of children from the communities outlying San Pedro actually attended the classes; a report sent to the mayor of Sololá in 1800 read: "All the Indians in general embrace with such repugnancy the establishment of schools that, even persuading them that they do not have to give anything to the teachers, they resist sending their children" (in Aguirre 1972: 381).

In the late 1870s, after primary education was declared "free and compulsory" under the Barrios regime (see Gonzales Orellana 1960), the town of San Pablo received authorization to establish its first school. Although Marqueños were assigned to this school, intercommunity antagonisms were so great that they refused to help finance the construction of the school or to send their children there for classes.

Around 1920 San Marcos opened its first public school. It was built in the valley, across from the church and to the west of the municipal building. The adobe building had two rooms, one for girls and the other for boys. At first there was no division made by grade or attained skills, but later, during the Jorge Ubico period, the groups were divided into Castilianization and first grade. Castilianization, first instituted in rural Guatemala prior to World War II, was intended to be a preparatory year for teaching indigenous children oral Spanish and for introducing school culture.

Villagers who were schooled during this period report that because school was obligatory they attended, but always under orders of the mayor and in fear of the willow switch. Marqueños remember that on the mornings when the teacher would actually show up (alcoholism seems to have plagued teacher attendance) pupils spent hour after hour learning to write their names and practicing their signatures. The afternoons were dedicated to making "toe weavings" for the girls and maguey string for the boys, both skills that Marqueños today exploit as sources of secondary income. Many of the classroom hours were also spent in such tasks as cultivating the teacher's corn, cutting his firewood, and washing his clothes.

In 1949 the school was destroyed by a mudslide and subsequently relocated on the eastern flank of town. Not until 1961, when the school was moved into a three-room concrete construction, was second grade added to the curriculum. Third grade was added in 1969, fourth grade in 1970, fifth grade in 1974, and sixth grade in 1975.

Students attending school during this twenty-five-year period fared little better than their predecessors. One Marqueño remembers spending an entire year drilling five phrases: *Tengo una botella, tengo una lima, tengo una naranja, tengo una silla, tengo un vaso* (I have a bottle/lemon/orange/chair/glass). Another recalls learning only the days of the week and the months of the year; still another only learning to write his name and the numbers from one to ten. In brief, villagers relate that during this period the teachers did not teach much of anything, and what was taught was taught poorly.

As part of a government plan for the expansion and improvement of public schools, the National Committee for School Construction contributed funds in 1975 for the construction of a new school. The school was supposed to have been built through donated community labor; however, townspeople's general resistance to the project, and specifically their reluctance to donate free labor, was such that the school was constructed almost in its entirety by the mason contracted by the government to supervise the project. Despite threats of coercive action from the village mayor (under orders from the municipal secretary), at most one or two Marqueños appeared each day to help in the construction. Finally, after almost two years, the six-classroom red brick school building was completed.

In 1975, the first year all six grades of primary were taught, a bilingual promoter (*promotor bilingüe*) was sent to San Marcos to teach Bilingual Castilianization (Castellanización Bilingüe). This new rendition of Castellanización had been instituted in rural Guatemala in 1965, but it had not yet been initiated in San Marcos. Although Castellanización Bilingüe, like its predecessor, was clearly acculturative in design and was established to facilitate the transition from home to school (see J. Richards 1989), the crucial addition to the Castellanización Bilingüe program was the use of the native languages as media of classroom instruction. The *promotor bilingüe* sent to San Marcos was an Indian from San José Chacayá, a nearby Kaqchikel-speaking community. Although he used the bilingual method when he first began his tenure in San Marcos, he soon abandoned it in favor of a monolingual Spanish instructional method. His reasons for abandoning native language instruction were that (1) his variety of Kaqchikel, that of the students, and that of the primer were too disparate to use as a medium and object of classroom instruction; (2) parents were skeptical about instruction in the vernacular because they had sent their children to school to learn how to read and write Spanish, not the home language; and (3) the students needed as much exposure as possible to Spanish. Consequently, he no longer "wasted his time" teaching in or about Kaqchikel.

Until 1975, when the *promotor bilingüe* came to teach in the community, all San Marcos schoolteachers had been Ladinos. For the most part they lived out of suitcases and traveled home as frequently as possible. In 1980 the first teacher from San Pedro La Laguna was assigned to teach in the community. Although he was Tz'utujil, all his interactions in the community were conducted in Spanish. Additional Pedrano teachers were added to the teaching staff as enrollment increased; today all ten teachers are from this community. They commute daily back and forth from San Pedro. Since 1986 San Marcos has been incorporated under the National Bilingual Education Program as an "incomplete bilingual school," with the goal of providing bilingual education during the preschool year of primary (now called Preprimaria Bilingüe) and extending the use of the mother tongue for concept facilitation purposes through the sixth grade. Nevertheless, only rudimentary use of the native language occurs during the first years of schooling, and the only concerted attempt at instructing Kaqchikel consists of teaching the Kaqchikel alphabet in Preprimaria in order to facilitate the children's transference to Spanish literacy skills.

According to the 1965 Basic Education Law, children ages seven through fourteen must attend school. The intent is that children will enroll in Preprimaria at the age of seven and complete the six grades of primary by age fifteen. In San Marcos, as throughout most communities in indigenous areas of Guatemala, the ideal of total enrollment and homogenous class age-grading is far from reality. In 1980, for example, only 75 percent of the San Marcos school-age population was officially enrolled in school. Now teachers say that enrollment in San Marcos is considerably higher, ostensibly due to greater societal importance placed on formal education.

Once children are enrolled in school their attendance is often very poor, mostly because child labor is needed for household economic subsistence. Consequently, children's attendance at school depends upon their response to the demands of the agricultural and domestic cycle. Unfortunately, peak agricultural demands coincide with the months of school attendance while the slack production months coincide with the months of vacation. Because child labor is needed for the many domestic and agricultural tasks, parents pull their children out of school for days, weeks, and even months at a time.

The effects of low attendance are reflected in high grade repetition rates and limited school progress. In the history of schooling in San

TABLE 4.1. 1980 School Enrollment

Grade	Total No. of Students	Students Repeating Grade	
		Number	Percent
Castellanización	62	30	48.4
First	55	28	50.9
Second	29	14	48.3
Third	8	1	12.5
Fourth	5	0	0
Fifth	2	0	0
Sixth	1	1	100.0
TOTAL	162	74	45.7

Note: Some individuals cited more than one source.

Marcos, no one has ever progressed through schooling at the expected rate of one grade per year. In 1980 just under 90 percent of the children attending school were enrolled in the first three years of schooling (Castellanización, first grade, second grade), and half of these students were repeating the grade in which they were enrolled (see Table 4.1).

In 1994, 87 percent of the children attending school were enrolled in the first four years of schooling; at the close of the school year 44 percent of these students were not promoted to the next grade (see Table 4.2). Because some pupils enter school years behind schedule, others repeatedly fail, and still others are persistently absent, there is often a substantial spread of ages in each of the grades, sometimes reaching five or more years' difference per grade (see J. Richards 1987b).

In 1975 no Marqueño had progressed beyond the fifth grade of primary. By 1981 three children had graduated from sixth grade. One of these boys was immediately nabbed by the army, but subsequently returned to San Marcos, where he is attempting to establish a bread-making business (the trade he was taught during his conscription). Another graduate now is in the business of contracting fellow Marqueño laborers and constructing adobe houses; the third is a senior catechist for the San Pedro Catholic parish. By 1995 an additional twenty-five persons had graduated from sixth grade. One of the students, a woman, went on to study outside of the community and will soon receive her

TABLE 4.2. 1994 School Progress

Grade	Enrolled	Dropped Out	Retained	Promoted	Percent Promoted
Preprimary	100	14	28	58	58.0
First	81	19	20	42	51.9
Second	51	4	14	33	64.7
Third	53	11	15	27	50.9
Fourth	22	3	6	13	59.1
Fifth	12	0	2	10	83.3
Sixth	9	0	0	9	100.0
TOTAL	328	51	85	192	58.5

Bilingual Secretary certificate; ten others (nine men and one woman) are currently studying in secondary school in Sololá; one has enrolled in the teacher training course of study.

LANGUAGE USE

The Regional Context

There are approximately 100,000 Maya Indians who inhabit the greater Lake Atitlán region. They reside in fifteen *municipios* that extend from the shoreline of the lake to the mountain ridges that surround the basin. As a result of administrative policies implemented after the Conquest (see Richards and Richards 1993), the *municipio* functions as the primary locus of Indian orientation in the lake region, as it does in greater or lesser degree throughout all the Kaqchikel language area (see Tax 1937). The formation of municipal political boundaries demarcated by rigidly punctuated geographical boundaries historically has contributed to cultural and linguistic isolation among the communities of this region.

The residents of San Marcos, like those of the other lake communities, consider themselves to be a distinctive people, united and defined by common origin. The notion of a *municipio*-based ethnic cohesiveness and distinction is signaled by a relative uniformity of cultural style, dress, and language that varies from *municipio* to *municipio* within the region. Although the political, social, and cultural circumscription of the *municipio* has dissipated within the past several decades, the restrictiveness of its orientation is still reflected in varying degrees of *municipio*-based allegiance to civil hierarchies, community endogamy, postmarital residence patterns, and separate household economic reliance.

The inhabitants of Lake Atitlán's western shore refer to the *municipio*-based language varieties spoken around the lake as *tzojob'äl* (in the case of San Marcos) or *tzijob'al,* 'the medium of speech'; those who live on the eastern shore utilize the term *chab'äl.* They refer to their own specific language variety as *qatzojob'äl* or *qachab'äl,* 'our language,' and to the language variety of other municipios as *kitzojob'äl* or *kichab'äl,* 'their language.' Lake inhabitants readily confirm that "in each town it is different the way they speak."

Although the language varieties spoken in the Lake Atitlán region correspond to three distinct languages—Kaqchikel, Tz'utujil, and K'iche'—rarely do their speakers use these terms to identify or classify the varieties. For the inhabitants of the lake area, who rarely have occasion to refer to their speech by any name, these labels are of little significance. Marqueño schoolchildren, who in the 1970s and 1980s were unfamiliar with their language's name, now sometimes refer to it as Kaqchikel because, they report, their teachers participating in the Ministry of Education's National Bilingual Education Program use that name from time to time.

Lake area inhabitants in general are uncertain as to how to label their own language variety and that of the surrounding lake communities or how to group the varieties by linguistic affinity, partly because Lake Atitlán is a linguistic convergence zone for the three closely related, yet distinct languages (J. Richards 1983). The persistent borrowing among the dialects for long periods has created similarities in linguistic structures that have tended to obscure the genetic distinction. What this means is that within the Lake Atitlán Basin what constitutes K'iche', Kaqchikel, and Tz'utujil is basically a matter of fine distinction.

The phonemic inventory for all of the Lake Atitlán dialects is the same, with the exception of some variation in vowels. The Tz'utujil dialects spoken on the southern and western shore and the K'iche' dialects spoken on the western ridge have vowels with a long-short distinction, while the Kaqchikel dialects spoken on the eastern shore and ridge have vowels with a tense-lax distinction. Even the most linguistically divergent dialects of the region share at least 83 percent of their lexical forms as cognates and 40 percent of their lexical forms as phonemically identical (J. Richards 1983).

Although many features of language are shared across the language and dialect boundaries, the language variety spoken in each *municipio* is distinguishable from all others by pronunciation and other linguistic features. Lake area inhabitants regularly use features of pronunciation, grammar, and vocabulary to mark their own cultural identity as well as to identify the origins of others. The San Marcos language variety is viewed by other lake area inhabitants as being one of the most distinctive and most difficult of the lake varieties to understand (Richards and Richards 1987). Indeed, from a structural linguistic perspective, the San Marcos dialect is the most independent lake dialect. San Marcos shares most grammatical structures and some phonological correspondences with the eastern Kaqchikel dialects. It shares many phonological correspondences and lexical patterns with the western Tz'utujil dialects. Nevertheless, the Kaqchikel of San Marcos has many unique phonological, morphological, and lexical variations, some being relic features of earlier K'iche'an forms (see Campbell 1977).

The strong identification that Marqueños perceive between language and community-bound cultural identity is signaled by the fact that community members claim that, with the exception of greater or lesser degrees of interspersions of Spanish, everyone in the town speaks the same. When specific instances of intravillage variation are brought to their attention, the differences are usually disregarded as insignificant or at best fleeting transgressions of the normative code.

Many villagers believe that the language variety spoken in San Marcos today is identical in form to the variety spoken by generations of ancestors before (again with the exception of increased intrusions from Spanish). According to oral tradition, when the patron saint San Marcos founded the community and entrusted the language to the founding fathers, he advised them to cherish the language and pass it down from generation to generation in its unaltered and pure form. Marqueños assert that this is what they have done.

Because membership within the *municipio*-defined cultural group is indelible and determined by birthright, slight in-group speech variation is tolerated. Perhaps because San Marcos lies at the juncture of the Kaqchikel-Tz'utujil-K'iche' boundaries and its inhabitants regularly carry out economic transactions with members of all three language communities, Marqueños are keenly aware of linguistic alternatives that are characteristic of other community varieties and indeed use them for purposes of marking subtle social distinctions within the community. The vaguely demarcated sociolects that are found in San Marcos are based on gender, age, and socioeconomic networks.

What is striking about San Marcos is that within permissible limits individuals accommodate different pronunciations and lexical choices in their intercommunity interactions (for example, making their speech more "western Kaqchikel–like" when talking with a person from Sololá) and even in their intracommunity interactions (for example, softening certain consonants when speaking with older community members). Nevertheless, while the potential for using speech alternatives in San Marcos exists, and is practiced to a degree, alternatives are generally repressed. Marqueños mostly communicate in their own specific forms because it is this variety that defines them as a cultural group. Indeed these dialect differences are retained and manipulated for purposes of marking Marqueño cultural identity.

To illustrate this point, one of the oldest living Marqueños told me how around 1920, as a result of debt peonage, his parents had been subjected to enforced residency on a coastal plantation near Patalul. Later, when President Ubico abolished debt peonage, he decided to return to his ancestral village:

> I grew up on a coffee plantation near Patalul where there were several Marqueño families. My father died, then my mother died, and then General Ubico freed us by lifting our debts. I left to find my parents' town, but I didn't know where it was. I only knew that it was on the lake. I climbed up the back of the volcano and finally came to the town of San Pedro. In San Pedro I greeted the men with *d'ata'* [sir] and the women with *yawa'* [madam], and the people there, the Pedranos, knew from the way I greeted them that I was Marqueño. They pointed to the other side of the bay and said that was where my town lay.

Marqueño Ways of Speaking

Language and speech play a significant, if not central, role in Marqueño culture and society. Within their world view, language distinguishes Marqueños as human from nonhuman. As speakers of a Mayan language, language also distinguishes them as Indians from Ladinos. At a finer level, speakers of the San Marcos variety of Kaqchikel are distinguished culturally from other Indians. Marqueños believe that with the capacity to speak comes the capacity to think and to reason. Because Marqueños perceive life to be structured and controlled through language, they emphasize the importance of verbal competence; learning to speak persuasively and elegantly is a highly valued skill. Indeed, the ability to manipulate speech is seen as an ability to wield power. For men and women, each advancement through the rungs of Marqueño social structure requires a concomitant increase in language presentation skills.

The Kaqchikel word *tzij* is used by Marqueños to refer to nearly all forms of verbal behavior and oral tradition. In its various modified forms *tzij* can mean word, language, verbal lore, argument, dispute, subject, topic, truth, gossip, authority, and even witchcraft.

These genres are Marqueño 'ways of speaking' or *ruwäch tzij*, which literally means 'the face of the word.' The genres fall within a conceptual continuum of style that extends from 'plain, ordinary, everyday speech' (*xa tzij*) to emotional speech (*ruk'u'x tzij*) to formal ritual speech (*ojer tzij*). This continuum of style is very similar to that noted by Gary Gossen (1974) for the Chamulas of Mexico: the three overlapping categories of verbal behavior are distinguished by varying degrees of stylistic formality, redundancy, adherence to prescribed syntactic structure, cadence, and content.

At one end of the continuum are the speech categories known as *xa tzij*: plain, ordinary, everyday speech (*xa jik chi tzij*) and casual conversation (*b'i'in tzij*). There are no restrictions on the style, form, or content for this category of speech, except that it be appropriate for the social setting, intelligible, and grammatical.

The second conceptual category along the speech style continuum—now entering the *choloj* or formal speech categories—is the genre known as 'words spoken from the soul' (*ruk'u'x tzij*). These genres are restricted with regard to their structure and form, displaying an elaborate repetition of words, phrases, syntactic structures, and semantic forms. However, the content changes because, the Marqueños believe, the words emanate from the soul of the individual speaker. By definition, these genres embody a sense of performance and display an excited, elevated, emotional attitude on the part of the speaker. Examples of this category are word games (*etz'anem tzij*); angry, drunken, emotional, impassioned, or argumentive speech (*kowilaj tzij*); court speech and political oratory (*ch'ob'ol tzij*); religious oratory (*konsagrado tzij*); and words that cause illness (*yab'ilaj tzij*). In San Marcos, as in many other societies, such as the Trobriand Islands of Melanesia (Malinowski 1961: 428–464), words are held to possess qualities of supernatural power. Indeed, certain types of disease and illness (such as epilepsy, tuberculosis, and those causing "soul loss") are believed to be caused by the utterance of evil words (M. Richards 1987).

The most formal end of the speech style continuum consists of what

Marqueños call 'pure words' or 'ancient words.' *Ojer tzij*—which includes the genres of Marqueño oral tradition—is 'authentic' and 'genuine,' having been passed down through the generations. As the most ritualized and stylized category of speech forms, *ojer tzij* is constrained by both form and content. Speech genres included within this category are sacred rituals; interfamilial petitions (*qutunem*) used when asking for a wife, asking for the sponsorship of a baptism, and asking for forgiveness for a moral transgression; legends, folktales, and myths (*ojer taq tzij*); and prayers and orations (*orásiyon*). These genres are delivered in a slow, deliberate, redundant manner, with an emphasis on conveying a sense of mission, completion, respect, and dignity.

Given the attention focused on speech and the importance placed on words and their metaphorical usage, it is clear that Marqueños recognize an innate power of language and the importance of speaking well. Children—through the word games they play, the requests they are required to make in the community on behalf of their parents, and the opportunities they have to observe multiple speech contexts—begin to acquire some higher-level speaking skills such as direct, parallel, and nonparallel repetition in their school-age years. Because greater linguistic acumen is needed for the discourse structures of the stylistically more formal genres, Marqueños tend not to exhibit this prowess until late adolescence and early adulthood. Mastery of formal dyadic couplets and other parallel metaphorical structures characteristic of *ojer tzij* genres is acquired only well into adulthood, and even then very few villagers become recognized as possessors of true oratorical skill.

Both men and women can become 'good speakers' (*kamol tzij*); but at the time of my fieldwork in the 1980s and during return visits in the 1990s only men were cited by men and women alike as examples of 'good speakers.' Among both men and women there was a remarkable uniformity of opinion as to which men in the community spoke well in *tzojob'äl*: all who were named were over forty and all commanded considerable community position. To be considered a good speaker, one must have a concomitant degree of community status, but speaking well also affords one elevated community stature. In a community not marked by overt wealth and social differences, oratorical skills figure as important markers of status and prestige.

Incipient Bilingualization

Although Kaqchikel is the language code among Marqueños for all language interactions in the community, interspersed within the *tzojob'äl* frame are borrowed elements from Spanish. The density of borrowings from Spanish substantiates the political, technological, economic, and cultural influence that the Spanish-speaking society has had on the indigenous cultures of Guatemala.

Most of the lexical borrowings from Spanish are loanwords: words of Spanish origin that have been phonologically or morphologically adapted into the San Marcos dialect of Kaqchikel. Some have been directly transferred from Spanish (see Heath 1984). However, due to the fact that Marqueños historically have had very little direct contact with Spanish speakers or the Spanish language, many of the loanwords have diffused into the San Marcos variety as secondary borrowings from the other Mayan language varieties in contact.

Although loanwords are found integrated into all word classes of the San Marcos variety of Kaqchikel, the majority of the borrowings are nouns. The very earliest Spanish lexical items were borrowed into the Mayan languages of Guatemala at the time of the Spanish Conquest and the period of colonial rule. These language borrowings consist mostly of words representing Christian themes, Spanish political offices and concepts, introduced foodstuffs, and certain material artifacts. These early introduced words, now fully adapted to the phonology and morphology of the San Marcos dialect, are regarded by even the most bilingual Marqueños not as borrowings from Spanish at all, but as being *puro tzojob'äl,* 'words of native origin.'

At the time of early contact with Spanish, to accommodate the wholesale importation of the Spanish-derived words, phonemes from Spanish that did not occur in the San Marcos dialect were assimilated to the closest occurring phonemes. For example, the three voiced stops from Spanish, *b, d,* and *g,* were assimilated to native sounds, sometimes including their glottalized counterparts. Spanish *b* usually became either *b'* or *w*—for example:

> *b'ara* '30 inch measurement' < Sp. *vara*
> *wakax* 'bull' < Sp. *vaca*

Spanish *d* usually became *d', t,* or *g*—for example:

> *d'yox* 'God' < Sp. *dios*
> *alkalt* 'mayor' < Sp. *alcalde*
> *pagr* 'priest' < Sp. *padre*

Spanish *g* usually became *k*—for example:

Amikel 'Michael' < Sp. *Miguel*

The Spanish word final voiced resonants assimilated to the voiceless native language counterparts—for example:

[*a·mi·kéeḷ*] 'Michael' < Sp. *Miguel*

In addition, Spanish *s* was replaced by an alveopalatal fricative (represented by *x* in Kaqchikel orthography)—for example:

patux 'duck' < Sp. *patos*
xil 'chair' < Sp. *silla*
lixton 'hair ribbon' < Sp. *listón*

The alveopalatal fricative *x* also replaced the velar Spanish fricative *j*—for example:

kaxon 'crate' < Sp. *cajón*
xab'on 'soap' < Sp. *jabón*

In contrast to old, fully integrated loans that Marqueños regard as words of native origin, they clearly identify recently incorporated loanwords as words derived from Spanish. These words exhibit the adoption of a greater degree of Spanish features into Marqueño pronunciation. For example, in recent loans Spanish *b*, *d*, and *g* are not accommodated by native language phonemes; the Spanish phoneme itself is imported into the San Marcos phonemic repertoire.

To illustrate the perception of language authenticity, the traditional San Marcos dialect word for 'nail' is the loanword *klawx* < Sp. *clavo*. In recent years the original Spanish word has been reborrowed into the dialect. Speakers who have greater familiarity with Spanish (and depending on the sociolinguistic context) use *kláwo*, a new lexical variant that is phonologically closer to the Spanish model. When asked to distinguish the two variants, Marqueños say that *klawx* is 'true' *tzojob'äl* but *kláwo* is 'a word taken from Spanish.'

For all speech borrowings, there is competition among the various phonemic shapes of the loan, displaying greater and lesser degrees of linguistic assimilation. For example, the Spanish word *doctor* can be variably pronounced [d'ok·tóoṛ] or [dok·tóor]. The extent to which a speaker uses one variant or another depends on his or her familiarity with the Spanish model and the sociolinguistic context of the speech act. In daily intragroup interaction among monolinguals, the competing variant chosen is nearly always that which is more fully assimilated within the native phonology. Among bilinguals, the variant chosen depends on an array of sociolinguistic factors, such as speaker, hearer, topic, setting, and intent. Whereas in certain contexts using a variant that more closely corresponds to the Spanish model can provide prestige and recognition of greater bilingual ability, in other contexts the use of this variant can be interpreted by listeners as pretentious and inappropriate.

Although Spanish lexical borrowings for newly introduced material culture items and concepts are incorporated into Marqueño speech with seemingly little resistance, borrowings that are used as progressive replacements for existing *tzojob'äl* words are marked as linguistic intrusions. Depending on the social context and the interlocutor, the use of extensive speech borrowings—particularly those variants that show minimal adaptation to the native phonology—is checked with subtle mechanisms of social control.

In addition to lexical borrowing, a fair amount of code-switching also occurs in the native language context. Whereas borrowing represents the use of partially or fully adapted forms from the host language in the recipient language, the language-contact phenomenon of code-switching involves the alternate use of two languages or language varieties within a given stretch of discourse, presumably involving the prerequisite intention to switch languages (Jacobson 1982). Generally the switch into the alternate language occurs at major discourse junctures, but it may also occur at phrasal or word boundaries. In San Marcos code-switching mostly occurs as a brief interspersion of a Spanish word or short phrasal form into an otherwise consistent *tzojob'äl* frame.

Although Marqueños on the whole possess low levels of Spanish proficiency, code-switching, called *xolon tzij* (mixing words), is a rather common communicative strategy in San Marcos. When Marqueños discuss why they themselves switch, their reasons are straightforward and context-bound; most often they say they use Spanish (1) to quote what a Spanish speaker said or to describe something that took place in Spanish and (2) to convey a meaning more accurately or more easily expressed in Spanish ("there is no word for this in *tzojob'äl*"). When these same persons discuss why others switch to Spanish, they say they do it "to show off," "to make themselves sound important," or "to exclude others." The reasons they give for their own code-switching are thus largely situational or contextual; the reasons they give for others' code-switching are largely metaphorical (Blom and Gumperz 1972; Gumperz 1982).

In San Marcos almost all switches, be they contextual or metaphorical, convey social meanings. Because most community members have only limited communicative proficiency in Spanish and because norms governing Marqueño speech are defined through the use of *tzojob'äl*, any violation of these norms is certain to have a metaphorical impact. Spanish is clearly the language of power in Guatemala; in San Marcos the restricted use of the power code of Spanish in the native language context works to evoke the instrumentality, status, power, prestige, and dominance of the Spanish-speaking Ladino society. The momentary switch to Spanish, under appropriate psychosocial contexts, thus lends authority, force, and credence to the *tzojob'äl* utterance.

Although Spanish code-switching can involve alternating a phrase or a sentence (or even several sentences), most code-switching in San Marcos consists of the interspersion of single lexical items. The greatest percentage of these Spanish interspersions are nouns and some adjectives and adverbs. Spanish function words (determiners, prepositions, conjunctions) are also found in Marqueño discourse. A great deal of code-switching in San Marcos also involves the use of Spanish slogans or emblematic tags, usually placed at the beginning or the end of a narrative. These formulaic expressions are learned as a unit and are applied as a unit in rather restricted linguistic and social environments.

Those speakers who have little proficiency in Spanish and little experience in Spanish language contexts generally confine their code-switching to single noun and tag switches. These linguistic categories can be inserted quite easily in a narrative because they have few syntactic constraints. They thus can be used even by speakers with little bilingual ability for metaphorical or stylistic reasons. In contrast, those who make more within-sentence switches require substantial knowledge of both languages since the switch must conform to precise grammatical rules. Extensive code-switching is a learned skill that requires a relatively high level of bilingualism and a rather sophisticated command of the syntactic systems of both languages.

Although code-switching is a discourse strategy used to some extent by all villagers, as a general rule, most consider the extensive "mixing" of languages to be a corruption of *tzojob'äl*. As with other social behavior that deviates from the norm, Marqueños criticize others' code-switching, but they tend to underplay their own. Because *tzojob'äl* is the language of the community—the code of ethnic solidarity—there are subtle sanctions against inappropriate and overextended use of speech borrowings and code-switching. "Heavy" users in the public domain are commonly chided and accused of acting Ladino-like (*puro mo's nub'än*).

In Marqueño society, there are basically two strata where considerable speech borrowing and code-switching occurs. But it must be remembered that in San Marcos the density of "hispanization" (or the use of Spanish interspersed within the native language code) is minimal compared to that found in biethnic communities where language and culture contact is high and both Kaqchikel and Spanish are used in nearly all domains of community and family life.

One group that engages in exaggerated code mixing is young single men, roughly those between the ages of sixteen and twenty-two. Because of their age and economic and marital status, these *muchachos* (boys, as they are called) have less entangled social commitments to the community. Many do not engage in traditional family-based agricultural economic pursuits, but rely on income derived from day labor on nearby coffee farms or on lands purchased in San Marcos by Pedranos or Atitecos or from making crochet balls for sale to regional entrepreneurs. With fewer family economic responsibilities, they can use the cash they earn to purchase durable consumer items such as watches, radios, sunglasses, jeans, tennis shoes, and even televisions, which they conspicuously exhibit. Because of their newly assumed posture in the community and their sometimes forthright disregard for traditional mores, older, more traditional or more established community members tend to look upon these youth as unabashedly self-serving and disrespectful. As one Marqueño elder said:

> It was really hard in the old days and the people suffered a lot. We worked hard and we gave our money to our fathers and we listened to them and respected them. Now the youth of our community don't know how to work. They only work a day here and a day there. They don't care about doing their job well. All the youth do is sit around and walk around the streets. They make their money and buy their beer, their bread, and their canned juices, their pants and shirts. And when the money is gone, well, they work again. They don't plant corn, and they don't have wives and children. These youth just think about themselves. They don't care about or understand their parents' suffering.

That young men use a number of nonintegrated, stereotypical, and often vulgar Spanish words and phrases in their speech only reconfirms the elders' belief that *xkijal kina'oj,* 'their way of thinking has changed.' Indeed, the familiar, authoritative, and abrupt Spanish employed in their language interactions with one another is reminiscent of the register of Spanish used sometimes by Ladino men when directing Indians or the in-group code used among male Ladino peers. Hispanisms are used by this young adult cohort (particularly in the mildly obscene joking context) to define and maintain the group, but their use also signals to the other community members the supposed preparedness and willingness of this cohort to deal with the larger society beyond San Marcos. This espousal of a wider orientation was expressed by one young adult:

> Before, people never went out of San Marcos. People never left. They were afraid to speak to others, and they would hide when they saw someone from the outside. I remember when my mother would hustle me into the house when some stranger came walking up this path. But now some are leaving; we are starting to go out. We can talk a bit to Ladinos and gringos. But those old people, they can only work with hoe and machete. We are learning things from other places because we are leaving this town to work and some now go to study.

The second stratum displaying higher levels of Spanish speech borrowings and code-switching consists of older, more prominent community men. Over the years these men have increased their exposure to Spanish, but more importantly they have acquired prestige and status through their association and advancement in the status-conferring community hierarchies. Because of their age and elevated social status, these community leaders are accorded the "right" to use hispanisms (although limits again are carefully monitored). In their public speech they rarely use the pejorative, often crude, and combative Spanish expressions characteristic of young men's Spanish code-switching. Rather, their code-switching is usually done in more formal contexts for purposes of lending authority, deliberation, and eloquence to their *tzojob'äl* utterances. Interestingly enough, bilingual individuals who have learned the art of skillfully integrating a tempered amount of Spanish into their various discourse styles are generally regarded by community members as the better village *tzojob'äl* speakers. Evidently, the careful integration and manipulation of Spanish words in their native language utterances serves to enhance the perception of their oratorical prowess.

The use of hispanisms in public speech is thus more a reflection of social process than of actual Spanish proficiency or even exposure to Spanish. Indeed, there are men and women, children and adults, who possess a fair degree of Spanish proficiency and familiarity with Spanish-speaking contexts and yet tend not to intersperse Spanish in their speech. Women and children, overall, have low rates of hispanization. Women especially are expected to adhere and definitely do adhere to a solidarity code defined in terms of "pure" *tzojob'äl*. Those who do interject hispanisms are criticized in the community as being self-serving and even morally suspect, an attitude similar to that noted by Hill and Hill (1980a, 1980b, 1981) among women of the Malinche Volcano region of Mexico. Presumably in response to this expectation and in reaction to social sanctions against presumptuousness, women monitor down their usage of Spanish speech borrowings and code-switching.

The existence of self-regulation mechanisms among both men and women to contain the use of hispanisms in *tzojob'äl* speech demonstrates the high degree of language loyalty to *tzojob'äl* that exists among community members. In essence, those who use too high a density of Spanish borrowings or code-switching in their speech are perceived as raising a flag of linguistic and cultural disloyalty. This is made even more apparent when one observes drunken speech (*q'ab'arel tzij*). Again as Hill and Hill (1980b) described for Nahuatl speakers, more Spanish is used by both drunken men and women, old and young and of high and low social standing, than among those same speakers when they are sober. Drunken speech is essentially unmonitored; in the right context, inebriated Marqueños assume an authoritative Ladino posture and allow repressed, not uncharacteristically vulgar and abusive Spanish to come forth.

Spanish Use in the Community

Aside from the blaring of Mexican country *ranchero* music and disc jockey chatter emanating from transistor radios, little elaborated Spanish is heard in San Marcos. With few exceptions, all interactions among *legítimo* (legitimate) community members are in the Mayan language. Although speakers intersperse Spanish borrowings and even momentarily code-switch, the discourse frame is without question Kaqchikel. As mentioned above, *tzojob'äl* is also the language code used by Marqueños with other Indians who come to the community. Within the Lake Atitlán Basin all the language varieties are mutually intelligible; with only small speech accommodations any transaction can be accomplished in the Mayan language varieties.

Within the community Marqueños use the limited Spanish that they know only with non-Indians and certain "state-sponsored" Indians. Until the late 1980s few non-Indians, however, came to San Marcos. An occasional political party member came to organize a platform; a health official came to encourage vaccinations; a member of the national rural electrification system came to fix a power line; an adventuresome tourist stopped in San Marcos on a trek around the lake; and so on. Because so few Spanish speakers actually visited the community, intracommunity Spanish language usage was limited to interactions with the representatives of the national government who resided in the community—the schoolteachers, the municipal secretary and treasurer, and the postal agent—and the priest who celebrated Mass in the community one Sunday per month.

Prior to the introduction in 1989 of the Live Better development project referred to earlier, Spanish speakers who resided in the community lived in San Marcos only during the week and returned to their homes on the weekends, and the degree of their integration within the community was minimal. With the establishment of Live Better, Spanish speakers have become full-time residents of the community, yet the range of their interaction in the community is still largely restricted. Because the school, the municipal building, and the telecommunications office (buildings where the representatives of the national institutions can be found Monday through Friday) are centrally located in an area rather distant from most of the community's dwellings, and because these government functionaries basically have little interest in interacting with Marqueños, communication is quite restricted.

It is important to note that the town mayor, secretary, and treasurer are Mayas from larger, more cosmopolitan communities; nevertheless, these persons still are addressed in Spanish by all who know even a minimal amount of Spanish, and they themselves use Spanish in their dealings with Marqueños. The town mayor, elected in 1991, came to San Marcos in 1975 as a bilingual promoter of the Ministry of Education's Bilingual Castilianization Program. From his first days in the community he refused to speak to adult community members in Kaqchikel, although he himself is a Kaqchikel native speaker. In his words:

These people need practice. They don't know Spanish because they never talk it . . . they are afraid to talk it . . . they never talk to anyone—they just hide in their houses. Their children don't learn Spanish because their parents won't talk to them in Spanish. How are these people supposed to learn Spanish if everyone keeps talking in *lengua?*

This man eventually married a Marqueña and had children with whom both he and his wife only speak Spanish. Although his children are considered Marqueño (and eventually learned Kaqchikel "in the street"), he has never been considered anything other than an outsider, despite being elected mayor of the community.

Currently all ten schoolteachers are Tz'utujil Indians from the neighboring community of San Pedro La Laguna. Traditionally teachers made it a point to speak Spanish in their assigned communities, as the case described above suggests. Although the current teachers embrace an Indian consciousness instilled within the profession since the mid-1980s, when the National Bilingual Education Program became institutionalized (J. Richards 1989), they still tend to speak Spanish in the community, and community members—especially men—speak Spanish to them.

To Marqueños, "public servants"—Indian or not—are considered outsiders, holding positions of authority traditionally filled by Ladinos. The prescribed role-relationship both from the Marqueños' perspective and from that of the government officials defines the language of interaction as Spanish. The fact that the mayor, secretary, and treasurer (and to a lesser extent the teachers) are addressed in Spanish and that they themselves use only Spanish within the community minimizes their ethnic identification with a local Indian people they regard as *menos desarrollado* (less developed) and *menos despierto* (less awakened). This paternalistic and deprecatory attitude—one commonly held by Ladinos toward Indians in general, but one also held by more cosmopolitan Indians toward more traditional ones (see M. Richards 1985)—is encoded in the use of Spanish.

Marqueño Spanish Proficiency

Outside the community, as a rule, Marqueños who possess a degree of proficiency in both *tzojob'äl* and Spanish use *tzojob'äl* with Indians and Spanish with non-Indians. Even as far away as the K'iche'-speaking communities of Chichicastenango and Totonicapán, where mutual intelligibility is decidedly low, Marqueños speak to other Indians in *tzojob'äl* as much as the interaction allows. There are, of course, factors that mediate language choice, but generally the ethnicity of the interlocutor determines the language of communication. When ethnicity is in question, the choice of language is determined by other sociological characteristics of the interlocutors that suggest ethnic membership and language appropriateness. In a sociolinguistic survey undertaken in 1981, all Marqueños—regardless of gender, age, or oral Spanish proficiency—reported that they normatively use the Mayan language with Indians and Spanish with Ladinos regardless of other factors, such as the setting of the interaction, the degree of formality of the situation, or the topic. Whether or not they do, and at all times, is another question. The immediate point is that, for Marqueños, the prescribed use of the Mayan language establishes the ethnic boundary between Indians and non-Indians. Vis-à-vis Ladinos, the Mayan language is the marker of Indian identity.

In all of the 222 San Marcos households surveyed during fieldwork in 1980, household respondents were asked to report the degree of their communicative proficiency in Spanish as well as that of other family members age seven and above. The scale of bilingual ability was coded on a zero to four scale, monolingual Maya (*majun tzij pa kastiya*) to substantial bilingual proficiency (*kongan ütz ntzijon pa kastiya*). In order to determine the relation of self-report data with tested bilingual proficiency, I tested a sample of children and adults using a dual language proficiency instrument (see J. Richards 1987a). Overall, the test results corroborated the self-report estimations: for the sample of schoolchildren, the correlation between tested performance and parents' report was .63 ($P < .001$) and for the out-of-school sample the correlation was .77 ($P < .001$). It is interesting to note that the correlation between the two measures was slightly higher for the male out-of-school sample than for the female out-of-school sample ($R = .83, P < .001$ and $R = .56, P < .004$, respectively).

The fact that women showed less correspondence between their reported performance and tested Spanish proficiency than did men or schoolchildren has to do with the role of women in the community and norms concerning their behavior. The general consensus among Marqueños is that women, in comparison to men, are more likely to be monolingual, to intersperse few Spanish words in their native language discourse, and to display substantial native language interference in the Spanish they do control. While this characterization is true, women possess more Spanish language competence than is generally recognized by men or even admitted by women themselves. Several women who insisted that they could speak no Spanish at all were actually surprised by their own performance on the Spanish test. Some said that, although they learned a bit of Spanish in their years at school, they had soon forgotten it all, especially after they began to have children and their mobility was even more restricted by the demands of childrearing and domestic chores. Others confided that all their lives they had avoided speaking Spanish because they were too embarrassed to speak it in front of others and too afraid of being laughed at for their attempts.

By exhibiting little working knowledge of Spanish some women can avoid assuming even more burdens that would fall on their shoulders if they did know Spanish (these tasks often being passed on to their school-age children). Moreover, by displaying few Spanish language skills they also have the advantage of being able to circulate within contexts that would be denied to them if they admitted knowing Spanish. It should be mentioned that men take advantage of this perception of women's linguistic lag as well. If a man with limited bilingual ability needs to discuss some matter with the school director or the mayor, for example, he will send his wife. Because women are not expected to know Spanish, these Spanish-dominant Mayas will address the women in *tzojob'äl,* whereas men would be expected to undertake the same interactions in Spanish.

In Figure 4.1 we see the distribution of Spanish proficiency among community members stratified by ethnographically relevant age categories, data derived from the 1980 household survey. Among school-age children, boys and girls possess roughly equivalent proficiency across the Spanish proficiency categories. In the next age bracket, males and females aged fifteen to twenty-four, a clearly divergent trend emerges between the two gender categories. There are no females with moderate bilingual ability, and in relation to males the category of females possessing incipient or minimal bilingual ability is quite large. In the next age category, men and women aged twenty-five to thirty-nine, 25 percent of the men are moderately bilingual, while only 4 percent of the women fall in this category. Conversely, 75 percent of the women are either monolingual or possess only minimal Spanish proficiency, in contrast to only 13 percent of the men. In the last age grouping, individuals older than thirty-nine, the rate of monolingualism is higher for both men and women. Nevertheless, the proportion of women in this category remains substantially larger than for men.

In tests of Spanish proficiency carried out among school-age children in 1980, the girls displayed as much bilingual ability as the boys. This was also the case in a study of second language proficiency among

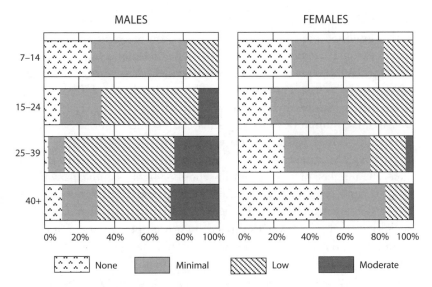

FIGURE 4.1. Spanish Proficiency by Age and Gender Categories

school-age children undertaken twelve years later by the Ministry of Education (Richards and Cojtí 1992). Although the school laid the foundations for bilingualism during the 1980s, most children upon leaving school (the vast majority not progressing beyond second grade) possessed little more than very elementary proficiency in Spanish. Generally these young people could use some stock or memorized school expressions, but their ability to create language was minimal. They had almost no control of Spanish syntax, largely communicating through the juxtaposition of certain words and using a vocabulary only adequate for limited interactions in restricted contexts. Those children, however, who did remain in school beyond the second grade showed definite increases in Spanish language skill, controlling Spanish to a level comparable to that displayed by the average adult Marqueño male.

Based on the 1992 test performance and recent observations, Marqueño children are now entering school not monolingual in Kaqchikel as was the previous generation, but possessing incipient bilingual skills. While the Spanish language skills possessed by these young children are still largely limited to the production of nouns, some nominals are inflected for plurality and others are modified by a quantifier or a stative positional adjective, and the range of vocabulary extends to several semantic domains. The fact that children have been entering school possessing greater communicative competence in Spanish is largely attributable to the preschool program of the Live Better project, where the focus of early childhood education has been placed on teaching Spanish word names through a general Castilianization methodology. Indeed, in 1992 Marqueño children enrolled in Preprimaria who had participated in the Live Better development project tested at higher levels of Spanish proficiency than children living in some of the *aldeas* of Comalapa, Tecpán, or Patzún, communities showing substantially higher levels of societal bilingualism (Richards and Cojtí 1992: 127).

Although Marqueños are justifiably critical of their schooling experience, the number of years spent in school is highly significant with regard to both school-age and adult bilingualism. The relationship between self-reported Spanish proficiency and a number of independent sociological variables was examined. In a multiple regression analysis executed for the 1980 study, results indicated that the number of years spent in school had the highest association with Spanish ability: $R = .43$, $P = .000$ (see J. Richards 1987a). This was greater than the association between Spanish ability and a number of other variables, including gender, age, frequency of migration to coastal plantations, frequency of trips made to other towns, religious affiliation, household economic production potential index, and household "modernity" index.

In the 1980s most children dropped out of school after second grade; in the 1990s many children are continuing through the third and even fourth grade. Children who graduate from fifth and sixth grade possess linguistic proficiency in Spanish comparable to that possessed by the community's most bilingual adult males. What these children lack, however, is sociolinguistic proficiency in Spanish; that is, they lack familiarity with the cultural norms and constraints governing acceptable Spanish language use in diverse social contexts. Because Marqueño schoolchildren participate in few appropriate Spanish-language contexts outside the confines of school, the opportunity to develop and extend their Spanish language skills is limited. Whether these children ultimately acquire more bilingual skills in their lives (or even maintain their school-acquired skills) is largely determined by the structure of economic and cultural opportunities open to them as men and women in the local and wider society.

Although gender was not shown to be a statistically significant variable with regard to school-age bilingualism, it is highly significant with regard to the out-of-school population. Because of their domestically restricted role, women tend to acquire few additional communicative skills in Spanish beyond those learned in school. Once women assume the home-confining duties of domestic maintenance, childbearing, and childrearing, much of their school-acquired second language proficiency, as minimal as it may have been, is sublimated. Although many women do leave the community on a regular basis to sell domestically grown foodstuffs, they travel exclusively to nearby indigenous markets where transactions are executed through *tzojob'äl*. If they work as seasonal laborers, they are always accompanied to the plantation by either relatives or peers from the community, and thus their interaction with outsiders is limited. The fact that women in general interact infrequently with Spanish speakers—coupled with the cultural expectation held by women and men alike that women are to function within the "internal sphere" of home and community, defined and encoded in Kaqchikel—leads most women to underplay and denigrate their Spanish language ability (or at times deny and even mask their actual proficiency). In the household survey I undertook, respondents were asked whether they knew more Spanish at that time or at some point in the past. Without exception, female heads of household said they knew more Spanish at an earlier point in their lives; male heads of household, on the other hand, said they knew more Spanish at present than previously.

It remains to be seen whether girls today who are remaining longer in school and passing into the higher primary grades will retain or increase their Spanish language skills to a greater extent than did earlier cohorts of women. Although I have not undertaken formal language testing of young adults in San Marcos since 1981, the conversations that I have had with women during repeated return visits suggest that the pattern is still one in which Spanish communicative skills decrease after women leave school, marry, and begin their childbearing years. Their language skills appear to diminish to about the same degree that they did fifteen years ago.

Adult males, in contrast, are expected to function within the public arena and to acquire greater communicative competence in Spanish during adulthood. From my over twenty-year perspective on the community, I have noticed that school-based communicative skills tend to lie dormant until men reach the age of about twenty. At this stage in their social development they begin to display the highly respected public speaking skills in *tzojobäl,* and these skills of discourse competence tend to transfer to their production of Spanish. Within the structure of Marqueño society, as men assume both familial and community stature, more economic and social opportunities are available to them to interact in Spanish-defined contexts. Their role in society lies more in the public domain, and their participation in civil, religious, and economic affairs more readily places them in contact with Spanish-speaking government and religious officials and economic entrepreneurs.

The overall language proficiency of Marqueño men is at the level of subordinate bilingualism, but it is generally sufficient to get basic messages communicated in a variety of Spanish-language contexts. In 1980 less than 1 percent of the Marqueño population was substantially bilingual and at best only 5 percent was moderately bilingual. At present perhaps 5 percent of the population is substantially bilingual and an additional 5 percent possesses a moderate level of Spanish skills. All the community's most bilingual males are gainfully employed in the community in nontraditional jobs, the majority of which have arisen from the extension of national or nongovernmental institutions within the society. In positions such as village mayor, Catholic Action president, cooperative officer, military commissioner, health promoter, and chalet guardian, these individuals require higher levels of Spanish proficiency, not only to make their messages more potent in the local context, but also to be positively accepted and evaluated by their Ladino patrons. These men secured their prestigious and comparatively lucrative positions because they knew Spanish, but their acquired positions have also allowed them to increase their mastery of the language.

CONCLUDING COMMENTS

This chapter has presented the dynamics of language in San Marcos La Laguna, a small, relatively isolated town in the extreme western region of the Kaqchikel language area. Marqueños have undergone a diasporic history, rooted in a trajectory of multiple resettlement brought on by cataclysmic events. Today the inhabitants of San Marcos, largely due to the cycles of multiple debt that they have accrued, clearly remain in a disadvantaged economic and political position within the region, leading to their blatant exploitation by Indian and Ladino neighbors and others. The shortage of land, the lack of economic alternatives, and the high prevalence of malnutrition and disease place Marqueños in a precarious survival position. To borrow the words of R. H. Tawney, the situation of Marqueños is like "that of a man standing permanently up to his neck in water, so that even a ripple is sufficient to drown him" (Tawney 1966: 77).

Within the regional societal framework, Marqueños' primary identification revolves around an image of themselves vis-à-vis other Indian *municipio*-based cultural groups. As is characteristic throughout the entire Highland Mayan language area, Marqueños use and maintain their specific variety of Kaqchikel to demarcate the boundary between themselves and other Indian groups. The San Marcos variety of Kaqchikel is quite distinct from the other major dialect groupings of Kaqchikel or even the other community-based varieties of Kaqchikel spoken in the Lake Atitlán Basin; this is due largely to the community's historical pattern of migration and its geographical proximity to Tz'utujil and K'iche' speech communities.

Within the community, there exists a high degree of language loyalty to the mother tongue: indeed *tzojob'äl* is the prescribed language of interaction in every domain of community life. Verbal competence is an extremely valued skill in San Marcos, and the ability to use the mother tongue in its diverse speech styles and genres grants recognition and power to the speaker and provides an important marker of social identity in the community.

While *tzojob'äl* represents to Marqueños the language of hearth and home and a resource for obtaining and securing goods and services within the community, Spanish, the language code of Guatemala's politically dominant group, represents the language of oppression and power. Collectively, Marqueños have acquired only marginal levels of Spanish ability. This reflects the limited exposure they have had to the Spanish language historically, the lack of meaningful communicative interaction between Marqueños and Spanish speakers, the limited utility of Spanish in their immediate lives, and the traditionally perceived threat to Indian ethnic identity encoded in the acquisition of Spanish.

Twenty-five years ago San Marcos could be classified as a monolingual Kaqchikel community; fifteen years ago it was an incipiently bilingual community. With the changing economic, political, and social pressures of the recent decades, however, most Marqueños have begun to view the acquisition and manipulation of Spanish as a prerequisite strategy for survival. In San Marcos, as throughout the Americas, redefinitions of Indianness have come to incorporate the ability to use two language codes for instrumental and symbolic ends.

Although all language interactions among community members are conducted in San Marcos in Kaqchikel, interspersed within the native language frame are word borrowings from Spanish. These lexical borrowings mostly represent terms for new cultural concepts and items, but they are also used to replace native terms that have lost their "communicative power." In the context of code-switching, the tempered use of these "power words" and other tag expressions is largely for metaphor-ical reasons—that is, to draw upon the power of Spanish to give the *tzo-job'äl* utterance an added degree of authority and elevation. Within the community men and to a lesser extent women manipulate the Spanish language for a variety of economic, social, and political ends, while out-side the community Spanish is mostly used to negotiate economic op-tions. Among Marqueños at large, the addition of Spanish to the Mayan language repertoire is associated with factors including the number of years spent in school, gender, age, frequency of travel outside the com-munity, frequency of seasonal migration episodes, household economic status, and religion.

Schooling functions in San Marcos as the most strategic institutional interface between the community and the state apparatus; indeed, this national institution has brought about the most significant changes in community-wide levels of Spanish language proficiency. Although Mar-queños are critical of the quality of the education they have received, for-mal schooling has provided the foundations of societal bilingualism. Un-til the late 1970s no Marqueño had ever graduated from the six grades of primary school. Now there are a handful of sixth-grade graduates who are studying in secondary school outside of San Marcos. It remains to be seen whether bilingualism remains additive in San Marcos or whether San Marcos will begin to experience an accelerated language shift, following the pattern of other Kaqchikel Highland communities.

5. CASE STUDY TWO
San Antonio Aguas Calientes and the Quinizilapa Valley

R. McKenna Brown

THE COMMUNITIES

San Antonio Aguas Calientes is perhaps the most renowned Indian community of Guatemala today. Its polychrome textiles and easy access from Antigua have made it a popular visiting spot for tourists from all over the world. As Sheldon Annis (1987: 12) notes, "the image of the San Antonio woman at the loom—clad in her (multi-colored) huipil— has become a national icon for use on tourism and export promotion brochures."

Most visitors to San Antonio start their trip in the nearby town of Antigua, Guatemala's tourist center. If economy is more important than speed, they might board one of the buses behind the market that, once full, leave for San Antonio, costing less than a U.S. quarter. Travelers with more money than time to spend might prefer a taxi, which costs at least forty times more, but leaves immediately and offers more comfort.

The road first passes through Ciudad Vieja, which enjoyed brief glory as the colonial capital, then leaves the pavement behind as it enters a triangular valley along a hillside overlooking coffee plantations. At the valley's southern point the road tops the crest of the hill; far below, San Antonio appears in the midst of the Quinizilapa Valley.

The view from this valley entrance is worth contemplating, since it allows the traveler to appreciate San Antonio in relation to its setting. Tanned mountains surround the valley, cross-hatched almost to their peaks by the neat plaid patches of sand-colored cornfields dependent on the seasonal rains. Turning left, one faces south, along a rumpled line of hills tapering down to the point where a small river exits the valley on its way to the Pacific. The peak of Agua Volcano is visible, and behind it hang the coastal skies of another world.

Two volcanoes, Fuego and Acatenango, dominate the view to the west. Barely visible in the northwest corner, the thin line of a rough dirt road winds up the mountainside, passing through the village of Chima-choy and later descending in the town of Parramos. Below spreads the lush green of the valley floor, tilting slightly to the south, dissected by the Nimayá River. Toward the southwest corner a few ponds and marshes remain from the lake that was drained decades ago in the time of President Ubico. The ample water nourishes patches of garden vege-tables, watercress, and coffee plants shaded by *Gravilea* trees.

Sounds float up in waves from the valley floor with the smoke of household cooking fires. Music from radios and Protestant services is punctuated by bus horns, church bells, roosters crowing, children laugh-ing, dogs barking, and the belch and roar of the motorized corn mill.

From the valley's entrance, the first impression is of a single settle-ment, all of which is frequently presumed to be San Antonio.[1] Actually, there are four neighboring communities, including San Antonio's two hamlets, which are largely out of sight: Santiago Zamora in the far west corner and San Andrés Cevallos, most of which is tucked behind a hill to the south. A fourth community, Santa Catarina Barahona, forms a physically contiguous extension of San Antonio to the northwest and is not easily recognized at first as a separate entity. Many visitors, includ-ing Guatemalans, spend a few hours shopping and leave the valley un-aware of its other constituents.

From our observation point, the road descends the valley's steep northern wall. Pavement returns and simple stalls festooned with tex-tiles for sale adorn both sides. Women vendors nursing babies watch passing traffic with a practiced eye, knowing which vehicles to shout to and which to let pass. Dogs and younger children run about; older kids circle on bicycles. Rounding a bend, the final stretch of the road crosses the town's main street heading for the side of the Catholic church then veers to the right into the plaza. The plaza, a sloping, rather uneven dirt field, is lined with more textile booths to attract tour buses. Looking round, one's eye is first caught by the church, whose lovely, if slightly cracked, facade dominates the scene. Directly across from it, women wash clothing at the community laundry sinks, known as *pilas*. To the left sit the mayor's office, a new town library, and the health post. To the right is the public school where children study in grades one to six.

The town spreads west from the plaza along three main streets that are crossed by about ten smaller ones. Houses along the main roads tend to be single constructions of concrete block, built right at the curb with interior patios. Along the side streets, corn-cane fences surround household compounds of multiple corn-cane buildings. The valley's climate is gentle year round, and most yards are brightened by flowering bushes and vines.

Almost seven thousand people live in this valley, six thousand of them in San Antonio. Yet, as Annis (1987) notes, the town has few resources serving its citizens. There are no hardware or feed stores, no furniture stores, no book or school supplies stores, no weekly markets. People make the short trip to Antigua for many of their needs. The first high school and restaurant opened in 1994.

Valley History

The four communities of the Quinizilapa Valley share a common historical, economic, and cultural heritage. All were founded by the Spaniards about 1528, immediately after the Conquest, and populated with Indian slaves captured in combat, who represented many different ethnic and linguistic groups. Each was entrusted to a conquistador who, in exchange for tribute payments, was to oversee the Indians' religious instruction and general welfare. All of the communities are referred to in colonial documents as "the *milpa* of" the particular Spaniard to whom each was awarded. For example, Santa Catarina Barahona was called "la milpa de Sánchez Barahona." San Andrés Cevallos and Santiago Zamora also preserve the names of their original landlords. San Antonio was founded as the "*milpa* of Juan Chávez," but changed its name years later, when the Spanish Crown revoked the Spaniard's privileges and transferred Santa Catarina to the care of the Dominican order and San Antonio came under direct ownership of the king.

The four communities shared a common orbit as economic satellites of the Spanish metropolis, charged with the supply of *sacate* (fodder) to the capital. In 1641 San Antonio and Santa Catarina purchased some nearby land from a Spaniard to be used communally, which suggests a relative level of prosperity. A century later the communal holdings were split due to tax disputes (Lathbury 1974).

For at least a century, high literacy and education rates have distinguished the Quinizilapa Valley, and San Antonio in particular, within rural Guatemala. José María Navarro reported in 1874, at a time when most communities contained no schools at all, that San Antonio had two. One of the first United States missionary schools in Guatemala was built at the border between San Antonio and Santa Catarina.

Life in the Quinizilapa Valley

Traditionally, the economy of the valley towns has been based on *milpa* agriculture—small-scale cultivation of corn, beans, and other plants for household consumption—complemented by cash crops and artisanry. However, in the past decades far-reaching economic changes have affected valley life. Over the past forty years improved roads and regular bus transportation, radio broadcasting, and public schools have inundated Mayan communities with new goods and ideas. The increasing incorporation into the national and international economies brings changes in economic, cultural, and language behavior. This chapter describes the four towns in the Quinizilapa Valley and examines how changing economic forces alter language use patterns, thus affecting the vitality of the Kaqchikel language.

I first visited San Antonio in 1983 and returned two years later for repeated visits while taking Kaqchikel language lessons in Antigua. The contacts established then with local families and school and health post staff enabled me to embark on a fourteen-month field project researching Mayan language maintenance and shift in the Quinizilapa Valley in 1984. Data collection took several forms, including extensive interviews with parents, midwives, teachers, and elders, participant observation, and household surveys. Over five hundred surveys were carried out by *promotores de salud,* volunteers from the community experienced in vaccination campaigns and census-taking. Households were selected randomly in the two largest communities, San Antonio and Santa Catarina, where, respectively, 20 and 50 percent of households were surveyed. In the two smaller communities all households were included. Surveyors were instructed to speak to the housewife, asking a list of

TABLE 5.1. Number of Respondents by Community

Community	Households	Percent
San Antonio	222	42.4
San André	78	14.9
Stgo Zamora	83	15.8
Sta Catarina	139	26.5
TOTAL	524	100.0

questions about language abilities and practices as well as other household characteristics. By looking at certain features of valley households, and how they vary according to the age of the head of household, we get a sense of how life in the valley is changing. Table 5.1 provides a glance at the survey sample by community and the percentage of the total that each represents.

The Valley Household

Despite the contact with outside populations that comes from the proximity of urban centers and a tradition of regular commercial travel to other regions of the country, relatively few Quinizilapans have married outsiders. Immigration to the valley towns is very low. Over 84 percent of the respondents and spouses surveyed are from the community they reside in. The largest segment of immigrants—8.3 percent of respondents and spouses—comes from other valley communities. Less than 5 percent are from non-Kaqchikel towns. Thus, the role of non-Kaqchikel-speaking immigrants seems to be very limited in the case of Kaqchikel loss in the valley. Table 5.2 illustrates the small percentage of outsiders in the valley.

The single-family household is the modern norm in the valley and the most common. Multiple-family compounds generally result from some disadvantage. Older, infirm parents may share an offspring's compound; a newly married couple may reside with parents until they get on their feet; compound space may be rented to another family in cases of acute need of either or both parties.

In the Quinizilapa Valley most family compounds contain multiple

TABLE 5.2. Number of Respondents and Spouses by Place of Origin

Origin	Respondent		Spouse	
	Number	Percent	Number	Percent
Local	442	86	386	82.5
Same Valley	42	8	40	8.5
Kaqchikel	9	2	18	4.0
Elsewhere	22	4	24	5.0
TOTAL	515	100	468	100.0

structures: a principal residence and various outbuildings serving discrete functions as kitchen, latrine, storeroom, and additional sleeping area. Catholic households may also dedicate an outbuilding as a family altar. While the construction materials of the principal residence may vary, outbuildings tend to be of cane, corn stalk, and mud daubing. Cane construction uses local materials and requires more time and local expertise than cash inputs. Among the house construction types extant in the valley, cane is the most traditional and lends itself to the multiple single-room structures that customarily occupy a traditional family compound.

Cinder blocks are produced by large factories close to the capital and may be purchased in nearby Antigua. Cinder block houses are admired for their permanence and resistance to vermin. Because cinder block must be purchased outside the community, its use is a sign of wealth and necessitates participation in the cash economy. There are also lesser numbers of houses built of board or mixed materials.

It is important to keep in mind that the earthquake of 1976 interrupted any gradual architectural evolution that may have paralleled other aspects of cultural change. Massive reconstruction campaigns were organized and financed by international relief organizations that brought in outside technical advisors and materials such as corrugated aluminum roofing. Thus, current house constructions to some degree reflect the agenda of international relief efforts and must not be interpreted solely as an indicator of cultural maintenance on the part of the household.

Most Quinizilapa households operate in several economic realms. It is not uncommon for a family to have a daughter earning wages in Antigua, a son in the military, a father growing corn on family land and renting an irrigated plot to raise cash crops, and a mother weaving textiles for the tourist market. Families may exploit several niches along the spectrum from traditional *milpa* agriculture to the modern cash economy rather than occupy a single point along an economic continuum.

Most households supplement commercial, handicraft, and wage earnings with a *milpa* plot whose size and productivity may depend on the household's available cash and time inputs. The trend among Quinizilapa households is economic diversification, not a uniform drift into the capitalist economy. Surplus outside earnings may be invested in fertilizer, seed, land purchase or rental, or hired labor to increase *milpa* production. Higher levels of *milpa* production are more likely to signify

**TABLE 5.3. Mean Corn Production
(in Months) by Age of Respondent**

Age Group	Production	Households
Under 30	4.27	110
30–42	5.04	155
Over 42	5.62	143
TOTAL	5.04	408

successful exploitation of the cash economy than exclusive reliance on *milpa* agriculture. Lower levels of *milpa* production probably signify unsuccessful exploitation of either the formal or *milpa* economies.

Survey respondents were asked for how many months of each year did the corn that they grow feed the family. Data demonstrate a modest but constant decrease in corn production over time. In Table 5.3 the average corn production (in months) per household is given by age groups. From the oldest group to the youngest, yields drop about 11 percent, from about five and a half months to just over four. The decline in corn harvests seems to indicate a progressive, collective withdrawal from the *milpa*—that is, the younger people grow less corn. Reasons probably include shrinking availability of land for a growing population as well as increasing involvement with the cash economy. However, these data may also reflect individual productivity gains with age, as accrued expertise, capital, land inheritances, and the help of older offspring enhance yields.

Rising demands for land have led to increasingly skewed distribution, as some families acquire substantial tracts of lands while others are left with little. As a result, many individuals are forced to leave their towns in search of supplemental income. The proximity of Antigua and the capital to the Quinizilapa Valley allows daily commuters to take advantage of wage markets without disengaging from community life. They can also escape the seasonal migrations to the coffee and cotton plantations on the Pacific coast that have enmeshed many other Highland towns. Thus, for those Quinizilapans who report having lived outside the valley for any length of time, such a move was more likely a voluntary individual response to specific opportunities than a necessity. And

TABLE 5.4. Mean Levels of Temporary Outmigration of Respondents by Age Groups

Age Group	Stationary		Temporary Emigrants	
	Number	Percent	Number	Percent
Under 30	78	58.2	56	41.8
30–42	118	65.2	63	34.8
Over 42	130	79.3	34	20.7
TOTAL	326	68.1	153	31.9

the great diversity of destinations throughout Guatemala that they report does not suggest a monolithic reaction to broad economic pressures. The most common destinations, Antigua and the capital, each account for no more than 12 percent of reported emigrations. Kaqchikel-speaking communities represent less than 5 percent of destinations. Length of departure also varied greatly, from one to thirty-five years.

Nonetheless, outside residence intensifies contact with the Spanish-speaking world and the Ladino value system, neither of which places much value on Indian culture. Accommodating the outside world may lead to adopting its values, in some degree, and the returning prodigal Quinizilapan may prove the most effective conduit for the transference of these attitudes into the household and community psyche.

Almost one-half of the households surveyed report that either the respondent or spouse has emigrated and returned, and younger individuals are more likely to have emigrated than older ones (see Table 5.4). There is a progressive increase in the proportion of each age group that reports returned emigration, from 20.7 percent of the oldest age group to 34.8 percent of the middle group and 41.8 percent of the youngest, suggesting that returned emigration is increasing over time.

The high incidence of temporary emigration among younger respondents may reflect a combination of the lessening dependence on *milpa* agriculture and income generation within the community and the increased work opportunities available due to rising educational levels. At any rate, progressively more Quinizilapans are leaving the valley to study or work in, and return from, the outside world, a place where Spanish fluency is a requisite for survival and an overt Indian identity is often a handicap.

TABLE 5.5. Mean Age of Respondent by Respondent and Spouse Education Levels (Last Grade Attended 0 – 7)

Last Grade Attended	Respondent Age		Spouse Age	
	Mean	Number	Mean	Number
0	46.63	27	44.46	22
1	42.08	26	44.91	22
2	43.32	120	43.45	77
3	39.06	129	41.64	184
4	34.70	56	37.80	53
5	30.63	27	36.30	30
6	30.44	62	30.01	87
7	26.13	8	30.45	11
TOTAL	38.30	455	39.12	486

Education and Literacy

San Antonio enjoys a reputation as a Mayan community with unusually high educational and literacy rates. As Annis (1987: 27) notes, "San Antonio is exceptional for . . . any rural Guatemalan community—because of its high rate of literacy, particularly . . . female literacy. According to my field data and the 1973 census, about three-fourths of the adult population is literate."

In my survey of valley households, 82 percent of the respondents reported having attended school, and over 54 percent of these reported three or more years of schooling. On the average, women reported slightly fewer years (3.10) of schooling than men (4.08). School attendance has increased throughout the valley over the past forty years, as illustrated by the average educational level of respondents between twenty and sixty years of age, a level which decreases with age: the younger the population, the more educated. Table 5.5 displays the respondents' mean age according to the educational level of both the respondent and spouse, calculated by the last school grade completed (the value of 7 is any level beyond sixth grade). With a few minor exceptions, each succeeding grade level was achieved by a younger population. Thus, the average age of respondents with no formal education was about forty-seven, while the average age of respondents with post-primary education was about twenty-six.

San Antonio's reputation for exceptionally high literacy rates reflects a valley-wide phenomenon and may actually be more deserved by the other Quinizilapa towns. On the average, San Antonio respondents reported slightly lower literacy rates than those of the other communities in the valley.[2]

Clothing

One of the most visible indicators of cultural change among the Highland Mayan communities is clothing (Hendrickson 1996a). Fifty years ago every Indian of the valley wore the traditional outfit specific to the Quinizilapa communities. Men were the first to adopt Western clothing, and now there are only a handful of elderly men who still dress in the old way. Women's dress has changed greatly in style, but still remains distinctly Indian and distinctly Quinizilapan. The two principal articles of the woman's outfit are the *huipil,* a traditional hand-woven blouse, and the *corte,* a length of foot-loomed fabric wrapped as a skirt. The *huipil* serves as the woman's chevron, giving visible testimony to her birthplace, ethnicity, skill as a weaver, and individual tastes. It may also serve as a savings account for the owner, in which she invests her time and expertise and which she may sell or hock in times of need. The intricate *huipil* of San Antonio, which incorporates a brocaded weaving technique, is one of the most colorful and distinctive designs of the Highlands.

Since the *huipil* is very costly to produce in terms of time and material inputs, many women, especially those earning wages outside the home, find it difficult to maintain a traditional wardrobe. The flooding of local markets with cheap manufactured blouses provides an alternative to wearing the *huipil* daily. Thus, the Indian woman must make a choice between the culturally rich visual symbolism of the *huipil* and the economy of the manufactured blouse. This choice need not be definitive. A woman may reserve her *huipil* for use outside the home or for certain household occasions and wear a cheaper blouse while doing chores.

During the data collection for the present study, the surveyor noted whether the respondent was wearing a *huipil* or not. Such an observation cannot be interpreted as an absolute measure of an individual's whereabouts along some continuum of cultural change for the reasons discussed above; but, taken collectively, these data may reveal trends.

The general trend in the valley is away from *huipil* use. Older women tend to wear the *huipil* at all times, whereas many young girls do not

TABLE 5.6. Mean Age of Respondent by Use of Traditional Blouse

	Mean Age	Number of Respondents
Not wearing *huipil*	34.81	118
Wearing *huipil*	39.99	350
TOTAL	38.68	468

even own one. Local teachers remark that ten years ago most female students came to school every day in a *huipil* and now most do not except for special occasions. This trend can be seen among adults as well, although to a lesser degree, as indicated by Table 5.6. During the survey interview, only 25 percent of the women respondents were not wearing a *huipil,* and as a group they were about five years younger than those wearing the *huipil.* This does not mean the women wearing manufactured blouses are dressing as Ladinas; most wear *cortes,* the traditional Mayan skirt, and the blouses are often embroidered in a style reminiscent of certain *huipiles.* The shift away from hand-woven *huipiles* may reflect a move away from the traditional *milpa* economy in which there is time for women to weave *huipiles* for themselves and other women in their households.

In conclusion, an examination of the correspondence between the ages of respondents and selected characteristics of their households suggests certain trends in the Quinizilapa Valley. Younger people show higher school attendance and literacy rates. Returned emigration rates are also higher among the young, suggesting either that the younger population is more mobile or that those who leave the valley are now returning in greater proportions. The use of the *huipil* decreases among younger women. In a similar trend, the number of families per household and the months of corn consumption supplied by the household *milpa* are greatest among the older valley residents.

The Valley Towns and Intercommunity Relations

During the Colonial Period, the communities forged a common Kaqchikel identity. Yet each town today has a stronger sense of its individuality than of a collective valley association. Its residents do not generally perceive the valley as a separate, cohesive entity and do not even possess a name to refer to it as such. Relations among the towns are not always harmonious. The years of close coexistence have produced mild rivalries which occasionally erupt in brief conflict. Intermarriage among the communities is not common and accounts for only about 8 percent of valley households. While the four communities share a common heritage, each has its individual character, resulting from and contributing to its unique adaptation to changing conditions. The following sketch gives a picture of life in the valley. A clearer picture emerges by comparing aspects of village households, including composition, economy, education and literacy, and clothing.

San Antonio Aguas Calientes: Giant of the Valley

By size, location, and administrative role, San Antonio dominates the Quinizilapa Valley. Its population is more than double the populations of the other three communities combined. According to valley folklore, the founders of San Antonio consulted a shaman who gave them magical seeds to plant under a tree, which assured the town's proliferation.

San Antonio's command of the valley's main entrance grants it control over access to most transportation and the flow of many goods and services into and out of its surrounding communities. Its dominant economic status in the valley is reflected in the generally disparaging attitude of its people toward their neighbors; sentiments expressed, for example, through *apodos* (nicknames) bestowed upon each town and its inhabitants. Antoneros, as people of San Antonio are known, are famed for their generous and wily designation of individual *apodos* among themselves.

Generally, the other towns are disdained for being less worldly. For example, in the 1980s the national government built a public swimming pool in Santa Catarina, taking advantage of natural springs in the valley head. But, joke the San Antonio youth who frequent it, no one in Santa knows how to swim, so they can only watch enviously through the fence.

The Antoneros do not seem eager to share their tourist trade with other valley towns. For example, after a stop in San Antonio, where most passengers get off, local buses arriving from Antigua continue on to Santa Catarina, though mention of such a destination never appears on the vehicle. Gringos remaining seated at this stop are often told by local women, who do not generally engage in spontaneous, noncommercial exchanges with foreigners, that they have indeed arrived at San Antonio—that this is where they want to get off. Nor are directions to Santa Catarina warmly given. Such inquiries in the streets of San Antonio are likely to be answered simply, "¿Busca tejido usted?" (Are you looking for weavings?).

Differences of linguistic form and usage are also mocked, especially with regard to Santa Catarina. Though traditionally classified as the same regional group separated by a "subtle variation in dialect" (Annis 1987: 22), the varieties of Kaqchikel spoken in the two towns exhibit some of the feature contrasts that distinguish the major Kaqchikel dialects (Chacach 1987). There are also commonly acknowledged differences in language use patterns. While *novios* (sweethearts) in San Antonio now court in Spanish, Kaqchikel remains the language of such pursuits in Santa Catarina. Youth in San Antonio joke that they must learn Kaqchikel well to look for a *novia* in Santa Catarina, implying that Santa is more rustic. In general, San Antonio is considered more Spanish-speaking than Santa.[3]

Large families are common in San Antonio; almost 20 percent of the respondents have six children or more. The average number of children for women forty-five years or older, 3.99, is above the valley mean (3.75) and ranks second behind Santa Catarina. Just over 63 percent of the households surveyed were single-family compounds, a portion larger than that of Santa Catarina, but smaller than those of both its hamlets.

San Antonio respondents and spouses were the most "local." Proportionately their sample contained the fewest outsiders: 92 percent of the respondents were from San Antonio. Only ten respondents came from outside the valley, and seven of those were not from Kaqchikel communities. Of the spouses, 10 percent were immigrants and 4 percent from outside the valley. Only two spouses were not from Kaqchikel-speaking towns. Outsiders, then, compose less than 10 percent of respondents and spouses combined, and the risk of language loss due to non-Kaqchikel-speaking immigrants does not seem grave.

On the average, San Antonio households are the second highest producers of corn for home consumption, exceeded only by San Andrés. But there is considerable variation among households: 20 percent grow all the corn they consume, while about 17 percent do not grow any. The average household grows 4.97 months of corn for home consumption. San Antonio also has the lowest percentage of cane houses in the valley.

The proportion of returned emigrants among Antoneros is the second highest in the valley, behind Santa Catarina: 35.5 percent of respondents report that they or a spouse have lived out of town for more than six months.

The relatively exalted local prestige of San Antonio shows some recent signs of leveling. For example, in 1985 the national government apportioned funds to many *municipios,* including San Antonio and Santa Catarina, to improve streets with pavement bricks (*adoquinamiento*). In communities beset by mud during the rainy season and ubiquitous dust in the dry season, paved streets are a widely coveted hallmark of progress. Work in Santa proceeded without incident, and now all streets in the town proper are paved. In San Antonio, however, the project was besieged by delays and scandal, amid accusations that the mayor, shielded by his party affiliation with the national government, had stolen the funds with impunity. A local uprising finally succeeded in ousting the mayor, but the funds were never recovered; as of August 1994 only a few main streets in San Antonio had been paved.

Additionally, while cash-cropping has gained importance in the valley economy, climatic changes have disrupted the yearly rain cycles, making access to irrigation water crucial. The valley's only river, the Nimayá, has its source in Santa Catarina, and many conflicts have arisen about its management. In the past the river flowed fairly quickly out of Santa to nourish plots in San Antonio. But recent water projects have irrigated two large tracts of Santa's hillsides, converting them into prime real estate and lucrative green pockets of intensive cultivation. Though many of these irrigated plots have been bought by Antonero farmers, there is an undeniable shift in the valley balance of power away from San Antonio.

San Andrés Cevallos: Prosperous Modernizing Hamlet

In the surrounding communities, natives of San Andrés are referred to as "coyotes," with the following explanation. Shortly after the first inhabitants had settled San Antonio, the future citizens of San Andrés were wandering fearfully through the surrounding hills, like coyotes, lured toward the settlement, but afraid of fire. People from San Antonio had to go up into the hills to calm their fears and convince them to come down and settle. Given the massive population displacements and high vagrancy rates reported for the period immediately following the Conquest (MacLeod 1973), the story probably reflects some element of historical events.

San Andrés is geographically the *aldea* or hamlet closest to San Antonio. Indeed, they are physically contiguous. About five hundred people live here. According to Annis (1987: 22), the people of this hamlet were described by the Instituto para Nutrición para Centroamérica y Panamá (INCAP) field workers in the early 1950s as at a "lower economic level [than San Antonio] and not much interested in the betterment of their community." However, increases in available farmland and intensification of cash-cropping have converted San Andrés into a "tightly knit and widely envied pocket of affluence" (Annis 1987: 23). An indicator of the relative wealth of San Andrés is the proportion of cinder block houses—29 percent, the highest in the valley. Cash crops have not replaced but supplemented *milpa* agriculture. Corn yields are by far the highest in the valley, as families grow enough corn to feed themselves for an average of six months. San Andrés also has the smallest average family size in the valley—just over two children per completed family.

Santiago Zamora: The Poor Hamlet

The smallest of San Antonio's hamlets is also the most isolated. Santiago Zamora is tucked away in the far western corner of the valley, about three and a half kilometers from San Antonio. Santiagüeños must walk to Santa for public transportation. Only the spire of Santiago's church is visible in the distance as one enters the valley on the main road.

Santiago is situated between the marshy lake bottom and eroded mountainsides of the valley walls and is the most land-poor of the Quinizilapa towns. Based upon reports from the past century, Annis calculates that land available per family in Santiago has shrunk to about eight *cuerdas,* about one-tenth of the supply in 1874. Many individuals trade their labor for land use privileges in nearby towns and *fincas* or devote themselves to the manufacture of *petates,* mats of woven reeds. The work of harvesting the reeds earns general disdain because it requires lengthy mucking about in the soggy lake bottom. As Annis (1987: 47) observes, *petate* weaving is barely lucrative and "provides serious employment only for the poorest of the poor." In reference to their location and labor harvesting reeds, natives of Santiago are called *kär* (fish) by other valley residents.

Santiago's education levels are markedly below those of the other valley towns. None of the respondents reported schooling beyond sixth
grade. About three-fourths reached either second or third grade. The average level of education for respondents in Santiago is 2.7 years. Almost
10 percent described themselves as not literate.

In keeping with its scarcity of land, Santiago's *milpa* yield averages
are the lowest in the valley: 20 percent of households grown no corn at
all, and only one household reports year-round self-sufficiency in corn.
An indicator of Santiago's relative poverty in the valley is the high proportion of cane houses—about 70 percent, the highest in the valley.

Santa Catarina Barahona: Playing Second Fiddle

In the administrative hierarchy of the national government, Santa Catarina and San Antonio are on equal footing. Like San Antonio, Santa is
a *cabecera municipal* with its own patron saints, church, and ritual calendar. Santa also has its own school and health post. But because of its
smaller size and location at the rear of the valley, Santa has always been
literally and figuratively behind San Antonio.

Though their central plazas are located at opposite ends of the north-
east wall of the valley, San Antonio and Santa Catarina have expanded,
especially the former, until now they are separated only by a street with
no formal boundary marker. At present, there is a fairly free flow of
people between the towns, but older people tell stories of a time when it
was not so. The Antoneros call the natives of Santa Catarina *catucheros*
(probably a pejorative derivation of Catarina) and when asked why respond "because they throw stones at you." Reportedly, when intruders
from San Antonio or its hamlets were spotted on municipal territory,
Catarineros, jealously guarding their women and water, would chase
them out with stones. Several residents credited improved relations between the two towns to the establishment of a very large Protestant
church in Santa Catarina that is attended by worshipers from the entire
valley and outside towns. This has accustomed Catarineros, they say, to
large groups of nonthreatening outsiders in their midst.

Annis calculates a population of about 1,700 for Santa Catarina in
1987 (based upon tables in Poitevin n.d.). Santa families are by far the
largest in the valley—almost 20 percent report 6 or more children. The
average completed family size is 4.4 offspring. Santa also has the lowest
proportion of single-family compounds—56.7 percent. The average
number of families per household is 1.4.

Santa has the second highest literacy rate of the valley. Santa's education levels are by far the highest in the valley for both respondents and spouses—an average of 3.7 years of schooling.

Milpa yields in Santa are a bit below San Antonio's. Almost 30 percent plant no corn for home consumption, and about 17 percent are self-sufficient. Over 65 percent of the households observed were of cane construction, the second highest percentage in the valley. Santa has the lowest percentage of cinder block houses—15 percent. It has the highest levels of returned outmigration. Over 40 percent report a returned emigrant in the household.

LANGUAGE USE

Language Shift in the Quinizilapa Valley

Over the past two centuries the Quinizilapa towns have become increasingly bilingual. Although documented evidence of changing fluency in the valley is limited, some clues do exist. In the late eighteenth century, according to the archbishop Pedro Cortés y Larraz (1958), the valley was monolingual, speaking "a closed Kaqchikel without understanding any other." One century later, José María Navarro (1874: 149) wrote that the Indians of San Antonio spoke Spanish "as if it were their native language."

In this century, a report in the late 1940s by the Instituto Indigenista Nacional, cited by Annis (1987: 27), estimated "that about three-fourths of the population was bilingual." Annis (1987: 27) also cites a 1950s study by the INCAP stating that "all the inhabitants of San Antonio and San Andrés speak Spanish and Kaqchikel, except a few women in San Andrés who do not understand Spanish."

Forty years ago, it would seem, Spanish was already firmly established in the valley. Yet Spanish fluency among the residents did not immediately threaten the vitality of Kaqchikel. The majority of survey respondents, whose mean age is about forty, report that they learned Kaqchikel as young children. Thus, forty years ago Kaqchikel was still being passed on to offspring in most homes.

In the past forty years the linguistic situation of the valley has changed radically. Though most parents today are bilingual, many speak only Spanish to their children. In his study of seventy-four households, Annis (1987: 28) found that "none of the present group of one- to four-year-olds were learning Kaqchikel as their first language, while almost all children in the generation now over forty learned Kaqchikel first."

What Annis describes is a shift generation—parents who do not teach their native tongue to their children—whose legacy may return the Quinizilapa Valley to monolingualism, but this time in Spanish. The current decrease in Kaqchikel use is recognized throughout the communities. For example, teachers with long experience in the valley schools report that their students today speak less Kaqchikel than those of the past. The balance between Spanish and Kaqchikel has been shifting across recent generations. The decrease in Kaqchikel usage in the valley parallels the changes in education levels, household economies, and traditional clothing.

Kaqchikel Fluency by Age

Survey respondents were asked to evaluate their own fluency in Kaqchikel as good, fair, or none. The distribution of respondents by fluency rating is displayed in Table 5.7, which offers a fairly encouraging view of Kaqchikel vitality. Only 11 percent rate themselves as nonfluent (meaning monolingual in Spanish), and almost 70 percent as fully fluent. Husbands were rated as slightly more fluent than wives; almost 80 percent of them are rated as fully fluent in Kaqchikel, and less than 7 percent do not speak it.

Table 5.7 describes a population in which the majority of parents are fully Kaqchikel-speaking, and the threat to Kaqchikel vitality is not readily apparent. Not until these figures are broken down by age does a more sobering trend suggest itself.

The first analysis demonstrating the progressive loss of Kaqchikel in

TABLE 5.7. Kaqchikel Fluency among Respondents

Level of Fluency	Number of Respondents	Percent
None	49	11.0
Fair	90	20.2
Good	307	68.8
TOTAL	446	100.0

TABLE 5.8. Average Age of Respondent by Kaqchikel Fluency Level

Level of Fluency	Mean Age	Number of Respondents
None	34.53	49
Fair	35.19	90
Good	40.79	305
TOTAL	38.96	444

the valley population calculates the mean age of respondents at each of the three fluency levels. These data are presented in Table 5.8. The oldest of the three groups, at just over forty, is the most fluent. Their mean age is five years older than the semifluent group, which, in turn, is about six months older than the nonfluent group. In Table 5.9 the average Kaqchikel fluency for three age groups is calculated on a scale of 0 (does not speak it) to 3 (fluent speaker). Both Tables 5.8 and 5.9 illustrate that the lower the age, the less likely it is that the respondent will speak Kaqchikel fluently.

One possible interpretation of Table 5.8 is that respondents simply do not learn Kaqchikel until they are older. There are reports of other bilingual communities in which the traditional language is not acquired until adulthood. But this is not the case in the Quinizilapa towns. Most respondents who speak Kaqchikel fluently or semifluently report learning it as children. Additionally, 95 percent of the respondents who speak

TABLE 5.9. Average Kaqchikel Fluency Level by Age Groups

Age Group	Mean Fluency Level (1–3)	Number of Respondents
Under 30	2.34	121
30–42	2.65	170
Over 42	2.68	153
TOTAL	2.58	444

Kaqchikel report that they learned it at home. The possibility is remote, then, that the decreasing Kaqchikel fluency by age is a product of a static situation in which people do not learn the language until they get older.

Kaqchikel Fluency and the Semifluent Speaker

One result of language shift—valley residents who do not speak Kaqchikel—appears fairly evenly distributed among valley towns, as indicated in Table 5.10. About 11 percent of the respondents (and 7 percent of their husbands) are reported as nonspeakers of the language. Their percentages vary little—by 3 percent—from one community to another. However, the percentage of fully fluent Kaqchikel speakers varies a great deal from town to town—by 35 percent—suggesting that a decrease in fluent speakers and an increase in nonfluent adults are separate, though related, processes of the language shift.

As one language's various duties in a community become usurped by another, its full range of styles and forms is no longer given public forum. Thus, children have insufficient exposure to acquire the language completely and become less than fully fluent. The emergence of semispeakers has been documented in many language obsolescence scenarios (Dorian 1989; Hill and Hill 1986). Because semispeakers cannot

TABLE 5.10. Respondents' Fluency in Kaqchikel by Community

| Community | Fluency Level of Respondents | | |
	None	Somewhat	Fully
San Antonio	22	46	132
	11.0%	23.0%	66.0%
San Andrés	8	24	34
	12.1%	36.4%	51.5%
Stgo Zamora	7	4	69
	8.8%	5.0%	86.3%
Sta Catarina	12	16	72
	12.0%	16.0%	72.0%
COLUMN TOTALS:			
Cases	49	90	307
Percent	11.0%	20.2%	68.8%

fully transfer the language to a following generation, they exacerbate language shift in a community.

In the Quinizilapa Valley semifluent speakers are reported in every community and account for about 20 percent of respondents (and 14 percent of husbands). The percentage of semifluent speakers is greater in the communities reporting lower general levels of Kaqchikel fluency. Over 36 percent of the respondents in San Andrés self-identify as semifluent, compared to only 5 percent of those in Santiago.

Kaqchikel Use and the Shift Generation

Language use patterns for individuals in the valley, once established, seem to be stable. For example, respondents who report having learned Kaqchikel at home also report still using Kaqchikel with their parents. But new patterns are different from the old. Younger parents today are more likely to speak Spanish to their own parents and to their children, whether or not they speak any Kaqchikel. Since there is a strong correspondence between Kaqchikel use with offspring and offspring Kaqchikel fluency, the home appears to be the only current locus of Kaqchikel transference. Changes in language use in the home have wide-ranging implications for language vitality in the entire community. Kaqchikel is no longer the first language learned by most children in the valley. Most homes use at least some Spanish with children, and half report using mostly Spanish. Kaqchikel may be reduced from the language of hearth and home to a language used only with grandparents, whose end is thus in sight.

San Andrés reports the least pervasive Kaqchikel use by respondents with their parents, implying that the shift toward Spanish use began in the previous generation. The high percentage of semifluent speakers in that town fits such a hypothesis. Santa Catarina reports the highest degree of Kaqchikel use with parents and with offspring, making it the most stable and least shifting community (see Table 5.11).

A comparison of the differences between language use with parents and offspring suggests the severity of language shift at a particular moment. For example, Santiago Zamora shows the highest degree of Kaqchikel fluency in the valley, yet the lowest degree of Kaqchikel use with offspring. This suggests that Santiago Zamora is presently undergoing the most acute degree of language shift in the valley.

San Andrés shows the least change in language use between generations, signaling a more advanced stage of shift. Surprisingly, Santiago Zamora shows the greatest difference in use patterns, despite its rank as

TABLE 5.11. LANGUAGE USE WITH OFFSPRING BY COMMUNITY

Community	Language Used		
	Kaqchikel	Both	Spanish
San Antonio	27	78	102
	13.0%	37.7%	49.3%
San Andrés	10	23	33
	15.2%	34.8%	50.0%
Stgo Zamora	2	24	48
	2.7%	32.4%	64.9%
Sta Catarina	40	37	58
	29.6%	27.4%	43.0%
COLUMN TOTALS:			
Cases	79	162	241
Percent	16.4%	33.6%	50.0%

the most fluent community in Kaqchikel. This also suggests that Santiago is presently undergoing a very rapid language shift.

Gender, Fluency, and Economic Activity

Gender is repeatedly cited as a determining factor in language use patterns. Language use differences are usually attributed to the division of labor and role expectations that culturally distinguish the sexes. In particular, sustained economic activity outside the home, and especially outside the community, exposes the individual to linguistic varieties of wider currency and impels their adoption.

Women of Highland Mayan communities are generally considered to be more conservative than men in the maintenance of traditional culture. This conception may be partly due to the visible symbolism of the traditional dress, which women continue to wear more than men. However, the surveyed women of the Quinizilapa Valley rated their Kaqchikel fluency as lower than that of their spouses. The differential remains constant across age group and community boundaries. Though possibly due in part to respondent bias, the economic activity of these women is also worth consideration. Women of the Quinizilapa towns have become actively engaged in commercial activity outside their communities. The display and sale of textiles is now a well-known occupation, but the distribution and marketing of produce and low-cost manufactured goods in the markets of Antigua and the capital employ increasing numbers of Quinizilapa women as well. This commercial activity may in part account for their deviation from the expected pattern of greater fluency than men. The relationship between lower Kaqchikel fluency levels and economic activity deserves further examination.

Cultural Change and Language Use

In his interpretation of economic and cultural change in the Quinizilapa Valley, Annis argues that the "Indian" identity of the valley is the product of a tradition of successful participation in and exploitation of several economic networks, including both *milpa* agriculture and nearby metropolitan markets. Households most successful in straddling multiple systems were those most likely to remain Catholic and active in community/religious institutions and thus remain most "Indian." Conversion to evangelical Protestantism was most common among individuals on the fringes of village life, those who were least successful in both the internal and external economies. Protestantism's emphasis on the individual and the individual's direct relation to God and salvation releases the convert from the constraints of community religious obligations, thus paving the way toward individual prosperity in the outside economy.

The linguistic counterpart to the successful straddling of separate economic spheres would seem to be bilingualism. Participation in the cash economy has made Spanish acquisition increasingly necessary over the past century as a tool to deal with the outside world. But the use of Spanish inside the home with offspring is comparable to conversion to evangelical Protestantism. Both lie beyond merely gaining fluency in another medium and signify the taking to heart of foreign values.

The factors that Annis found relevant in distinguishing Protestant converts from Catholics are also applicable in the study of shifters. In agriculture, for example, Protestants tended to outperform Catholics in every aspect except corn production. Likewise, language shifters grow less corn than nonshifters, indicating less reliance on the traditional *milpa* economy. In textile production Annis found that Catholic households were more likely to produce traditional weavings for household consumption, versus commercial textiles for sale. In the present study the association between *huipil* use and Kaqchikel vitality is very strong.

Not only were women in *huipiles* more fluent, but they also reported higher levels of transference to offspring.

The role of Protestantism in cultural change in Mayan communities has been the subject of much debate and sharp criticism among Maya activists. Yet whether language shift and Protestant conversion are merely similar responses to changing economic conditions or causally related is not yet known. In a 1996 follow-up survey in Santa Catarina, I found no significant differences in Kaqchikel fluency by religious affiliation (Brown 1996b). Further research is needed to determine the impact of proselytizing sects on the vitality of Mayan languages.

Social Networks and Diffusion of Shift

The concept of the social network provides an appropriate instrument for the present account of the effects of modernization upon communications in the Quinizilapa towns. Karl Wolfgang Deutsch (1966) predicts that modernization will open up networks and realign them along a more global axis, making a medium of wider currency necessary. Such is the case of the Quinizilapa Valley, monolingual two hundred years ago and now, connected in many more ways to the outside world, completely fluent in Spanish.

Networks with a high proportion of interconnected points are described as dense; when interpersonal links in a network encompass multiple types of relationships (kin, neighbor, co-worker, etc.), the network is described as multiplex (Milroy 1987). The communities of the Quinizilapa Valley are examples of dense, multiplex networks. Studies of these kinds of networks, particularly in urban, working-class neighborhoods, ascribe to them an effective norm-enforcement mechanism. Also typical of dense, multiplex networks is a high value placed on the ethic of social solidarity.

Traditional Mayan communities place importance on the solidarity of the group, constraining individual deviance through customs such as endogamy and community-specific dress, as well as wealth-leveling mechanisms exemplified in the *cofradía* system. As described by Annis (1987), "*milpa* logic" favors the reinvestment of surpluses into expressions of community membership and thus strengthens an economic system that discourages individual enrichment.

When dense networks are disrupted (for example, due to urban renewal projects), the need for markers of individual status, including educational attainment for offspring, increases. Again, such trends may be found in the Quinizilapa communities. Annis (1987) interprets the rise in evangelical Protestantism as an exchange of the traditional communal value system for an impersonal metric rewarding individual achievement.

Network density has been proposed as a positive factor in the rate at which innovations diffuse in a community. Studies of Mayan communities report that the new technology that has been adopted has been incorporated fairly quickly. It is suggested, then, that network density will also be a positive factor in the rate of language shift in a community.

The Quinizilapa towns possess relatively dense networks, some denser than others. It is expected that higher network density in a community will coincide with a faster and more uniform language shift. Several characteristics of each community suggest the degree of network density.

An initial clue to network density is the total population of the community. It stands to reason that if a network is dense because points are interconnected then the probability of interconnection is greater in a smaller population, provided that outside contact remains constant across communities. Among the four communities, the percentage of immigrants remains fairly constant, and all communities have outside commercial ties.

Of the study towns, the two *aldeas*, San Andrés Cevallos and Santiago Zamora, have by far the smallest populations (under five hundred and under four hundred, respectively). The population of Santa Catarina is over three times greater than that of San Andrés; the population of San Antonio is over ten times greater. The multiplexity of a network is determined by the complexity of its links. In the two *aldeas* individuals are more likely linked to each other as neighbor and kin than in the two larger towns. In San Antonio not all residents are neighbors. The town is divided into four *cantones*, and residents do not necessarily consider themselves neighbors of Antoneros in other *cantones*. Santa Catarina has no official divisions such as *cantones*, but residents recognize three spatial divisions, sometimes called *barrios*, defined geographically by the head of the valley and a low hill protruding from the valley wall. In the two *aldeas* settlement is physically concentrated so that all residents are neighbors.

Both *aldeas* are described by residents and knowledgeable outsiders (e.g., health center staff) as composed of a few extended families ("Son unas pocas familias, no más"). Indeed, over 50 percent of the residents in each town share at least one of three last names. Residents of the *aldeas,* then, are more likely to be linked to their neighbors as kin than are residents of the two *municipios.* The fact that two randomly selected individuals from the *aldeas* are more likely to be neighbors and kin, regardless of any other links, argues for more multiplex networks in the smaller towns.

Language shift is most advanced and seems to have been fastest in the *aldea* of San Andrés, which has the lowest Kaqchikel fluency levels of all communities. The *aldea* of Santiago Zamora displays the highest fluency levels, but also the largest proportion of parents who speak only Spanish to their offspring. The speed of this shift is in part attributed to the density and multiplexity of networks in these communities.

According to Eric Wolf's model (1957) of the traditional Mayan community, cultural survival strategies such as communal land tenure and wealth-leveling mechanisms seek to maintain uniformity among the population. The forces of modernization tend to skew the distribution of resources in a community and to stress individual gain over communal welfare. From this perspective, if language competence is taken as a resource, increased variation in fluency levels within a population is one more reflection of the penetration of modernizing influences in a community.

The high proportion of semispeakers highlights the abrupt nature of language shift in San Andrés and corresponds with historical accounts of the rapid transition from relative poverty and isolation to recent wealth from cash-cropping. Moreover, the cohesion of the town's small population and its compact settlement would serve to accelerate the shift. Language shift in the valley towns, then, may be accompanied by a progressively greater diversity in the distribution of fluency levels within each community, due to differences in the strength of social networks.

Although it still remains to determine the ranking of causal factors in triggering a language shift, once that shift has been triggered, social network features appear to play an important role in determining the pace and scope of the shift. Further research is needed in Highland Mayan communities to better define social networks and the progression of changes in language fluency and use along network paths.

CONCLUDING COMMENTS

Despite a century-long tradition of bilingualism, the past few decades have seen a radical change in the status of Kaqchikel as a mother tongue in the Quinizilapa Valley. Statistics corroborate what is widely recognized throughout the valley: the Quinizilapa communities are becoming progressively less fluent in Kaqchikel. The two communities representing the extremes in Kaqchikel fluency, San Andrés Cevallos and Santiago Zamora, also demonstrate the fastest shift, characterized by increased variation of fluency levels within their populations.

The data from household surveys describe Kaqchikel vitality in the two areas of fluency and use. In each area a subset of the surveyed population that wields an important impact on Kaqchikel vitality is identified. In terms of fluency, it is those who fail to achieve full fluency. Regarding use, it is those bilingual parents who speak only Spanish to their children (i.e., the shift generation).

Further research should trace the progression of language usage with parents and offspring over time to profile language shift in a given community. Language use might be represented numerically as it is here, in the form of an average between the two languages. Thus, in cases of rapid and fairly uniform shift, the difference between the mean of language use with parents and of language use with offspring should expand quickly, climax, and then quickly dwindle. On the other hand, in communities where the shift is more erratic and scattered throughout the population, the difference in usage means should fluctuate and show less linear development. At the individual level, respondents who report speaking Kaqchikel with parents but Spanish to offspring are classified as members of the shift generation, and they make up about one-fourth of the surveyed population. The identification of a shift generation is one of the paramount tasks in evaluating language vitality. Discovering the number and distribution of shifters reveals the precise degree of shift and helps predict future vitality.

The prognosis for the future of Kaqchikel in the Quinizilapa towns is not bright. In all the towns combined, half the respondents do not speak to their children in Kaqchikel, and Spanish is used to some degree in over two-thirds of the valley households. Should present trends continue (for example, if the 20 percent decrease in fluency from the respondent generation to the next repeats itself), within two generations Kaqchikel will no longer be spoken in the valley.

However, even though Kaqchikel loss is verifiable, the valley is still strongly bilingual. Although more people speak Spanish now than in the past, substantial portions of every sector examined (respondents, spouses, and offspring) are still fluent in Kaqchikel. Sufficient resources should persist for the next twenty years or so to permit a deceleration or even reversal of the language shift in the event that some intervention program or other factor effects widespread changes in language behavior.

NOTES

1. The complete names of the communities are rarely used in local reference. The "Aguas Calientes," "Cevallos," and "Zamora" are dropped from the names of San Antonio, San Andrés, and Santiago, except in formal use. Santa Catarina is known simply as "Santa." For the sake of conciseness, local terminology is used when convenient in the discussion here.

2. The cultural impact of national education incites heated controversy. Though touted by the government as a benevolent promoter of economic development and as a necessary tool of national unification, state education is frequently accused of ethnocide by Mayan activists and is one of the culprits most blamed for language loss (for example, Cojtí Cuxil 1987; Sam Colop 1983).

3. There has been, as yet, no systematic analysis of the linguistic differences between San Antonio and Santa Catarina, nor an explanation of how two communities with similar origins and centuries of coexistence could develop characteristics typical of towns separated by much greater distances. Such an investigation could shed light on the linguistic origins of the valley as well as address central questions concerning the development of Indianness during the Colonial Period. For if, as Annis suggests, the language, like the cultural identity of the valley, is a reflection more of an externally imposed economic system than of indigenous tenacity, the preservation of prehispanic elements should also be taken into account.

6. CASE STUDY THREE
San Juan Comalapa

Susan Garzon

THE COMMUNITY
Arriving in Comalapa

Several times a day a bus leaves Guatemala City heading for the Mayan town of San Juan Comalapa. The passengers boarding the old buses are mostly country people. The men wear the polyester shirts and dark pants and the straw Western-style hats typical of rural Central Americans. Some of the women wear dresses, but many wear brightly colored Mayan clothing: richly brocaded or embroidered *huipiles* with straight ikat-dyed *cortes*. The bus streaks along the Pan American Highway, heading for Chimaltenango, the departmental capital, where it pulls off the road and takes on more passengers. By this time, it is usually full. On market days in Comalapa (Sunday, Wednesday, and Friday) people are packed in together, standing room only. A few minutes outside Chimaltenango, the bus leaves the Pan American Highway and heads for Zaragoza, a nearby Ladino town. After skirting the plaza and dropping off several riders, the bus begins its journey into the mountains along a winding dirt road that climbs up pine-covered mountainsides overlooking deep ravines. It stops to pick up riders from neighboring villages and occasionally young soldiers from a nearby garrison. The bus squeezes past an occasional truck along the narrow, bumpy road, but cars are rare. About three hours after its departure, the bus rounds the shoulder of the last hill, descending into more level terrain, and Comalapa comes into view.

The town sits in a sheltered, level area among the surrounding hills. All readily accessible land is tilled, and what remains is covered with pine, oak, and cypress trees. On the outskirts of town the bus passes small houses and a large neighborhood *pila* where women gather to do the family washing. Spring-fed *pilas*, some with ghostly legends, are found in various parts of the town. The bus passes the public elementary school for boys, its one-story buildings lined up in rows. Nearby is the Instituto de Educación Básica, a public high school consisting of a two-story building with a basketball court. Soon the bus passes the ruins of Calvario, a former church now being restored, where townspeople go to celebrate Easter. Across from it is the gate to the town cemetery. As the bus approaches the center of town, the houses become more numerous. Painted in various colors and wedged in side by side, they show only a front wall of wood or cement block, with a door or dark entryway. Nearer the center of town, the road becomes the Calle Real (Royal Street). In recent years the town has been gradually paving this section with cement blocks. Small stores appear among the houses, then a gas pump. A large concrete Catholic church dominates one block. This is Sagrado Corazón, the more orthodox of the two main Catholic churches in Comalapa. Finally, the bus pulls into the central plaza and stops in front of a small park with benches, flowering bushes, and a few pre-Colombian sculptures.

The plaza is the heart of Comalapa. At one end is the large indoor market. Even on nonmarket days women often sit outside, selling their goods spread out before them. On market days the area is crowded with people buying and selling fresh produce, colorful flowers, woven goods, and all kinds of manufactured items, from clothing to cassette tapes. On a corner of the plaza is the municipal building, where the mayor and other officials have their offices. San Juan Comalapa is the administrative center for eight villages and twenty-two hamlets (Gall 1976: 975). The town has a population of about 16,300, and the *municipio* at large has about 27,800. Comalapa's population is overwhelmingly Maya. Indians made up 95 percent of the population according to the 1973 census (Farber 1978: 35), and there has been no major change in the ethnic makeup of the town since then. At the time of my fieldwork the mayor of Comalapa was Maya. Across from the municipal building is the one-story public elementary school for girls. Classrooms are arranged around a central courtyard where the girls have recess and physical education. Outside the school, on the plaza, is a large basketball court where young men and women often congregate to play informal games after school and on weekends. Nearby, a colonial-style fountain adorns the plaza. Next to the school are two Catholic churches. The farther one is the colonial Church of San Juan Bautista. Almost totally destroyed by a massive earthquake that hit the Highland region in 1976, it is now under reconstruction. The nearer church is made of cement block in a simplified colonial style. It functions as the traditional Catholic church in Comalapa, the home of the *cofradías* responsible for honoring the saints in the fiesta cycle typical of Highland Mayan communities. A number of small Protestant churches representing around fifteen denominations serve the 15 to 20 percent of the population who are Protestant (Mejía 1985: 20).

Comalapa boasts a number of educational institutions, including the two public primary schools and the Instituto de Educación Básica Andrés Curuchich, where students can study from seventh to ninth grade, earning a diploma in Basic Education. For those students who want to stay in Comalapa and earn a more advanced degree, there is also a three-year program in accounting. In addition, Comalapa has both Catholic and evangelical elementary schools. Among the public institutions are a hospital and health center, where people can consult a doctor or dentist. There is also a cultural center, offering classes in music and art and housing a small auditorium. Electricity and potable water are available throughout the town, although running water is usually only available for a few hours a day during the dry season. The area where I lived had water from about four to eight in the morning during the dry months.

The Early History of the Town

The town of San Juan Comalapa dates to the period following the Spanish Conquest, when Franciscan friars resettled the defeated Mayas into centralized towns. The people of Comalapa were Kaqchikels who had taken refuge at Ruya'al Xot, 'River of the Comales.' In 1549 the new town was entrusted to a conquistador, Juan Pérez Dardón. Throughout the Colonial Period the townspeople were required to supply labor and various forms of tribute to the Spaniards and their descendants, first through the *encomienda* and later through the *repartimiento*. By the end of the Colonial Period Comalapa had attained the status of a curacy, with two churches, a ranch, and ten *cofradías* (Mejía 1985: 11–12).

A report from Archbishop Cortés y Larraz (1958: 89–91), who visited the town in 1770, provides some insight into ethnic and language relations in colonial Comalapa. At that time the curacy as a whole had a population of about 7,000, including approximately ten Ladino families. A school with eighty-nine students provided instruction in reading, writing, and Christian doctrine, all taught in Spanish. The archbishop examined the schoolchildren and found that many of the small children knew their letters, as well as the "Our Father," the "Ave Maria," the creed, and some questions of the doctrine. Some of the older students were learning to read, but he noted that they confused and stumbled over many of the words, and none of them had learned to write. Overall, the school was not very successful. The archbishop reported that none of the students could speak Spanish and that they immediately forgot what little they had learned as soon as they left school.

The students' failure to learn and use Spanish is probably partly attributable to pedagogical methods, but, beyond that, it indicates that the Spanish language played a very peripheral role in the life of most Comalapans during late colonial times. There was probably little incentive for children to learn the language, since it was not used in ordinary interaction among Mayas and social barriers would have precluded any substantial interaction with Ladinos inside or outside the town. The sharp division between Indian and Spanish societies has survived well into this century, although relations between the two groups have been slowly changing in recent years.

During this century, Comalapa has experienced changing conditions. Traditional life, based on the cultivation of corn, has become less feasible while at the same time Guatemalan society has become more open to the participation of Mayas. Although some of the changes have been gradual, many accelerated during the 1970s and the years that followed. In the following section I outline some of the events and trends that have affected life in Comalapa in recent years. I am fortunate to be able to draw on Anne Farber's 1978 dissertation, focusing on language choice and ethnic identity in Comalapa.

Changing Economic Patterns

Traditionally, the economy of Comalapa has been based on *milpa* agriculture. The principal crop is corn, with black beans and lima beans also raised. Since this is the subsistence base for families, each family tries to grow and process enough corn and beans to feed itself throughout the year. Squash, pumpkin, and edible greens are also sometimes raised for family consumption. In addition, cash crops such as wheat and potatoes may be raised (Mejía 1985: 17). In recent years more exotic export crops, such as broccoli, have been added. The population of Comalapa has been growing steadily, from 3,500 in 1890 to 7,400 in 1950 to 27,800 in 1997. At the same time the land base has not increased. There are almost no communal lands, so families must depend on small landholdings; in the countryside around Comalapa 72 percent of the farms consist of fewer than 3.6 acres (Mejía 1985: 17). Since there are many people in Comalapa who own little or no land, townspeople must find income elsewhere. In some cases, individuals are able to rent enough land to supplement their own holdings or to work part-time as agricultural day laborers. Even those men who identify themselves as farmers often have a secondary source of income, including trades such as baker, mason, tailor, shoemaker, carpenter, or artist (Farber 1978). Comalapa is a center for folk art, mainly paintings of traditional scenes from Comalapa's past, such as the saint's day fiesta, Easter, or weddings. In some families painting has become an inherited occupation. The interest in painting traditional scenes has probably helped to keep alive a knowledge of older customs and lifeways, especially among young people.

Textile production is the main source of income in some households. Women usually weave on a backstrap loom, while men are more likely to use a treadle loom. The 1970s were a high point for the weaving industry in Comalapa, as evidenced by the existence of two active weaving cooperatives. Their activities were disrupted by the violence of the early 1980s (Mejía 1985: 19–20). However, weavers continue to work. In recent years Guatemalan textiles have been popular internationally. To meet the demand, many women weave small items at home, such as coin purses or wall hangings. Women also continue to weave fine *huipiles*, often for the use of women in their own household.

Women also engage in trade. Some buy produce from villagers and resell it in town or in Guatemala City, while others buy goods in Guatemala City that they resell in Comalapa. A number of families have opened small house-front stores that sell items like soft drinks and eggs to their neighbors, and it is often the wives who handle customers.

Men sometimes leave Comalapa in order to find employment, often in Guatemala City. Married men may take their families with them or leave them in Comalapa and come home on weekends.

Increased Integration with the National Society

In recent years the town of Comalapa has become more open to the influence of Guatemalan society. For example, many Mayas have left their traditional Catholic form of worship to adopt a more orthodox form. Evangelical Protestant churches have also gained converts, as evidenced by the large number of churches distributed throughout the town. A number of Indians have become affiliated with national political parties and have gained access to local power through them. Many of these changes began during the 1970s, when Mayas began joining cooperatives and participating in organizations beyond the local level. These changes resulted in considerable polarization in the town, with families divided according to their traditional or progressive orientations.

While individuals in both groups identified strongly with their Indian background, their values and behavior sometimes diverged. According to Farber (1978: 10–11), the progressive citizens of Comalapa held the idea that Indians needed to become involved in the world outside of Comalapa in order to ensure their survival as a community. They sent their children to school and taught them Spanish in the home to prepare them for dealing with the Ladino world. This was seen as the key to economic and social advancement. Not surprisingly, the progressive citizens were often bilingual, while their more traditional neighbors were likely to be monolingual in Kaqchikel. Today there seems to be less polarization in the town, probably due in part to the realization on the part of Comalapans that isolation and a return to traditional life are not really possible.

Earthquake and Political Violence

Unusual hardships beset the people of Comalapa during the years between 1976 and 1984. Adults in Comalapa all have vivid memories of the 1976 earthquake, which left some 1,500 people dead (Mejía 1985: 15). Everyone lost family members and friends. It is said that sometime after the earthquake ghostly specters were seen in the cemetery. In the account by Idalma Mejía de Rodas (1985: 16), animal ghosts (coyotes) appeared by the hill of Saint Anthony north of town. At first people thought they were there to dig up the recently buried. Later, however, they concluded that the spirits had come to warn them of the political violence that was soon to overtake the town.

Only a few years after the trauma of the earthquake, a new kind of devastation struck, a period of widespread political violence which people refer to simply as *la violencia*. Many of the town's leaders were killed, including those who had participated in organizations such as the cooperatives. At the same time, a great deal of the violence was more random and unpredictable; families and even whole villages were massacred, and some people fled the town to hide in the cities. Although the violence has largely abated in Comalapa since the early 1980s, many people in the late 1980s still lived in fear of its return. When I arrived in Comalapa in 1987, some individuals were profoundly distrustful of strangers, sometimes blaming foreigners for the violence they had suffered. These individuals were reluctant to interact with me as an outsider; they were understandably anxious to avoid any kind of public activity that might foster the return of the violence. However, I also met many people who welcomed the possibility of participating more fully in Guatemalan society, taking advantage of educational and employment opportunities. Although they had painful memories of the violent years, they had not retreated from involvement in the outside world. Indeed, this is not really an option for most people in Comalapa.

Formal Education in Comalapa

In the mid-1970s Farber (1978) found that some inhabitants held a negative view of education. Undoubtedly, parents had grown up with the expectation that they would spend their lives in hard physical labor, harvesting corn on the mountainsides and enduring privations as they raised their families. These parents felt that school was ineffective and encouraged laziness. Some also remembered teachers who were cruel or unsympathetic. Many of the adults, particularly the women, had received little or no schooling themselves (Farber 1978: 244–245). However, at that time, negative attitudes toward formal education were beginning to change; today, as a result of changing economic conditions, formal education is seen in a positive light by most Comalapans. Parents are aware that many of their children will not be able to support themselves and their families by growing corn and beans on a family landholding. Therefore, their prosperity, and even survival, depends on an ability to interact competently with members of the Spanish-speaking world. As a result, an increasing number of families are sending their sons and daughters to school and sending them for longer periods.

Various opportunities for education exist in Comalapa, although this has not always been the case. Maya boys were first able to complete primary school in the 1930s, while girls were not able to attend until the 1940s. In the late 1960s and early 1970s educational opportunities began to expand further. The Catholic primary school, Medalla Milagrosa, opened in 1967, and an evangelical primary school, Bethlehém, opened in 1973 (Gall 1976: 474). The Instituto de Educación Básica, offering grades seven to nine, opened one year earlier, and the program in accounting was added later. In 1988 there were over 1,800 children in the public primary schools, with over 400 in the Catholic school and almost 300 in the evangelical school. The number of students in secondary school is smaller but steadily growing (see Table 6.1). In 1975

TABLE 6.1. Number of Graduates from Third Year Básico in Selected Years

Year	Men	Women	Total
1975	14	9	23
1980	38	34	72
1985	38	20	58
1990	49	28	77
1991	55	48	103
1992	75	37	112

Note: Includes both Indian and Ladino students.

only 23 students graduated from Básico: 14 boys and 9 girls. In 1980 the number had increased to 72, with 38 boys and 34 girls. Although this is not a large number for a town the size of Comalapa, it should be remembered that 1980 was one of the worst years of the violence, and it is noteworthy that this many young people were willing to continue their educations at a time when educated Mayas were viewed with suspicion and any kind of public activity was somewhat dangerous. In 1992, 112 students graduated from Básico, 75 men and 37 women. The students in the graduating classes have been both Maya and Ladino, with Mayas outnumbering Ladinos. A number of young people go into the accounting program, which is also housed at the Instituto; in 1988 there were 62 students enrolled.

Educated Young Adults

For the first time in Comalapa's history there is a sizable group of adults with an education beyond secondary school. They constitute a minority in a town where most children still do not complete primary school. Nevertheless, they represent a growing trend, as families increasingly see education as a means of survival. In order to understand what is happening to this group, and whether they are likely to maintain their use of Kaqchikel, I carried out a study on Básico graduates from the years 1979, 1981, and 1982. At the time of the study, in 1988, the graduates were in their early to mid-twenties. I employed three female graduates of these classes to assist in data collection. They compiled informal lists of

TABLE 6.2.

Occupations for Maya Básico Graduates in Their Twenties (1988 data)

Occupations	Women	Men	Total	Percent
Education				
Administrator	2	1	3	
Teacher	15	15	30	
TOTAL	17	16	33	29
Traditional				
Farmer	0	7	7	
Homemaker	22	0	22	
TOTAL	22	7	29	25
Business				
Independent	1	1	2	
Accountant	3	2	5	
Secretary	2	0	2	
Other Employee	2	2	4	
TOTAL	8	5	13	11
Students				
Medical	1	3	4	
Architecture	0	1	1	
Other	3	2	5	
TOTAL	4	6	10	9
Security				
National Police	0	4	4	
Treasury Police	0	2	2	
Army	0	3	3	
TOTAL	0	9	9	8
Technical Fields				
Agronomy	0	1	1	
Aviation	0	1	1	
Health	4	0	4	
TOTAL	4	2	6	5
Skilled Trades				
Baker, Bus driver, etc.	2	4	6	5
Unemployed	0	2	2	2
Insufficient Data	1	5	6	5
TOTAL	58	56	114	

their former classmates then interviewed the graduates or their families to collect information such as whether the graduates had received further education, what kinds of employment they had found, where they were living, and whether they had married.

The survey revealed that the majority of those students who finished Básico (ninth grade) in Comalapa went on for further education. Of an estimated 114 Indian students who graduated in 1979, 1981, and 1982, approximately 85 percent continued their studies, many of them receiving degrees in primary education. In fact, over one-fourth (29 percent) of both men and women were employed in education (see Table 6.2). The experiences of this group offer insights into the opportunities and obstacles facing young Mayas who wish to gain entry into middle-class Guatemalan society.

Opportunities for Teachers

In 1988 none of the young people with backgrounds in education had found jobs in the Comalapa public schools. This is not unusual since positions in the public schools are awarded by the National Ministry of Education and are scarce. Those openings that exist are sometimes in remote villages, requiring teachers to commute by motorcycle. Kaqchikel speakers may find themselves teaching in a different language region, where they must communicate in Spanish. Due to the scarcity of jobs in the public schools, eleven teachers took positions in the private religious schools in Comalapa or one of its villages. Although these schools are well regarded, they pay poorly and lack benefits. Another man found work in literacy training. In addition, two women were directors of the private primary schools in Comalapa, although by 1993 one of them had given up her position as director to take a teaching position in one of the public schools in Comalapa. In 1988 twenty-two graduates had educational positions outside of Comalapa, including a woman teaching for the army and a man working in Guatemala City for the ministry program for bilingual education.

Not all the young people trained in education found jobs in that field. Other men's jobs included plumber, bus driver, and member of the Treasury Police. Women's jobs included secretary and staff member at a museum. Other graduates found themselves without formal employment. Nine women, six of them single, were listed as homemakers, performing *oficios domésticos,* which probably often included weaving. None of the men with a background in education was listed as a farmer, the traditional male counterpart to homemaker, although one man was identified as unemployed.

When teachers I knew found positions, even many hours' travel away from their homes, they did not hesitate to accept them. Some of the women who were initially unemployed found jobs later on; by 1993 four of the women who had previously been listed as homemakers had found teaching jobs, two of them outside Comalapa.

According to these data, the young people trained in education faced four main options upon graduation. The most favored option, a position in the Comalapa public schools, was initially closed to all of them, although with time more may be offered such a position. The three alternatives included accepting a poorly compensated job in a local private school, which would usually enable them to stay in Comalapa and live at home, returning to traditional work in their homes, or taking a formal job outside education, which often meant leaving Comalapa.

Employment and Residence among Básico Graduates

For educated young people in Comalapa, opportunities for employment often lie outside the community. Almost one-half of the Básico graduates in the survey, 54 out of 113, have moved away from Comalapa. A number of occupations, such as those in some technical fields and in security, often require residence outside Comalapa. For example, a person trained as an aviation technician must work near an airfield. The members of the National Police work in Guatemala City, while both employees of the Treasury Police live in another department. It remains to be seen whether people trained in medicine and other professions will choose to return to their hometown. Sometimes young people who move to other areas to study or work find spouses there, increasing their ties outside of Comalapa.

While some kinds of employment require outside residence, others, such as skilled trades, enable individuals to remain in Comalapa. Young people may also remain in Comalapa by returning to the traditional occupations of farmer or homemaker; one-quarter of the graduates surveyed had followed this course. As these individuals set down roots in Comalapa, they may choose to carry on traditional aspects of Mayan culture, including the Kaqchikel language, but it is too soon to tell. For some, residence in Comalapa is not permanent. By 1993 three of the married homemakers had left the town, and employment may eventually draw others away.

Predicting future residence is complicated by the high percentage of the graduates who are still single and thus have probably not established a permanent household. In 1988 approximately one-third of the class of 1979 was single. Among the 1981 graduates a much higher percentage was single—73 percent of the women and 69 percent of the men—while in the 1982 group 90 percent of the women and 77 percent of the men were single. These percentages are surprisingly high, given that most Comalapans traditionally marry at an early age, often in their teens (Mejía 1985: 16). The delay of marriage may be partly due to the period of violence, which made courting more difficult. It may also reflect young people's wish to become established professionally before marriage or their difficulty in finding acceptable partners. Individuals who marry late are likely to have more opportunity to meet and marry partners outside the town. They may also be more independent economically and better able to establish a household separate from their families. In both cases, the married couple may have limited contact with parents and grandparents who might still speak Kaqchikel on a regular basis.

Young people who leave Comalapa to study and work may return periodically. Over one-third of the graduates in the survey who had moved away from Comalapa regularly went home for weekends. In this way individuals are able to receive support from family members and assume family responsibilities themselves. They may also participate in the social life of the community, with its religious and secular celebrations and ongoing activities. Although not affluent, Comalapa is a bustling town with an energetic atmosphere. While many young people are willing to go almost anywhere to find a good job, there are definite advantages to living in Comalapa or at least to maintaining strong ties there, especially given the chronic instability of the Guatemalan economy.

LANGUAGE USE

The changes affecting Comalapa have had an impact on language use. The town as a whole is undergoing a shift toward ever greater use of Spanish, while the use of Kaqchikel is in decline. The course that this shift is taking can be seen by comparing data on language use from two studies: one carried out by Farber (1978) in 1974 to 1975 and another that I carried out with a group of colleagues in 1987 and 1988. During the approximately twelve years that elapsed between Farber's study and my own, trends that Farber observed have accelerated sharply, to the extent that the position of Kaqchikel seems much less secure than it did a short time ago.

Language Use in the Mid-1970s

Farber's (1978) study looked at language use and its relation to ethnic identity in Comalapa. Her research included an in-depth survey of forty households selected at random as well as a period of participant observation. At the time that Farber completed her fieldwork in Comalapa, she felt confident in asserting that all adult Indians spoke Kaqchikel (Farber 1978: 9). Since 90 to 95 percent of the population of the town claimed Indian ethnicity, this meant that the great majority of the town was Kaqchikel-speaking. At the same time, there was growing bilingualism. Reportedly, the increase had begun in the 1880s when a rising population made arable land scarce and forced townspeople to seek nontraditional means of support (Farber 1978: 15). However, the percentage of bilinguals was still probably low in the early half of the century, when the adults in her survey were growing up (Farber 1978: 244). In contrast, by 1975 over half of the adult population had some ability in Spanish. Although Farber's survey indicated that 54 percent of the population was still monolingual in Kaqchikel, this number included many women who claimed they were monolingual but actually had the ability to speak Spanish in certain limited contexts. The percentage of individuals describing themselves as bilinguals was 38 percent, and this group consisted largely of men. Finally, 8 percent of the survey group consisted of Ladinos who were monolingual in Spanish or Mayas who were bilingual in Spanish and a Mayan language other than Kaqchikel (Farber 1978: 33).

Farber's study offers limited information on the extent of bilingualism among children in the 1970s, since her focus was on adult proficiency. However, I was able to get some idea by questioning adults who were children at that time. The data come from interviews with women in their mid-twenties who graduated from Básico in 1979, 1981, and 1982 and who therefore were starting school in the mid-1970s. Out of 39 women, 26 (or two-thirds) said they already knew Spanish when they started school. A minority, one-third, reported knowing little or no Spanish. These women, who completed ninth grade and sometimes beyond, do not constitute a representative sample; their families were probably among the more progressive segment of the population. However, these numbers indicate a changing trend in language use. Many children, including girls, were starting school with some knowledge of Spanish, while others still faced the hurdle of studying in a nonnative (and structurally very different) language.

Language Use in the Late 1980s

By 1988, some thirteen years later, bilingualism had spread considerably. Although there were still older people, particularly women, who were monolingual in Kaqchikel, I met many women middle-aged and younger who spoke both Kaqchikel and Spanish. In addition, a knowledge of Kaqchikel had ceased to be an infallible concomitant of being Indian; some young adults admitted they had never learned the language. In view of this shift, one of the questions that concerned me was to what extent children in Comalapa were continuing to learn Kaqchikel, since the answer would have major implications for the future viability of the language. In order to answer this question, I worked with a team from the Universidad Rafael Landívar on designing interview-style proficiency tests in Kaqchikel and Spanish and administering them to children in the public primary schools. The testers were Kaqchikel-speaking women in their twenties, most of whom had a degree in education.

The test results indicate that while many children still learn Kaqchikel, Spanish now serves as the common medium of communication among school-age children. The continuing strength of Kaqchikel is demonstrated by the fact that approximately three-fourths of the students were able to complete the Kaqchikel test. Among the remaining one-fourth, some were unable to produce any responses in Kaqchikel; they either remained silent or answered the questions in Spanish. In other cases, the children produced a few words or phrases in Kaqchikel at the beginning of the test but switched to the exclusive use of Spanish when more complicated responses were required. The lowest rate of completion was recorded for the first grade girls; only 57 percent completed the Kaqchikel test. Among the remaining children—the first grade boys and the students in second to sixth grade—the rates of completion ranged between 67 percent for the fifth grade boys and 87 percent for the fifth grade girls. It is possible that a few children declined to speak Kaqchikel because they were uncomfortable using Kaqchikel in a school setting. For these students, failure to respond to the questions in Kaqchikel may reflect an unwillingness to use Kaqchikel in a public place normally associated with Spanish rather than lack of proficiency.

While one-fourth of the children tested failed to respond adequately in Kaqchikel, nearly all the children were able to converse in Spanish. Only one child failed to complete the Spanish test. Not all the students' responses conform to standard Spanish. Some responses are typical of a nonstandard variety of rural Guatemalan speech, while a few others have errors of a developmental or transfer nature. In general, however, the participants were able to respond adequately to a variety of questions. A first grade teacher from the private Catholic school also revealed that most children entering the first grade there already know Spanish; all but one of her fifty-three students knew the language at the beginning of the year. The evangelical school may be somewhat different. A colleague who had previously taught there reported that more Kaqchikel is used among the children. In general, though, the data on Spanish indicate that there are now very few school-age children in Comalapa who are monolingual in Kaqchikel. Almost all start school with an active knowledge of Spanish.

Intergenerational Shift

The data from the Básico graduates indicate that by the mid-1970s a number of Maya children were starting school with a knowledge of Spanish. This can be attributed to a trend that had already begun when Farber was in Comalapa: Indian parents were speaking Spanish with their children, so that many children were learning both Spanish and Kaqchikel as their mother languages. In fact, not only did progressive families choose to speak Spanish with their children, but traditional parents also encouraged their children to learn Spanish (Farber 1978: 11). Farber discusses this shift:

> There is recognition by Comalapans that the ability to speak and understand Spanish is an asset. Therefore, even parents with only slight bilingual ability prefer to speak to their children in Spanish. Since they report that their children will naturally learn to speak Cakchiquel by virtue of living in Comalapa, speaking Spanish with their children in the family setting increases their chances of learning to speak it. Indeed, it accords positive value to Spanish to have it spoken with the most intimate family contexts. This usage helps counteract the usual association of Spanish with Ladino values and norms. During my stay in Comalapa, I consistently observed parents speaking with their small children exclusively in Spanish. As the children

become older and attend school, the initial conscious effort to speak only in Spanish is often abandoned, giving way to the struggle of control and balancing the degree of culture change the child experiences. (Farber 1978: 177)

We can see the effects of the intergenerational shift by examining data on women in their twenties, since their parents were among the group experiencing pressure to speak Spanish with their children. Female Básico graduates from the classes of 1979, 1981, and 1982 were asked what language or languages they had learned first; their responses, summarized in Table 6.3, indicate that almost half identified Kaqchikel exclusively as their mother tongue. One-third claimed Spanish as their first language, while about 18 percent considered both Kaqchikel and Spanish to be their mother tongues.

Among the women who learned both languages at home, six out of seven mentioned that their fathers had spoken to them in Spanish while their mothers spoke to them in Kaqchikel. This is not surprising in view of Farber's observations that more men than women were bilingual in the 1970s. In other cases both parents spoke Kaqchikel with the girls, but their older siblings spoke Spanish with them; four women mentioned siblings as being instrumental in teaching them Spanish. This indicates that within some homes patterns in language use were gender related or age related. According to these data, the intergenerational shift was well underway in the early 1970s, although the majority of families still used some Kaqchikel with their children.

The progress of the shift since that time can be traced by comparing

TABLE 6.3. First Language Learned among Female Básico Students and Graduates

First Language Learned	Básico Graduates (Women in Twenties)		Básico Students (Women in Teens)	
	Number	Percent	Number	Percent
Kaqchikel	19	49	4	12
Both	7	18	10	30
Spanish	13	33	19	58
TOTAL	39	100	33	100

the first language learned by women in their twenties (the Básico graduates) with that learned by women in their teens. The teenagers were first year Básico students (equivalent to U.S. seventh graders) who filled out written questionnaires concerning their language use. Their ages ranged from twelve to eighteen, with the majority falling between thirteen and sixteen. The average difference in age between the Básico graduates and the students was only about eight years, far less than a generation, but long enough to indicate the progression of language shift. In the questionnaire the students were asked which language they had learned first: Kaqchikel, Spanish, or both. The results, summarized in Table 6.3, indicate that a clear majority, 58 percent, learned Spanish as their first language, while the number who claimed Kaqchikel as their sole first language was only 12 percent. Nearly one-third of the teenagers learned both languages as mother tongues. These figures demonstrate that the number of women learning Kaqchikel as a first language, either alone or in conjunction with Spanish, was still fairly high, about 42 percent. However, this was a much lower proportion of native Kaqchikel speakers than was found among the women eight years older. In that group the percentage of women who learned Kaqchikel either alone or in conjunction with Spanish was about 67 percent.

The trend toward teaching children Spanish as a first language is accelerating, at least among families who provide a secondary education for their children. Since there is an increasing community-wide trend toward sending children to school for longer periods, it would not be surprising if the shift in language use was widespread as well. Like Farber, I found that even parents with limited ability in Spanish were anxious for their children to learn the language.

Kaqchikel as a Second Language

Due to the intergenerational shift in language use currently underway in Comalapa, many children learn Spanish as a first language. In order to judge the effect of this shift on the future viability of Kaqchikel, I needed to know whether those children who learn Spanish as a first language will be able to learn Kaqchikel as a second language. As a first step in answering this question I examined the experience of women in their twenties who had learned Spanish as a first language. Their ability or failure to learn Kaqchikel indicates something about the strength of the language in the community at the time they were growing up. If children were successful in learning Kaqchikel, this suggests both that there were adequate domains to enable children to learn Kaqchikel and that they were motivated to do so.

The female Básico graduates in their twenties were not asked to evaluate their mastery of Kaqchikel. However, out of thirty-nine women, two remarked that they only knew a few words, and one reported that she understood but could not speak the language. This still leaves a large group of women who did manage to learn Kaqchikel. In the course of my fieldwork, young adults occasionally confided to me that they had learned Kaqchikel as a second language.

The women in their twenties who learned Spanish first had often learned Kaqchikel outside the home (see Table 6.4). These women cite townspeople and schoolmates more often than family members as the people from whom they learned Kaqchikel. This finding affirms the belief held by adults in the 1970s that a person who did not learn Kaqchikel in the home would still have opportunities to do so in the community. Among those women who mentioned family as their source of Kaqchikel, three specifically mentioned their mothers. One woman revealed privately that her father had been quite strict about speaking only in Spanish to his daughters; but as the girls got older they and their mother would sometimes speak Kaqchikel together privately.

Another woman whose first language was Spanish explained that she had learned Kaqchikel indirectly from her mother. Although the mother addressed her daughter in Spanish, the daughter listened to her mother speaking Kaqchikel with visitors and other Kaqchikel speakers and

TABLE 6.4. Source of Kaqchikel for Women Who Learned Spanish First

Source of Kaqchikel	Básico Graduates (Women in Twenties)	Básico Students (Women in Teens)
Family and Home	6	15
Townspeople	6	4
Schoolmates	7	0

Note: Some individuals cited more than one source.

learned the language in this way. Among the women who said they had learned Kaqchikel from nonfamily members, one had been obliged to learn it in order to interact with women at the market, while another woman, whose family owned a store, had learned the language in order to communicate with monolingual customers. The latter admitted that her Kaqchikel was limited. Finally, seven women in their twenties mentioned the school as a place where they had learned Kaqchikel. Three explained that they had learned the language in order to talk to girls who were monolingual speakers. One woman said that she had felt obligated to speak Kaqchikel with them, an indication that the rule of accommodation may have still favored Kaqchikel speakers at that time, at least in certain contexts. Another woman learned Kaqchikel because the girls at school had made fun of her for not knowing the language. Clearly, when the women in their twenties entered school in the early 1970s there was still pressure on young women to learn the Mayan language, and it could be learned both inside and outside the home.

The teenage girls differ from the older group in terms of where they learned Kaqchikel. Data on the teenagers who spoke Spanish as a first language suggest that they were more dependent on the home as a domain in which to learn Kaqchikel (see Table 6.4). The teenagers cited family and home more than twice as often as women in their twenties. Of the fifteen native Spanish speakers who said they had learned Kaqchikel from their families, six identified their parents as the primary source, while nine mentioned their grandparents. Although grandparents are a valuable language resource, it is noteworthy that other members of the household, such as parents or older siblings, were not seen as important sources. This indicates that those families had largely shifted to Spanish. In general, the fact that the Spanish-speaking teenagers often reported learning Kaqchikel from their families is probably not a favorable sign for the survival of the language, since many of the homes in question are largely Spanish-speaking. In order to gain competence in Kaqchikel, many Spanish-dominant children probably need additional contexts in which to use the language actively. For most girls, the peer group no longer acts as a primary agent of Kaqchikel language socialization, although this may be less true for the boys.

The inadequacy of current Kaqchikel domains for ensuring acquisition of the language can be seen by looking at Kaqchikel proficiency among the teenage women. The Básico students were asked if they knew Kaqchikel, and those who claimed to know the language were asked if they spoke "well" (*bien*) or "just a little" (*sólo un poco*). Among the

TABLE 6.5. Mastery of Kaqchikel among Teenage Women

Level of Kaqchikel Mastery	Kaqchikel		Both		Spanish	
	No.	%	No.	%	No.	%
Little or None	0	0	4	40	14	74
Good	4	100	5	50	5	26
Not Indicated	0	0	1	10	0	0
TOTAL	4	100	10	100	19	100

nineteen young women who had learned Spanish as a first language, almost three-fourths, or fourteen, indicated they spoke little or no Kaqchikel (see Table 6.5). Only about a quarter of the teenagers whose mother tongue was Spanish felt they spoke good Kaqchikel. Naturally, this is a subjective measure, since it is based on the students' self-appraisal rather than observed behavior. Nevertheless, it does indicate that many of the young women who learned Spanish first feel insecure about their proficiency in Kaqchikel or recognize that they use the language very little.

The School as a Language Domain

When adults in Comalapa talk about learning Spanish they often bring up the influence of the schools and the pressure they felt from teachers to abandon the Mayan language and speak and write only in Spanish. However, there may be a number of years during the language shift process when the school functions as a domain in which knowledge of both languages is expanded. In the school setting many children come into close contact with children from other parts of town for the first time. As a result, they may be exposed to children with language backgrounds different from those of their families and neighbors. They are also placed in an environment in which peer group relationships take on heightened importance. While the dominant language is taught formally by the teachers, both dominant and subordinate languages are used as media of communication by the students on the playground and elsewhere. In Comalapa, as late as the early 1970s, children who arrived at school deficient in Spanish could gain ability in that language through the formal educational process carried out in the classroom, while students who arrived deficient in Kaqchikel could learn that language through interaction with their peers.

In the context of the school, as in other domains, Kaqchikel and Spanish have sometimes taken on opposite functions. Kaqchikel has often been perceived as the language of closeness and solidarity. A colleague who previously taught at the evangelical school reports that when children enter that school they speak Kaqchikel with children with whom they are already acquainted—family and neighbors. With strangers they use Spanish. Similarly, young men and women may use Spanish with each other when courting, since this is the language of formality, even if they use Kaqchikel in less formal situations.

Gender Distinctions in Language Use

Farber observed a sharp distinction between the language use of men and women in the 1970s. Among adults, men learned Spanish as a second language, while women remained largely monolingual in Kaqchikel (Farber 1978: 13). Until that time, women's access to Spanish had been limited partly by their lack of access to schooling. In Farber's survey of forty households, she found no women over age thirty who had any formal education. Although an increasing number of girls were being sent to school at the time of the survey, only one-fifth of the women surveyed had attended school compared to three-fourths of the men (Farber 1978: 244–245).

In addition, women at that time were restricted in terms of the kinds of employment they could accept without putting their reputations at risk. This was in direct contrast to men; Farber notes that many of the "respectable" occupational choices open to men required some knowledge of Spanish. In order to work in trades such as baking, carpentry, masonry, or shoemaking in Comalapa, or to seek employment in Guatemala City, it was helpful to know Spanish. As a result, parents could see some utility in providing formal education for boys. However, for the most part women were expected to have little interaction with Ladinos, so education was seen as less important for girls. Farber discovered that women who had jobs that required them to travel and interact with Indians and Ladinos outside of Comalapa suffered from low social status in the community. They were suspected of being dishonest, of neglecting their children, and of being unfaithful to their husbands (Farber 1978: 250). Thus, in terms of job opportunities, there were few rewards for women who became proficient in Spanish in the mid-1970s. Even within the town of Comalapa women's participation in certain spheres was restricted. Public interactions involving Ladinos or dealing with nonlocal topics, such as national politics, were often conducted in Spanish. Since women did not speak Spanish, they could not participate in these events (Farber 1978: 13).

While women's failure to learn and use Spanish was due in part to restrictions placed on them, there was sometimes an element of volition involved. Some women shunned the use of Spanish, even if they knew the language. If they pretended ignorance of Spanish, they could avoid involvement in unpleasant situations, such as contact with Ladinos (Farber 1978: 249–250). According to the women, they claimed to understand and speak less Spanish than they actually did in order to avoid the extra work that would result from being bilingual. Men, on the other hand, tended to overreport their ability in Spanish (Farber 1978: 159). For them, a knowledge of Spanish carried prestige.

Today the relationship between language use and gender has changed considerably. The great majority of both young men and young women are bilingual, while a minority are monolingual in Spanish. In some ways, women in Comalapa continue to serve as bearers of the traditional culture; even those with a formal education may be expert weavers, and nearly all Indian women wear Mayan clothing on a daily basis. Adults in their twenties grew up in a world in which the use of Kaqchikel was heavily associated with women, and their attitudes toward women's use of language are consistent with this. In discussing their years in Básico, the female graduates remembered speaking Kaqchikel among themselves, but they reported that all but one of their male classmates avoided its use. Judging from the remarks of young adults, teenage men in the 1970s identified with the Spanish language to a greater extent than did the women.

Today, however, the association between women and linguistic conservatism may be breaking down. In 1993 I interviewed ten Básico students between the ages of fifteen and twenty-one, asking them about their use of Spanish and Kaqchikel. One of my questions concerned whether men or women in Básico used more Kaqchikel. Two of the students from outlying villages asserted that the female students spoke more Kaqchikel, an opinion that accords with the traditional view of women as more conservative. However, among the students from Comalapa the responses were different. The three women were mixed in their assessment; two felt that men and women in Básico used the same amount of Kaqchikel, while one felt the men used more. But all five of the men felt that the male students used more Kaqchikel than the females. It would be unwise to give too much importance to these findings since no attempt was made to measure language use objectively and in some cases the students were hesitant in their judgments. However, the students' answers do suggest a major change in the perception of linguistic behavior. Among these young people, women are no longer automatically associated with greater use of Kaqchikel. In fact, it may be the men who will be seen as the more faithful speakers of Kaqchikel. This does not mean that young men will shift back to a predominant use of Kaqchikel. It is more likely that they will use the language in certain contexts—for example, as a marker of solidarity (Garzon 1994).

Language Shift and Ethnicity

Farber noted in the 1970s that increased bilingualism in Comalapa was not accompanied by a shift in ethnic identity. Bilingual Mayas, even Western-oriented ones, continued to identify themselves as Indian (Farber 1978: 10–11). This trend, continuing today, is a significant one for the maintenance of both language and ethnic identity in Comalapa. While in some places in Mesoamerica adoption of the Spanish language and other Western traits and orientations has resulted in a loss of Indian identity or a blurring of ethnic lines (Garzon 1985), this has not been the case in Comalapa. There, as Farber noted, "a range of cultural behaviors, including many which are characteristically defined as Ladino, fit under the rubric 'Indian'" (Farber 1978: 242).

Although social and economic changes continue to propel the people of Comalapa into more active involvement in national life, in some ways it is now easier to maintain identity as an Indian than it was in the recent past. In earlier times Indians who wanted to advance themselves in Guatemalan society often had to give up their Mayan identity along with all outward signs of being Indian, such as wearing traditional clothing and speaking a Mayan language. Often they had to leave their home community as well. Today the young Maya professionals of Comalapa often speak Kaqchikel as well as Spanish and, in the case of the women, continue to wear Indian clothing. They identify themselves unequivocally as Indian, although what it means to be Indian, or Maya, is changing.

CONCLUDING COMMENTS

In 1978 Farber wrote:

> Cakchiquel . . . continues to maintain its linguistic hegemony in
> Comalapa. The aboriginal language is preferred in speaking with
> family members, especially kinsmen in successive generations, such
> as grandparents, parents and parents-in-law. In local public settings
> (market, shops, on the street), both Cakchiquel and Spanish are heard.
> However, it is primarily women who speak Cakchiquel and men who
> speak Spanish. When men and women speak together, the language
> of choice is Cakchiquel, since women tend to be monolingual. (Far-
> ber 1978: 252–253)

Today, some twenty years later, it is not possible to make the same as-
sertion about the linguistic hegemony of Kaqchikel. The intergenerational shift to the use of Spanish noted by Farber has progressed to the
point that nearly all children enter school knowing Spanish, and the
great majority of young adults are bilingual in Kaqchikel and Spanish.
A generation ago, parents could confidently predict that their children
would have enough exposure to Kaqchikel to learn the language even if
it was not taught in the home. This proved to be the case for many individuals. Women in their twenties report having learned Kaqchikel
from their schoolmates, as well as in their daily interactions in places
like the market. This is much more difficult for children today, as young
people come into contact with fewer monolingual speakers of Kaqchikel on a regular basis. The peer group no longer acts as a source of Kaqchikel, at least for many girls, and sources within the family will continue to diminish. Some children today speak the language with
monolingual grandparents. However, in a generation or two, grandparents will mostly be bilingual, and children will no longer need Kaqchikel to communicate with them. Certainly, there is very little chance that
the current group of first graders will be strongly Kaqchikel-dominant
when they are grown.

In the 1970s many parents foresaw better opportunities for their children if they spoke Spanish well. They were proven correct, as those children attained a formal education and left to look for jobs in other
places. Certainly not all the graduates of Básico have been able to reach
the level to which they aspire; a lack of money and shortage of opportunities limit the advancement of many young people in Comalapa, as
well as elsewhere in the country. However, for many families, educating

their young people may be the best strategy open to them, as traditional life becomes less feasible and the old social barriers come down. As young people seek education and jobs outside Comalapa, their ties to the town and its traditional culture are likely to weaken, and this change has important implications for the future viability of Kaqchikel in Comalapa.

From the standpoint of language use, those young adults who settle in distant cities will have few opportunities to speak Kaqchikel. They are unlikely to pass the language on to their children, particularly if they marry a Spanish speaker or even a speaker of another Mayan language. For those who find jobs in nearby cities like the capital or Chimaltenango, the situation is less clear. Some may wish to maintain ties with Comalapa, visiting regularly or maintaining a residence there. This is particularly likely if they have inherited land in the area or if they find opportunities outside the community to be limited or insecure. Some students with a secondary education remain in Comalapa, whether by choice or by force of circumstances, and they may return to a traditional life as farmers or homemakers or go into some kind of business such as weaving or another skilled trade. Those individuals who remain in Comalapa or return periodically can probably avoid speaking Kaqchikel if they wish. However, if they want to assert their identity as Mayas and residents of Comalapa, they may choose to continue their use of Kaqchikel, at least in certain contexts. Certainly a number of the educated young women take pride in designing, weaving, and wearing Mayan clothing, one sign of a continuing allegiance to Mayan tradition.

In the past, even when young people rejected Mayan traditions, it was often temporary. Reportedly, young men sometimes went through a period in their teens and early twenties when they identified with the outside world and demonstrated this through exclusive use of the Spanish language. However, as they grew older they returned to more traditional local values and a willingness to speak the Mayan language. Whether young men and women continue to assert their Indian identity as adults will depend on a number of factors, including the strength of traditional Mayan culture in Comalapa, the young adults' need for economic and social support from the community, and the prestige ascribed to Mayan identity inside and outside Comalapa.

Hopeful signs exist for the continuing viability of Kaqchikel. Although young, educated Mayas experience pressures to assimilate to Ladino society, many are maintaining their identity as Indians. This behavior is reinforced by a widespread movement to revitalize Mayan culture in Guatemala. There are several individuals in Comalapa with backgrounds

7. MAYAN LANGUAGE REVITALIZATION IN GUATEMALA

R. McKenna Brown

INTRODUCTION

Drop in at almost any corner store in a Mayan town, strike up a conversation about the changing times, and a spirited discussion is likely to ensue. Most everyone has something to say about how life among the Mayas is changing at an unprecedented rate. Farming, markets, customs, young people—nothing seems impervious to outside influences, including the weather. So it is not surprising that the increasing shift to Spanish language use and the subsequent decline of the Kaqchikel language have not been lost on the Mayas. It is widely recognized that the younger generation speaks less Maya than the preceding one: they are increasingly oriented toward the cultures and language surrounding the Mayas and are every day less fluent in the ways and speech of their elders.

One response to this cultural and linguistic threat has been a growing Mayan nationalist or pan-Maya movement whose central pillar is promotion of the Mayan languages. The movement is broad and complex and has received attention in both the popular and scholarly press (Fischer and Brown 1996b; Rohter 1996; Wilson 1995). This chapter briefly describes the movement then discusses four specific aspects: domestic language use, Mayan language literacy, bilingual education, and religion. Efforts in all these areas seek to deter and reverse the loss of language and culture and gain for them a broader, more formal, legitimized institutional role in Guatemalan national life. The final section looks at the important role that Kaqchikels play in the movement and the role of language in the Guatemalan Peace Accords.

THE MAYAN MOVEMENT

The movement is led by a mostly young group of Maya intellectuals, many of whom pursue studies at the university level in order to regain control over their linguistic and cultural destinies. They are developing an ideology emphasizing self-determination, cultural pride, and pan-Mayan unity in the belief that a rejuvenated Mayan culture can peacefully lead Guatemala into a truly culturally pluralist future.

Mayan history, especially as recovered through epigraphy and archaeology, enables the movement to reconstruct the bonds that unite all Mayas through time and space (Sam Colop 1996; Warren 1996). Municipal, linguistic, and national borders become secondary to the distinction between non-Mayas and all Mayas together. The tools of linguistic reconstruction are further employed in the quest to develop standardized codes and invent neologisms to replace Spanish loans (England 1996; Kaqchikel Cholchi' 1995; Maxwell 1996). Thus, the scenario today is one in which the Mayas are putting Western sciences to use in the struggle to find strength in unity.

One right the Mayas aim to reappropriate is the authority to define their own culture and what it means to be Maya. They reject the externally imposed metrics of Western academics, which have often read like grocery lists of cultural traits (e.g., type of housing, clothing, religious practices). As Gaspar Pedro González (1995: 96) writes in the first modern Mayan novel: "The word *Indian,* my son, can't be explained and there's nothing we can compare it to. Rather, it's a feeling that grows inside of you to a greater or lesser degree, according to your own experiences."

Maya activists see important differences between Western approaches to Mayan studies and their own. Where Western scholars might focus on elements of Mayan culture that have been lost, the Mayas seek to emphasize what remains, celebrating the resilience and courage demonstrated by five centuries of cultural resistance, exemplified in the continued use of traditional dress, *traje* (Hendrickson 1996b; Otzoy 1996). As Raxche' Demetrio Rodríguez (1996: 87) has written:

> Today, Mayan identity and culture remain strong. The Mayan pueblos maintain in large part their cosmovision and technology, their spirit of service toward community, and, above all, their languages which are unmistakable symbols of their identity and existence. The Mayan pueblos maintain their ethnic loyalty, and the current awakening of the more educated members has greatly strengthened the resistance of peasant and other Maya.

Despite Western academic claims of objectivity, many Mayas perceive that Western scholarship through language dialect studies or community-specific ethnographies has helped to divide and fractionalize the Mayas. Today the movement seeks to complement and supersede the political boundaries of municipality, department, and even nation with cultural borders that embrace all Mayas.

Ancient Mayan hieroglyphic, numerical, and calendric systems, salient symbols of the grandeur (and literacy) of precontact Mayan culture which had largely fallen out of use after contact, are now used to symbolize cultural awareness (Schele and Grube 1996; Sturm 1996). Modern Maya activists are using the Classic Mayan glyphic syllabary to spell modern Mayan words and names phonetically. Mayan numeration is widely used in personal writings and publications.

The history of the movement is closely linked to Guatemalan political history (Brown, Fischer, and Raxche' n.d.; Fischer and Brown 1996a). During the Arbenz Arévalo Revolution years (1945–1954), Catholic groups began mobilizing the Indian population around economic and political issues (Warren 1978: 88–93). Agricultural exports fueled rapid economic growth in the 1960s, producing a relatively well-off class of Indians, some of whom became active in cultural preservation issues. Population displacement resulting from the 1976 earthquake and political violence in the 1970s and 1980s, as well as the attraction of higher education and professional employment, led to massive Mayan emigration to urban centers, especially the capital. Mayan cultural groups were formed, eventually leading to a series of national meetings, called Indigenous Seminars, among local Maya leaders. Mayas began participating in local and national politics as never before (Ebel 1988: 177–178), except for a hiatus during the Romeo Lucas administration and the early 1980s, when government repression against all forms of popular resistance increased sharply.

In 1985, with the democratic opening reflected in Vinicio Cerezo's election to the presidency and the concurrent scaling down of the violent counterinsurgency campaigns, Mayan cultural activists once again began to pursue their agendas with renewed vigor. At the Second National Linguistic Congress in 1984 a resolution was passed calling for the creation of an institution to preside over the creation of a unified alphabet for writing Mayan languages. Toward this end a meeting of all the groups working on Mayan linguistics in the country was held in October 1986. At this meeting the Academy of the Mayan Languages of Guatemala (ALMG) was founded to promote a new unified alphabet for Mayan languages and to coordinate linguistic conservation efforts (see López Raquec 1989). The ALMG quickly rose to the forefront of the revitalization movement. The prominence of the ALMG reflects a general emphasis on linguistic issues for cultural activists, because speaking a Mayan language is the predominant marker of Mayan ethnicity and one which has been relatively well maintained during the five hundred years of Spanish contact. Demetrio Cojtí Cuxil writes that "Mayan people exist because they have and speak their own languages" (1990b: 12). Nevertheless, over the last several years cultural activists have increasingly focused on other aspects of Mayan culture, forming organizations to study topics ranging from economic development to modern maize rituals.

The Mayan language movement in Guatemala shares features of such movements around the world (Brown 1996a). First, it is led by a largely urban, educated minority of Mayas, some of whom are not fluent in a Mayan language. Although some claim that the Mayan language activists do not represent the great majority of rural Mayas, most of the educated Mayas grew up in Indian towns and villages and return to them regularly, staying in touch with the rural reality despite their current urban residence. A more representative Mayan voice is not likely to emerge, given that language revival movements commonly originate and have their greatest impact in cities.

Another feature of the movement is its apolitical nature, at least in the sense of the Left-Right dichotomy of Guatemalan politics. Edward Fischer (1992) and others have noted that the progress and survival of the revitalization movement are owed in large part to the ability of its leaders to carve out a new political space in which to agitate. The revitalist agenda carefully avoids explosive topics such as land reform and social-class ideologies and consistently maintains a discourse of cooperation with the state. In the Guatemalan context, linguistic and educational reforms may prove the safest and surest paths to real structural change.

Maya activists today also seek to mobilize the language-ethnicity link by raising the Mayas' consciousness of their roots and promoting the value of the languages as a link with the glorious past and a symbol of authenticity. They seek to mobilize affective factors in the struggle between language maintenance and language shift.

The movement also seeks to raise perceptions of the prestige of the Mayan languages in Guatemala. There is a broad consensus that many of the language-internal phenomena produced by intense contact—loanwords, for example—reduce the prestige of the Mayan languages for both speakers and nonspeakers. Many varieties of Mayan languages are disdained because they are perceived as "contaminated" or "diluted" by the infusion of foreign—most commonly Spanish—elements. However, a growing body of literature (England 1992; López Raquec 1989) argues that the Mayan languages possess rich structures that allow for subtlety not found in Spanish or other Western languages. Additionally, the publication of various types of grammars enhances the prestige of the Mayan languages (Oxlajuuj Keej Maya' Ajtz'iib' 1993).

Domestic Language Use

The Mayas active in the recovery and promotion of their cultures are particularly sensitive to the implications of a decrease in Mayan fluency among the young. One of the most urgent needs of revitalization is to reverse the trend toward language shift. Through the mobilization of ethnic identity, parents must be persuaded to speak regularly to their offspring in Mayan and must be guided in finding ways to help their children meet their future language needs. However, to date, there has been a lack of a detailed, cohesive prescriptive model for Maya parents much beyond the general exhortation to speak Mayan to their children. Maya activists themselves may present contradictory examples, since they are largely drawn from the more urban, educated Mayan population, and their fluency in the Mayan language—or, more importantly, that of their offspring—is often notably less than that of rural Mayas.

Maya parents recognize that Spanish language acquisition is necessary to prepare a child to deal with schooling, Spanish literacy, and mastering the intricacies of the dominant bureaucratic system. However, adequate opportunities outside the home for Spanish acquisition are lacking. Most parents do not see public schools as a good point to begin learning Spanish. Many parents recall their own traumatic experiences arriving at school with no command of Spanish and the abuse they suffered from Ladino teachers who did not respect their language or culture. They do not wish for their children to repeat this experience. And despite the improvements and expansion of bilingual education today, the great majority of classrooms are still not able to serve the monolingual Maya student adequately.

Despite the practice of speaking Spanish in the home, many Maya parents still recognize the value of Mayan languages and do not claim to be intentionally precipitating their demise. Parents may not speak Mayan at home for a combination of many reasons, including what Laura Martin (1991) has termed a "genetic" view of language—that it is such an essential part of the people, like skin color, that it need not be consciously taught or learned to be acquired. Many parents are not aware that language is only acquired easily during childhood and that if their children do not learn the Mayan language at home it will be much more difficult for them as adults. Other attitudes and beliefs affecting Maya parents' language use with their offspring include the following:

- Imperfect language output, including mixing languages, is pathological in children

- Stable, balanced bilingualism is not possible

- Mayan fluency will worsen school performance

- Mayan languages have low prestige, due in part to the presence of Spanish loanwords.

Additionally, in cases where parents speak different Mayan languages, confusion exists over which language to use at home.

Parents readily accept the value of intergenerational continuity for the Mayan languages. What is needed at present is a practical guide to raising bilingual offspring. Parents need to be assured that bilingualism is indeed feasible, and they need specific suggestions on how to distribute the two languages among communicative settings within the home. Specifically, they need strategies to teach their children Spanish in a Mayan-speaking household. Until recently, larger issues, such as the recently signed Peace Accords, have preempted language planning at this microlevel.

Literacy in Mayan Languages

Literacy in Guatemala is intimately tied to historical, economic, political, and ethnic circumstances. Illiteracy rates, some of the highest in the Americas, reflect the profound marginalization of much of the population. Although the majority speak a Mayan language as a mother tongue, most national literacy campaigns have promoted literacy in Spanish. In fact, almost all Mayas literate in a Mayan language have prior, and in most cases greater, literacy in Spanish. Since programs in Mayan language literacy involve the standardization of orthographies and the production of educational materials, their net effect empowers the Mayan population. The current movement for Mayan revitalization or nationalism has roots in efforts to promote literacy in Mayan languages. In fact, many of its leaders began their training and organizational experience in the study of Mayan linguistics. Today many Mayas speak of a personal process of *concientización,* which occurred as they learned more about their language, culture, and history. They came to appreciate the worth of Mayan culture and chose to dedicate themselves to its promotion.

For many scholars, the relation between writing and political power is quite direct. Some describe literacy—and, by extension, education—as the social space in which dominance is reproduced and hegemony established (Hogben 1965; Lankshear 1989). Paulo Freire (1987), on the other hand, sees literacy as liberating, enabling the oppressed to distance themselves from their oppressors and to perceive their situation objectively. Thus, the relation between literacy and political struggles can be two-sided. As Daniel Wagner (1987) notes, since the advent of printing (coinciding with the Reformation and the birth of capitalism), the written word has been used to intimidate those in power, as well as the other way around.

For the Mayas, literacy can be repressive or liberating, depending in part on the process and the product. In terms of process, one can compare literacy to the acquisition of oracy, which generally takes place under psychologically favorable conditions, and learning to write, which generally takes place in the authoritarian socialization process of the school. Spanish-language literacy almost always takes place in an environment that is foreign and unfriendly to the Mayas, while Mayan language literacy training, almost by definition, is a Maya-only enterprise since very few non-Mayas read and write a Mayan language.

In terms of product, one must ask what materials will be accessible to the newly literate reader, who writes them, and to what end. The literacy campaigns of the past five hundred years, motivated by religious or political agendas foreign to the Mayas, were foreshadowed in the last paragraph of Antonio de Nebrija's (1992) grammar, in which he wrote: "Soon Your Majesty will have placed her yoke upon many barbarians who speak outlandish tongues. By this, your victory, these people shall stand in a new need; the need for the laws the victor owes to the vanquished, and the need for the language we shall bring with us."

Arnulfo Simón (Wuqu' Ajpub') (1994) argues: "If the content is Western, comprehension is going to be very difficult." He offers an example: "Many have translated Apocalypse, chapter and verse into a Mayan language. What comprehension are Maya readers going to have of that? And the less one understands, the less interest there will be in literacy." One product of Mayan language literacy can be a new way of viewing the world. Jean Piaget (1995) established that new concepts develop as a result of challenges from experiences that contradict a person's existing conceptual systems. Becoming literate in a Mayan language provides just such a challenge by contradicting many of the myths used to justify Mayan oppression: that the languages are inferior, have no grammar, and are not fit to be written or used pedagogically.

The benefits of initial literacy training in the mother tongue of the learner have been widely recognized for many decades (UNESCO 1953). Nevertheless, arguments against wide-scale education in Mayan languages are common in Guatemala, and they point to the logistical complexity and expense of multilingual material production. Virtually all public education in child and adult literacy is carried out in Spanish. Lower educational rates among the Mayas are one result, not surprisingly, since initial literacy training in a second language has been shown to delay reading skills (Downing 1987). There are further implications: not only is the academic performance of Maya students affected, but also their self-esteem and cultural identity. The decreased use and prestige accorded Mayan languages by Maya youth are one result of this policy.

Mayan Language Literacy in San Juan Comalapa

During the mid-1980s, after the worst of the violence, an undetermined number of small literacy groups formed in several Mayan communities. In San Juan Comalapa the handful of organizers (alternating between two and five active leaders) had previously worked with the Proyecto Lingüístico Francisco Marroquín, where they had become literate in Kaqchikel Maya as well as learning the basics of linguistic analysis. For three years about thirty-five adults, mostly under forty years of age, voluntarily attended night classes once a week for about two months. In 1986 I visited one of the literacy classes, and I have since remained in contact with the organizers and several students. I spoke with several of them at length about the literacy classes in 1995 and present their recollections here. Although very small in scale, the group represents a radically distinct form of literacy training in Mayan communities, one of local initiative and control.

Four commonly cited functions of the educational process are socialization, acculturation, vocational training, and the formation of intellectuals. Of course, two months of weekly literacy classes constitute only a small part of an educational process. Nonetheless, each function merits a brief discussion of its relation to acquiring literacy in a Mayan language.

1. Literacy Training and Socialization. One way to appreciate how Mayan language literacy training imparts values is to contrast it with the national educational program, which has been described by Cojtí (1990a) and others as colonial in terms of content and effect. Values imparted by Mayan language literacy classes include an increased respect for the language itself and for the elders of the community, whose stock of knowledge is implicitly or explicitly denigrated in the public school classroom. Referring to the literacy class, one student comments, "It enabled me to value my language."

2. Literacy Training and Acculturation. Education not only transforms students, it often leaves them separated or alienated from their roots. In this way, national education has served to defuse many of the brightest potential Maya activists. In contrast, literacy training in a Mayan language can have the opposite impact. As Brian Street (1987) points out, identification and internalization act as mechanisms in the socialization process of literacy. As adults become literate in a Mayan language, they identify with and internalize the values associated with Mayan culture and then serve as models for their children to emulate. When individuals become literate, they enroll in a literate community and help shape its customs. As one student remarks: "I felt it was the most important step in my process of cultural vindication. I had suffered a terrible alienation."

3. Literacy Training and Vocational Training. Literacy has long been valued as an escape from drudgery. J. Goody and I. P. Watt (1962: 306) cite an ancient Egyptian motto: "Put writing in your heart that you may protect yourself from hard labor of any kind." Literacy training will only succeed if literacy will fulfill some useful function for the individual (Downing 1987).

The literacy classes started as a response to a need for teachers in the national bilingual education program. At that time, many Maya youths had pursued professional degrees in elementary education at normal schools but found teaching posts elusive. About twenty-five of the thirty-five students were trained as teachers, and the rest attended out of personal interest. Once they became literate in Kaqchikel, about twenty of the educators were hired as bilingual teachers. As one participant says: "At the same time, it gave me a source of work . . . I think that was the complement that consolidated literacy in my life. If they had taught me literacy just as a mechanical act, I probably wouldn't have developed the whole process."

Two of the organizers themselves had been recruited in 1984 to receive literacy training in Kaqchikel to prepare them for a specific job. As one reports: "I was looking for work, and they sought me out because I was a teacher, and they wanted me to give Kaqchikel classes to Ladino students from the capital who were going to do some fieldwork in Comalapa."

Employment opportunities are crucial to success in Mayan language literacy. As one former student says: "If there's no application, it has no meaning. To the degree that the need grows, so will the literate population grow."

4. Literacy Training as a Stimulus to Intellectual Growth. Mayan language literacy occurs within the context of threats to the languages and cultures from outside pressures. It is usually the most "contacted" Mayas, those with links to Ladino society through education, work, and urban residence, who are the most literate. As one organizer said: "For them it is a symbol of identity, like long hair for the Otavalos of Ecuador. The leading intellectuals have actually written and spoken more in Spanish, so Kaqchikel serves a symbolic value."

A fundamental change brought about by the literacy classes was in the students' language use. In Comalapa, as elsewhere, an educated Maya is expected to speak Spanish among peers. However, the literacy students developed a different norm for language use among themselves. As a former student reports: "After classes, we would leave, all of us speaking in Kaqchikel. And to this day, we still greet each other in Kaqchikel."

The students underwent a shift not only in behavior, but in attitude. An organizer remembers clearly the students' "change to speaking the language with no shame. For many it was tough to speak Kaqchikel in a meeting of professionals, even if they spoke it at home."

Another effect was a desire by the students for appropriate reading material in the language—material which did not exist. In response, several of the participants began interviewing community elders and succeeded in collecting fifty recipes for natural medicines in Kaqchikel. As one participant says, "The urge to rescue was born."

Literacy training in Spanish is an enormous social investment, producing jobs for Spanish speakers. For Mayas, who are often illiterate in Spanish, lack of training serves to maintain the unequal power relationship between Maya and Ladino. Currently, literacy in a Mayan language is a requirement for certain government jobs, yet the government seems to resist awarding the jobs to Mayas. One example comes from the Ministry of Education, which, due to accords with the United States Agency for International Development, agreed to hire 5,000 bilingual teachers. Only 1,200 have been hired, and there are reported cases in which these posts were given to monolinguals in Spanish.

Mayan Religion

Aside from language, one of the most frequently cited elements of Mayan identity is world view. The Mayan conception of the cosmos is intricately entwined with the Mayan calendar, which links the divine to the everyday. Mayan ceremonies marking the passage of time survived the Colonial Period by falling in step with the Catholic ritual calendar (B. Tedlock 1992; D. Tedlock 1985). Today these ceremonies are practiced unabashedly as a legacy of pre-Christian religion. For example, the closing of the 260-day cycle of the Mayan divinatory calendar, the Cholq'ij, is celebrated on the day Waqxaqi' B'atz' (Eight Monkey) as the Mayan New Year; over the last ten years thousands have attended the growing public celebrations at Mayan archaeological sites such as Iximche' and Saculeu (Blanck and Colindres 1996). Officiating at these ceremonies are growing numbers of Mayan priests (Ajq'ija'), who provide an important link between the ideology of a movement shaped among an urban elite and the common practice of the rural Maya majority. Mayan religion provides a crucial path in searching for the values of a modern Mayan identity (Zapeta 1996).

Mayan religion, referred to locally as *la religión maya,* offers an alternative to the existing Catholic/Protestant dichotomy in Guatemala. Some have criticized Mayan religion as an unauthentic, ahistorical pastiche of rituals (Morales 1996). However, many Mayas affirm that these practices have always formed part of Mayan life, although they were widely unknown, due to religious persecution and a lack of interest among non-Mayas. The more visible Mayan religious practices have been those most closely resembling Christian practice, such as household altars, while the more pre-Christian rites have taken place in secluded areas.

The ranks of Mayan priests have grown tremendously during the last decade. For example, the membership of the Association of Kaqchikel Mayan Priests (Asociación de Sacerdotes Mayas Kaqchikeles) headquartered in Chimaltenango is estimated at about five hundred. The call to priesthood generally manifests itself in two ways. One is by an individual's birth date according to the Mayan calendar. Certain days, such as No'j and Iq', in combination with high numbers (from 8 to 13) are considered very propitious. The other means by which individuals may become aware of their vocation are signs, which can include constant twitching of a particular body part, dreams, and messengers.

There are several types of ceremonies, including those to ask pardon, to ask permission, to ask favors, and to give thanks. This last ceremony, known as the *k'otz'i'j*, is generally performed by women in the home and takes its name from the symbolic use of flowers, which are traditionally sacred. Growing numbers of women are becoming Mayan priests as well.

Bilingual Education

Perhaps the most important training ground for Mayan revitalization has been in the institutional programs for bilingual education that are now called DIGEBI (the General Office of Bilingual/Bicultural Education), certainly the largest source of employment for Mayas within the state. What began in the 1960s as a rural education program and eventually grew into a General Office within the Ministry of Education has seen the conversion of about 1,200 rural Mayas into credentialed teachers (Richards and Richards 1996). Collateral effects included the creation of university programs in curricular development, linguistics, and sociolinguistics in which, for the first time in centuries, Mayan culture became a subject of study at Guatemalan universities. Maya professionals trained in these programs now represent most of the personnel in Mayan organizations such as the Academy of Mayan Languages.

DIGEBI has also made important contributions to the peace process. Many of the Mayan organizations participating in the process received technical support from DIGEBI in the publication of their own materials, and much of the discourse in the negotiations about "interculturality" and "peaceful and harmonic co-existence" comes from DIGEBI materials. DIGEBI is not without its critics, and many Mayas consider its position too compromised by dependency on the Guatemalan state and development funds from the United States to represent Mayan interests effectively.

KAQCHIKELS IN THE MOVEMENT

Perhaps due to their proximity to the capital and greater access to educational resources, Kaqchikels are by far the most represented Mayan language group in terms of institutional office and, in many cases, are the first Mayas to occupy such positions. Of the six Maya congressional representatives in 1996, three are Kaqchikel. Under the Ramiro de León administration, for the first time in history, two members of the cabinet were Mayas, one K'iche' and one Kaqchikel. Julio Otzoy Colaj, an ex–vice-minister of defense, is a Kaqchikel from Comalapa. Manuel Salazar, a Kaqchikel, was the first Maya dean in Guatemala, serving as head of humanities at the Rafael Landívar University. Martín Chacach is the head linguist at that university's Institute of Linguistics. The general director of DIGEBI, María Ernestina Reyes, is a Kaqchikel, as are the heads of curricular design and evaluation and research.

Many key leadership positions in nongovernmental organizations (NGOs) are held by Kaqchikels. The general coordinator of the Mayan Educational Counsel (CEM-G), Germán Curruchich, is Kaqchikel. At the publishing houses of Cholsamaj and Nahual Wuj, almost all administrative posts are held by Kaqchikels. A high percentage of NGOs were founded in the town of Chimaltenango, in Kaqchikel territory, such as the first Maya women's group, which in part accounts for the large Kaqchikel presence.

Kaqchikel intellectual leaders, such as Demetrio Cojtí, Raxche' Rodríguez Guaján, and Wuqu' Ajpub' (Arnulfo Simón), are quick to point out that competition among language groups is negligible and that advances made by Kaqchikels open doors for all Mayas. They also emphasize the contributions of Mayas from other language groups, such as Rigoberta Menchú, Enrique Sam Colop, Virgilio Alvarado, Gregorio Tum, and Alfredo Tay Coyoy.

THE GUATEMALAN PEACE ACCORDS

December 1996 saw the final signing of the Guatemalan Peace Accords, bringing to an end thirty-five years of armed conflict that had left over 150,000 dead and millions displaced, the majority Mayas. The peace process has taken years of negotiations and signals the first significant Mayan participation in national politics.

One of the first of the five sets of Peace Accords to be signed were *The Accords on the Identity and Rights of the Indigenous Peoples,* which were signed March 31, 1995, and subsequently published in Spanish and several Mayan languages (the translations here are my own). The document is organized under seven headings which fall into three general sections: an introduction establishing the context and terms ("Identity of the Indigenous Peoples" and "The Struggle against Discrimination"), the specific Mayan demands ("Cultural Rights" and "Civil, Political, Social, and Economic Rights"), and the implementation of the *Accords* ("Equal Representation," "Resources," and "Final Regulations").

The list of demands we find in the *Accords* has evolved from the work of many Mayas, including Enrique Sam Colop, Demetrio Cojtí Cuxil, Raxche' Demetrio Rodríguez Guaján, and Rigoberta Menchú. One widely read version of the *Accords* was published by the International Mayan League, centered in Costa Rica. The Mayas most centrally involved in shaping the *Accords* hold advanced degrees, some from universities in Europe and the United States, and live in the capital or overseas. While not "representative" of the economic status of the majority of Mayas, they nonetheless have emerged to speak for their fellow Mayas on a global scale.

The *Accords* are a marvel of political strategy: their tone is consistently conciliatory; the political demands are couched in cultural terms and, even when addressing potentially sensitive issues, avoid provocation. For example, when calling for the officialization of the Mayan languages, they first clearly establish that the Spanish language is not under attack with the pronouncement that "all languages deserve equal respect." Of the two headings containing specific demands, the less threatening cultural demands come first and receive as much attention as the social, economic, and political demands, which are all lumped into a single section. The language of the political demands is exceedingly circumspect given the topic and carefully couched in terms of the existing political structure. For example, in calling for increased local autonomy, one subsection begins, "Taking into account the State's constitutional commitment. . . ."

That the very first section of the *Accords* explicitly addresses the notion of identity points out the complexity of this contested topic. The Mayas for centuries lost the authority to define themselves, submitting to royal decrees labeling subjects as *indios,* mestizos, and other categories based on Western criteria. Later anthropologists and census takers devised their own lists of criteria including clothing, occupation, and residence to decide who was and who was not Maya. Today the Mayas reclaim that authority to establish their own identity, on the basis of:

1. languages that come from a common Mayan root

2. direct descent from the ancient Mayas

3. world view (*cosmovisión*)

4. culture

5. self-identification.

Nowhere in this list do we find "dirt floor" or "wears sandals." The first four criteria call upon the historic link to the ancestors, and the fifth is perhaps the most powerful, since it returns to the individual the right to name oneself. What at first glance may seem innocuous may be the most radical portion of the document.

Under the heading of "Cultural Rights," the very first topic is language, described as a pillar of culture and "a vehicle for the acquisition and transmission of world view." A list of specific measures to elevate the status of the Mayan languages follows:

1. constitutional recognition

2. bilingual education and Mayan language education

3. the use of Mayan languages in government services in Mayan communities

4. informing the indigenous peoples of their rights

5. training bilingual judges and interpreters

6. fostering appreciation of indigenous languages

7. promoting the officialization of indigenous languages.

That language remains central to Mayan cultural activism is evident by its placement in the series of linguistic demands and its relevance to many nonlinguistic demands. Language makes its first of many appearances in the accords in the very first heading on "Mayan Identity." Of the demands for cultural rights, language is the first to be made. Language is called a pillar of culture and the recuperation of the Mayan languages essential to a true Guatemalan nationhood. Language figures prominently in cultural rights demands, including names and place names, educational reform, and mass media. A central theme permeating all demands is that the Mayan languages retake their rightful place in all facets of national life.

The Accords on the Identity and Rights of the Indigenous Peoples show a sophisticated mastery of modern political processes. They establish a firm foundation in international legal precedents to construct a constitutional support for the protection and promotion of the Mayan languages and cultures. In doing so, they maintain a discourse of mutual

respect and interchange which asks us to rethink stereotypes of nationalist movements as necessarily divisive and to accept this Mayan proposal as a path toward lasting stability and peaceful coexistence.

CONCLUSION

Growing numbers of Mayas are acquiring the tools of Western education in order to defend and promote their history and way of life. Chief
among their concerns is the future health of their languages, which they
seek to promote in almost every facet of Guatemalan national life. The
Kaqchikels, perhaps in part due to their central location and access to
Western resources, play a predominant role in this movement. The future survival of the Mayas as we know them today may depend upon
their success.

NOTE

Parts of this chapter were presented at the American Anthropological Association Invited Session for the General Anthropology Division, "Language
and Identity among the Guatemalan Maya," Atlanta, 1994, and the Languages South of the Rio Bravo parasession at the 1995 Annual Meeting of the
Linguistic Society of America, Tulane University, New Orleans, January 9,
1995.

8. LANGUAGE CONTACT EXPERIENCES OF A MAYAN SPEAKER

Wuqu' Ajpub' (Arnulfo Simón)
Translated by Michael Dordick

PROLOGUE

There are several different ethnic groups within the borders of Guatemala, including the Xinca, Garífuna, Maya, and Ladino cultures. Guatemala is, then, a multicultural and multilingual nation. Most outsiders are familiar with only one face of Guatemala; they see it as just one of the many hispanic countries of Latin America. I wish to take this opportunity to present and expound upon some of the events in my life, thereby providing a sketch of part of both my own history and that of my people—the Mayas—the other, unknown face of Guatemala.

My name is Wuqu' Ajpub' (≔ Ajpub'), but the name on my birth certificate in the municipal office of San Juan Comalapa, my hometown, is José Arnulfo Simón, since the municipality is not a Mayan institution. I am thirty-four years old and I belong to the Mayan culture, my mother tongue being Kaqchikel Maya, one of the twenty-one Mayan languages still in use in Guatemala. Kaqchikel is spoken by more than half a million Mayas. Due to the close proximity of our territory to Guatemala City, the Kaqchikels are among the ethnic groups experiencing greatest pressure from Ladino culture. All social contact has its costs, and this is especially true when sociocultural, political, and economic inequality and injustice characterize the relations between the cultures sharing the same territory. Constant contact with the capital city and its culture has greatly influenced the daily life of the Mayas of this region, bringing major challenges to our culture over the last four centuries. Societal pressure has forced my people to choose between two paths: either to retreat within the confines of our world, not allowing outside influence to affect us, or to seek new horizons, demonstrating that our culture has a great deal more to contribute to Guatemala than we have hitherto been able to provide. I chose the second alternative, convinced that only by means of constant education can we achieve more and better development, allowing us to participate in a pluralistic government as a people, while at the same time avoiding the loss of our culture and Mayan mother tongue.

In the following pages I will share part of the Mayan reality, with the understanding that everything expressed is from my point of view and based on my experience—that of a member of a group which has traditionally had neither the opportunity nor the means to express our thoughts and way of life. I offer my autobiography as a testimony of the path one person has taken in the field of education. Only time will tell whether I chose the best path.

INTRODUCTION

The best way to identify a country as multicultural is by objectively observing the kind of interaction that actually takes place among the cultures sharing the same territory. In the last few decades the majority of Latin American countries with cultural diversity have acknowledged their multicultural nature. In the case of Guatemala, the constitution ratified in 1985 recognizes the Xinca, Garífuna, Maya, and Ladino cultures. However, it is not enough simply to recognize the existence of cultures. When one of the cultures is dominated and controlled by another, official recognition is not legitimate, authentic, or significant for the development of the country. In this case, changes must be made in the way the cultures interact.

To understand our reality better, the following narrative illustrates some of the difficulties encountered by Mayas in their effort to advance and prosper while submerged in a sociopolitical and cultural system which is foreign to their own culture. My purpose is to appeal to the sensitivity of the people and governments of multilingual countries so that linguistic policies may be created which generate the kind of effective two-way bilingual communication which permits sustained development. Change will never be initiated by the communications media, nor will it come about through the well-crafted speeches read at international conferences. Real development begins in each family, in an atmosphere of emotional and material security.

This chapter is organized around the different experiences and realities encountered by a Maya at different levels of the national school system, with the qualification that this case is not typical, since the great majority of the Maya people do not have access to school even at the primary level. Nevertheless, it allows the reflections of one Maya to be clearly heard, while inviting the reader to consider the fact that the original peoples of America, as a group, can offer alternative strategies to achieving a balanced relationship between people and nature—one of the basic requirements for continued progress. But first we must have the practical mechanisms necessary for consolidating these strategies, just as our ancestors did as they freely and systematically made discoveries and acquired knowledge. The original peoples of America have had a difficult time developing their knowledge, since they have been seen merely as products of the tourist industry, to be appreciated as lifeless objects of art. It is now time to change this traditional attitude and see that behind the colorful textiles there is a dynamic people with a real existence and presence.

The following account deals with the educational system and its effectiveness among the Maya people. The purpose is to provide insights which may be helpful in giving rise to a *genuine Mayan education:* one designed by Mayas and for Mayas.

FAMILY LIFE

Human beings commence their psychological and social development in the bosom of a family, a place usually synonymous with love and understanding. This uniquely human form of development is almost always achieved through the use of words, especially those expressed in the parents' language, which normally becomes our first language or mother tongue. The acquisition of the mother tongue in its whole, integrated form is fundamental and is achieved most easily and successfully when the mother and father share the same culture and language. In my case, I belong to a culture which has in most cases struggled to maintain the tradition of marriages between members of the same culture. For this reason, both of my parents are Mayas, and consequently I am also a Maya.

I was born in San Juan Comalapa—Chi Xot, in the Kaqchikel language. It has a population of approximately thirty thousand and is located eighty-three kilometers (sixty miles) from Guatemala City, about a three-hour bus ride. My family was very poor. My mother spoke only Kaqchikel and almost no Spanish; she could not read or write either language. My father spoke our tongue but could not write it. Although few Mayas manage to stay in school very long, my father was able to attend school for four years, where he learned to read and write Spanish. Traditionally, the Guatemalan educational system has operated entirely in

Spanish, since Spanish is the official language as well as the one used by those who govern the country. Imposing an educational system foreign to our culture and language makes learning difficult and leads to a high drop-out rate and frequent repetition of school years. In spite of these obstacles, it is important for Mayas to learn Spanish in order to have access to certain benefits and in this way mitigate the kinds of injustice and social inequality to which my people are subject. An example of this is the forced military conscription of young Maya men. My father was one such conscript.

Public school and military service are among the elements which lead to cultural decontextualization for Mayas—not to mention religion. These institutions affected my life, so that now I have to ask myself: "Was this a positive or a negative influence?" The answer is complicated, but I will use an example to help clarify it. Imagine you use a certain language to communicate with your grandparents, aunts and uncles, cousins, friends, and other people in your community on a daily basis. In addition, that same language is the one in which your mother speaks words of affection to you. Suddenly, there is a person speaking to you in a different language, and you cannot understand anything. The result is disastrous; at least that is the way I felt.

At home my emotional relationship to the Kaqchikel and Spanish languages was conflictive, since my parents had different views regarding the acquisition and use of these languages. Communication with my mother was in Kaqchikel and with my father in Spanish, while they spoke to each other in Kaqchikel. This complicated our family relations and interfered with communication, especially that of an affective nature. It is difficult for a young child to deal with a relationship with his father which is lacking in affection due to the need for progress. This is a particular case, one which typifies my childhood—namely, that my father spoke to me only in Spanish because of his good intentions to help me get ahead.

My father's attitude was the consequence of social and economic pressures exerted by the dominant group and, in particular, was the product of cultural discrimination springing from school and other government institutions. These were the sources of my father's good intentions, of his ideas about what was "best for his son." Experiences like this determine the future development of our society, limiting the amount of success people can expect in all aspects of life, including the social, emotional, material, and spiritual spheres.

LIFE AT SCHOOL

When I began school at the age of seven or eight, I was completely fluent in my mother tongue and knew a few odd words in Spanish. My first impression and mental picture of my future teacher when I saw him was: "This man has very long arms; he must hit really hard." None of my friends who attend or have attended this school have anything good to say about it; they always recount how difficult life was there. For example, if the teacher asked you something (of course, the questions were in Spanish) and you did not answer well or correctly, you would be punished. The "unforgettable" punishments were, for example, kneeling down on loose grains of corn with bare knees (corn is sacred in the Mayan cosmology), kneeling down on soda bottle tops with bare knees, making a bridge with arms crossed behind the back and head leaning on little stones, and others.

Similarly, our parents frequently used to say the following: "Study, son, because school is hard. You should see how it was when I went. They made me do a lot of things I did not know how to do. Or I did not understand what the teacher wanted of me." This was always said in Kaqchikel: "Nuk'ajol ta sik'ij ri awuj roma ri ti tijonik pa tijob'äl yalan k'ayew." With this image created, it is only natural that we saw school as a kind of punishment, and this impression of school became established among the members of our community so that today school is referred to as *tijob'äl* (punishment) in Kaqchikel.

Unfortunately, school is not what it should be for us or what some educators conceive school to be: namely, a "second home," a place to play, talk, and learn. But, frankly, are the teachers "bad"? Of course they are not. Rather, it is the ethnocentrism of the educational system which has caused them to take on this image. The fact that educators revert to corporal and psychological punishment is evidence of their failure. In this case, it is a sign of their powerlessness to deal with the cultural and linguistic barriers between the Maya children and their Spanish-speaking teachers. Nevertheless, as far as the Maya children are concerned, the teachers are indeed "bad" because of the role they play in imposing their own culture and language. In this way, the affective channel between Maya children and their teachers and school is broken. With it is lost an indispensable prerequisite for maintaining good conduct—in itself a necessary ingredient for academic success.

Classes begin, and on the first day we all arrive with our "best

clothes"—clean although mended—most of us with short haircuts, almost bald, like little frightened, cross ducks. (Our parents were aware
that members of the other culture often called us "hairy Indians" [*indios
peludos*].) The teacher walks in—"Good morning, children"—and no-
body answers. He sits down, cleans off his little wooden desk, and then
stands up. His next comment is "Here no *lengua,* here no *lengua,* only
Castilla. Understand? Understand?" [In this seemingly pidginized form
of Spanish, *lengua* (literally 'tongue' or 'language') refers to Kaqchikel,
and *Castilla* refers to *Castellano* or Spanish. The original Spanish is
"Aquí no lengua, aquí no lengua, sólo Castilla."—ed.] Each time the
teacher repeats this phrase, his voice gets louder. The expression "here
no *lengua*" simply means that from that day onward we have to forget
about our mother tongue; the most important thing at school is Spanish.

In Guatemala "tongue" or "dialect" refers to the Mayan languages,
since they are considered low in status and prestige, while Spanish is indeed a language, not a "tongue" or "dialect." As the official language,
it is commonly used in government offices, in religious institutions, and
in other public places. Of course the justifications for maintaining Spanish hegemony are social in nature and very subjective.

I have always been very shy, and at school my timidity became even
more pronounced. I remember the first lesson, which was repeated over
and over again for almost four hours. The teacher kept going in and out
of the classroom; each time he came in, he asked us to stand up and say,
"Good morning, teacher," in chorus. Then we changed places. He sat
down at his desk while each of us, one at a time, left the classroom, saying, "See you tomorrow, teacher."

This first Spanish lesson was hard for me, and it meant that I didn't
have lunch until two in the afternoon, since I was one of the last ones to
more or less learn the day's lesson. This forced immersion program only
ended up making pupils more reluctant to participate in class. Nevertheless, whenever the teacher left the room for a moment, we would
immediately talk in our language. This attitude strengthened our unity,
but it turned our classroom into a hostile place: "the kids against the
stranger."

As the days went by, many of my classmates dropped out of school
like soldiers fallen in battle. They could not stand the pressure which resulted from lack of communication, intolerance, and contempt for our
language and culture. On the first day of school the classroom was full
of children, with about 60 pupils per section (first grade consisted of two
sections), making a total of 120. Of the total number of pupils enrolled,

only half managed to pass to the next grade, while a sixth actually finished primary school or grade seven (about 20 children).

The school routine continued. In a few weeks the teacher initiated the reading process, and the first lesson dealt with identifying the five Spanish vowels (*a, e, i, o,* and *u*), using a textbook which my parents were able to purchase only through great sacrifice. This was the first book I was able to have in the first seven or eight years of my life, so I felt happy with it, knowing that it was mine, even though I could not read it. As we used the book with increasing frequency, I became more and more frustrated—to the point that I began to lose even that tiny bit of happiness that was in me, realizing that the lessons in that book constituted one of the reasons for my suffering and punishments at school. Besides this, the book mirrored a cultural and social reality which was alien to me. Nowhere could I find the image of a Maya boy or girl, nor any signs of those social and natural features familiar to us. Instead I found pictures of kiosks, oil lamps—things that had absolutely no meaning to us.

My frustration was so overwhelming that I failed the first year. All I learned were the five vowels, and I did this by memorizing them mechanically, without any meaning, singing them: *aeiouuuuuuuuuuuuuuuuu, aeiouuuuuuuuuuuuuuuuu.*

The next year I enrolled again, and the process was repeated. However, this time for some reason I passed, even though I did not know how to read and write in Spanish, nor had I mastered basic arithmetic (subtraction, addition, and division), the minimum requirements pupils must meet to be eligible for promotion to grade two.

I continued attending school, and we began to study history. Yet nowhere did my ancestors appear in the facts and accomplishments we studied. It seemed that the world had begun to exist only a bit over four hundred and fifty years before—in 1524, the year of the Spanish Conquest. One day the teacher said that before that time a group of people used to exist who were called Mayas and that they disappeared without leaving a trace. I did not understand very well what that meant and I felt that nothing about my history could be found anywhere; Arnulfo was the product of oblivion. This awakened in me the desire to know more about myself. It all happened while I was in the fourth grade, which, unfortunately, I also failed. My new educational failure almost eliminated me from school. Nevertheless, at the age of twelve I tried once more until I finally succeeded in finishing primary school at the age of fourteen.

My family consists of three children. Of the three, I was the only one able to finish primary school. My sister, the eldest child, dropped out of school in grade four, while my brother decided to go to work instead of continuing school when he was in grade three. Their withdrawal from school can be traced to the following fundamental reason: the cultural, social, and economic decontextualization of the school. Looking at my family in terms of percentages, this means that 67 percent of the children failed in the Guatemalan educational system.

During the eight years I was in school, I never found any logical relationship between school and my town; they were two worlds far apart. In the school setting, and in particular at the classroom level, "communication" was invariably in Spanish, resulting in total language immersion, just as the course content totally reflected the world of Spanish speakers. However, we only had to walk out the door of the classroom or school and communication was entirely in Kaqchikel. The contempt for my language at school contrasted with the prestige it held in the heart of local community organizations, such as the *cofradías* and neighborhoods, as well as in discussions of local events, such as marriages and other community activities. The hardest thing for me to understand as a child was the severity of the teacher's face as he entered the school, his "Good morning" contrasting with the affectionate smile with which my mother greeted me, along with her words—"Xatzolin pe wal!" (You're home now, son!).

To some extent, my reactions reflect the way any human being might feel in the face of unpleasant experiences, but especially a child, for whom this kind of emotional disorder is manifested in feelings of insecurity, timidity, apprehension, lack of self-esteem, and a sense of powerlessness to change the surroundings. I believe that the challenge for tomorrow is for the next generation to live together in harmony, sharing their emotions and understanding without fear.

The effort that Maya children make to remain in school until they obtain their sixth-grade diploma is praiseworthy. Likewise, the parents of these children deserve recognition for the economic sacrifice they make to keep their children in school. (Usually Maya children constitute a labor force for the family.)

Later, both parents and children face a new dilemma: what to do with the Spanish their child has learned. Most students who graduate from primary school do so at the age of fourteen or fifteen. Because of the exigencies of town life, these adolescents are already classified as full members of the community, meaning that they are given the same responsibility as adults. For this reason, young people have to make a decision:

to go on to secondary school or consider themselves finished with school. Often contradictions occur. When the children want to study, parents can no longer afford to cover the expenses that schooling requires. Or the opposite may occur: when parents are enthusiastic about keeping their children in school, the children are not interested in studying.

In my case, I wanted to continue studying, but my parents could not afford to pay for my schooling. Nevertheless, with the help of some secondary school teachers, I managed to continue for three years, finishing secondary school or Básico (ninth grade). At that point my way was obstructed. It was impossible for me to study further and enter a career due to the cost of leaving my town and moving to the city.

One of the social realities that had an impact on me had to do with the experiences of my classmates who could not continue their studies. Many of them were taken (captured) for military service, while the rest got married very young, had children, and became engulfed in poverty, thereby condemning their children to a very difficult life. All this made me more insistent in my efforts to look for support and move to the city to study. By observing the destitution in which my former classmates were living, I knew deep within me that they had not taken the best route—either for their own lives or for ameliorating the living conditions and the extreme poverty of my town. I had to find or create another option, yet I did not really have a clear vision myself of what kind of alternative to create. I hardly even knew what to do with my own life.

LIFE IN THE CAPITAL

Guatemala City, the capital, is the center for educational institutions, and it is there one can study in Diversificado (tenth to twelfth grade). Students graduate as accountants, primary school teachers, and related positions. The field that to some extent showed good prospects for me and accommodated my economic situation was teaching, with classes being held from 7:30 A.M. to 12:30 P.M. This schedule allowed me to work in a woodworking shop in the afternoons.

In 1981 I began classes at the Co-educational Normal School Rafael Aqueche, which specializes in teacher training for urban primary schools, and so a new stage in my life commenced. The city is huge, with a population of over two million, compared to my town with its population of approximately sixteen thousand. The move to a large metropolitan area had a negative effect on my academic achievement. Over

99 percent of the student body was Ladino. This was totally opposite to my previous experience. Before the only Ladino was the teacher, but now I was almost the only Maya.

When the school term began in January, two other Mayas from Comalapa were also attending. However, in June of the same year they were killed in front of their homes and families by a group of heavily armed men. According to some sources, the reason for their murders was that they were students. Since that time, some ideals concerning self-improvement have come at a very high price, and on this occasion it was my turn to feel the pain and fear close-up. As a result of the fear and insecurity that ensued from this tragedy, I stopped going to class for almost two months. Nevertheless, I still kept studying, though only at home. All of this happened during the time of the extreme *violencia*.

Not only did I think about the social and economic conflicts in Guatemalan society, but another type of conflict was looming in my mind—something unsuppressible—a kind of cultural identity crisis which had built up in me as a result of the alienation I had felt toward the Spanish-speaking world for about ten years and which began to have negative effects on my life. The school system and the racial, social, and cultural intolerance that prevails in society were causing me to want to deny my Mayan heritage and thereby hide my true identity. The following example may illustrate this. In the establishment where I was studying my classmates (Ladinos, of course) gave me the nickname of "Red Skin" (Piel Roja), which, in the Guatemalan context, is synonymous with "Indian." It is a kind of derogatory term used against those who belong to the other culture. The most serious aspect of this intolerance is the persecution of the Mayas, as evidenced by the thousands of refugees who have fled to Mexican territory as well as the thousands of dead people, among them my former classmates.

In 1983 I finished school, achieving my goal of becoming accredited as an Urban Primary School Teacher. I believed I had reached the world of success, though in reality I simply had begun a new stage in my life, that of joining the large pool of the unemployed. With my diploma under my arm, I found myself once again in a dilemma. This time it arose from my "ethnic shame," which condemned me to not want to go back to my town. My resistance was so strong that I decided to remain in the capital under the pretext of looking for work. I wandered about for over a year, looking for an opportunity in the private sector as well as the government, but finding absolutely nothing.

It is difficult to determine with any certainty why I failed in my search for a decent job, whether it was due to my social status (poor), my cultural status (Maya), or the high level of extreme poverty in Guatemala. Most likely it was for all these reasons. When the doors of the Ladino world with its economic system closed to me, I was forced to admit, with much anguish, that I only had one alternative: to go back to Comalapa and accept my defeat in attempting to flee from my real identity.

THE PAINFUL RETURN

During this time something very important happened in my life. I married a Maya woman, and her importance in the cultural sphere gradually grew. This proved to me that while the Western educational system was capable of transforming my mind, it could not change my heart. This event in my life marked the beginning of a new struggle—the restoration of my culture within myself. All human beings search for an ideal image of themselves (their identity), which generally can be found in their own family, as an essential expression of a people or culture. If we look for this ideal image outside the context of our own world, we begin to experience alienation and cultural decontextualization. This, in turn, neutralizes the potential of any human being.

When I returned to my hometown, signs of my alienation and estrangement began to manifest themselves as I felt a clash with the social and cultural dynamic existing among my grandparents, parents, friends, and other Mayas. I was no longer able to take hold of a hoe to work in the corn, bean, and wheat fields or in other agricultural activities because, according to my concept of a "professional and modern man" created by the school, all these activities belonged to traditional life and the "uneducated" people.

I began to feel the agonizing, emotional birth pains of assimilation as I returned once again to my cultural reality. Fortunately, with the help of my Maya brothers and sisters, I was able to find the door that would accelerate the process of rediscovery of myself and of the collective history of my ancestors. The ethnic shame which had developed in me was not sufficient to eradicate a fundamental element of my culture—the Kaqchikel language. From then on, my mother tongue turned into the lifejacket that saved the shipwrecked sailor tossed into the sea, that allowed him to live and breathe until he found land. That is how my mother tongue served me.

That "firm ground" began to materialize when I managed to land my first job with a nonprofit cultural organization, the Francisco Marroquín Linguistic Project (PLFM). This gave me the opportunity to teach the Kaqchikel language to a group of university students. My position required me to become literate in my own language, since hitherto I had only known how to speak it, as did most of my Maya brothers and sisters.

With that experience behind me, I competed for an opening as a bilingual teacher in Kaqchikel and Spanish in the National Program of Bilingual Intercultural Education (PRONEBI), a branch of the Ministry of Education. I began this new job in September 1985 in a small Kaqchikel community, where I was assigned as a first grade teacher to teach reading in Kaqchikel and Spanish to my little seven- or eight-year-old Maya brothers and sisters. It is very difficult to obtain employment with the government, so I felt very fortunate to have gotten that job. At the same time, I served as an example to my family and my people of how education can help us take advantage of certain opportunities in government.

The school year begins in January and ends in October. The months of November and December are vacation, in both the public and private sector of education. Government employees' salaries are very low in relation to the cost of living, so teachers often endeavor to find other employment during these vacations, and I was no exception. Fortunately, the institution which had supported me by offering me my first job again gave me the chance to work for a short period, this time teaching Kaqchikel to a foreign student.

This new experience marked the first step toward consolidating my culture, but this time it was with the sense of making the consolidation a collective one with a view to social action. This came about as a result of my acquaintance with a foreign student, a linguist, who shared his knowledge of that discipline with me, helping me to understand that the Mayan languages need to be worked on not only in the field of applied linguistics, but also in terms of description and the recognition of norms, in order to strengthen the languages and bring about their consolidation.

This experience of intellectual sharing gave birth to a desire in me to study at the university. Of course, this level of education is beyond the reach of the great majority of the population, especially Mayas, due to the exclusive and colonialist nature of university education. Nevertheless, the desire that moved me to study did not give up easily, and I kept searching for an opportunity until I was able to find one.

LIFE AT THE UNIVERSITY

There are five universities in Guatemala; one is public and the rest are private. Compared to the average income of government employees (even those few who are permanent), the cost of tuition at the private universities is extremely high. Since the central campuses of all five universities are located in the capital city, rural students have to pay room, board, and transportation in addition to the normal cost of studying, so neither private nor public institutions are readily accessible to them.

Luckily, in accordance with my own aspirations, a private school, the Mariano Gálvez University, created the School of Linguistics in the Faculty of Humanities for students from the rural areas of the country. Its classes met on the weekends: Fridays from 4:30 to 9:00 P.M. and Saturdays from 7:30 A.M. to 2:00 P.M. Opportunities were thus created for many people who wanted to study, provided, of course, that they had the minimum income necessary to meet the costs of transportation, room, and board for two days each week.

As a result of this new opportunity, I began my university level studies in 1987, three years after having graduated from Diversificado. My two greatest obstacles were always time and money. Time was a factor because the small Kaqchikel community where I worked was a two-hour hike from the municipal capital (there was no vehicle transportation), one hour from there by bus to the main highway (the only afternoon bus left at two o'clock) and another two and a half hours from the highway to Guatemala City. In total, it took me between five and six hours to get to the university when all went well. Then there were times when I could not get transportation. The other factor—economic—is one of the strongest and most immediate limitations for anyone with scarce funds, especially for someone like me with family responsibilities.

In spite of these hardships, I felt very happy and excited to have the opportunity to attend classes, although on occasion I encountered contradictions and deceptions which made me think more than once about leaving the university. There were several times when I only had enough money for one of two things: my studies or my family's sustenance. Of course, my family came first. Often I had to resort to borrowing money in order to pay for food and transportation. I was able to save on rent since I stayed in a kindergarten where the little tables served as my bed. One of the critical aspects of this experience is the fact that I did not want to admit that I was not a student like the rest—not a student who worked—but rather a worker who toiled simply to survive. The majority of the Mayas who began the program with me were in similar situations. Of the thirty-six enrolled in 1987, only eighteen regularly attended classes, and only about six have continued in the field.

Time marched forward, and I successfully completed one semester at a time, ever more eager to continue on my chosen path. Finally, I could see the light at the end of the tunnel. In 1990 two classmates and I completed the program in Applied Linguistics in Education. With this foundation, I transferred to the Rafael Landívar University, another private institution, in order to continue my studies leading to the degree of *licenciado* in the Linguistics Institute [the *licenciatura* is approximately equivalent to a five-year bachelor's degree with a formal thesis.—ed.].

By this time, I could feel and observe that the university could serve Mayas, either as a means of strengthening their culture or as a means of allowing them to flee from it. Usually Mayas strive to reach this academic level for one of two reasons. Either they wish to change their social and economic status, thereby hiding their true identity and looking for acceptance by the other culture, or they wish to consolidate their cultural self-esteem. Most people veer toward the first option, due to the individualistic nature of the Western system, which permits them to achieve material comfort rapidly. The tendency of individuals to seek escape from their culture is not accidental, but rather the result of years of schooling and of living in an atmosphere of social, political, and economic inequality. The second alternative implies accepting the great commitment to bring real development to Mayan towns, working within the framework of open competition and creating alternative options for the comprehensive development of each Maya family, the Maya people, and the nation itself. Development is grounded in the fundamental values of respect for others and a willingness to live together harmoniously—the essential pillars of real and lasting peace.

The option I chose was to take part in a collective commitment toward progress through education, carried out through a process of transformation and improvement of the sociocultural and natural surroundings, for our people and by our people. One should not think subjectively and expect a magic formula capable of rubbing out the imprint of five hundred years of socioeconomic, political, and cultural deterioration of the Maya people, but rather strive for and, above all, generate medium- and long-term strategies for development. A pluralistic and participatory society is needed, one capable of bringing about sustainable development as an alternative to our present reality. This viewpoint is in accordance with declarations of the United Nations to complete the final lap of the twentieth century and bring in the next century with a sure hope for a better tomorrow.

The fact that such a proposal for sustainable development has been made by the UN constitutes the clearest evidence that the efforts of international aid have not resulted in the changes hoped for, including qualitative improvements in the educational systems, basic education for all, eradication of illiteracy and extreme poverty, diminishing infant mortality, and much more. The reason there has been little progress in material development is that structural changes cannot be accomplished by outside agents or intermediaries who do not share in this reality and who get rich at the expense of the poor. Rather, change comes as a result of full, conscious participation and above all by relying on the unconditional commitment of the majority of the people affected and by giving them the opportunity to be the protagonists and agents of change—to freely choose their today as well as their tomorrow.

By viewing the situation and, indeed, life itself from this perspective, I was able to begin work on self-sustainable development projects with the parents of the children who attended my school. In addition, I began to collaborate with the Ministry of Education, which assisted me in contacting teachers from neighboring villages in order to cooperate on educational projects, giving us the option of improving our programs. I also wanted to increase the participation of parents as important actors in the educational process, since normally parents are not aware of what is going on in the schools. The scope of this activity continued to increase gradually, until in 1991 I formed part of the curriculum-designing team for the Section of Curricular Development of PRONEBI. This division is responsible for designing and making available Maya-Spanish educational materials for bilingual schools in the country. Materials include textbooks for Maya children, teaching guides for educators, and other secondary materials.

While I was progressing academically, I was also gaining practical work experience. This is the best proof that it is possible to both better oneself and bring about change. This is done by beginning with oneself, with the understanding that the process is a slow but sure one. As well as accomplishing my own dreams of academic advancement, I was equally concerned with applying my knowledge for the benefit of my people. In this way, I ensured that my thinking would not slip away from the correct path and objectives.

Finally, and in spite of many obstacles, I completed the fieldwork for my thesis and defended it at the end of July 1994, receiving the academic degree of *licenciado,* an accomplishment never dreamed of by a person who was born on a grass mat on the ground and grew up barefoot and who felt on more than one occasion backward and useless before the system. I attribute this victory to the Heart of the Heavens, to the Maya people, and to all the official and unofficial people who influenced me, whether directly or indirectly, in attaining my objective.

TRAVELING AND LIVING ABROAD

Due to my activities in interethnic and labor relations, I have been fortunate to travel to other Spanish-speaking countries and to the United States. The ability to speak Spanish facilitates interaction in the hispanic world; but in the United States Spanish loses its official status and becomes a language with very restricted domains of use, especially in the northern state which I visited.

I would like to share some relevant experiences and impressions from my stay in the United States. At first, I felt insecure because I did not know English, finding myself once again in a different and unknown world. This experience brought back to me the same feelings of isolation I had experienced as a schoolboy. At that time, my inability to communicate arose from my lack of Spanish; this time it was from my lack of English. This confirmed for me that when a person or people undergoes a disagreeable experience, one of being ignored by others (or by the system), the experience remains marked in one's mind and heart. This is especially true in the case of children, with their delicate and emotional foundations.

Nevertheless, at that stage of my life, as an adult under different circumstances and surroundings, the experience served to give me added impulse and incentive never to forget the reality of thousands of Maya children who at that very moment were feeling frustrated in their monolingual, Spanish-speaking schools, desiring to flee from school at the first opportunity that presented itself.

The truth is that until individuals actually live through this bitter experience they will not learn to be more tolerant, even though it should not be this way. I say this because I attended a school to learn English and found that the other students who attended, all from other countries, were facing the same difficulties in learning another language. This meant that they felt solidarity with me when I entered the course. Yet in spite of this, when the teacher asked me something in English the first time, I felt the same insecurity I had experienced as a schoolboy and I blushed like a child.

These are some of the reasons why I feel a responsibility to take on the goal of working together with government and private organizations in the field of Mayan education. For all the above reasons, I venture to write and make public a part of my life, sharing the results of my way of thinking. Behind any action, it is indispensable that there exist a reason, an objective, a vision, and better yet if it is based on a philosophy of life and ideals.

Dreaming is important, but it is even more important that dreams be accompanied by concrete action. My actions are probably not the best, nor exemplary. Nevertheless, I humbly share them so they may be of whatever service is possible. Until now, my actions have been sufficient to allow me to continue dreaming and, above all, continue acting, always in search of a tomorrow in which the sun shines brightly for everyone, just as Ruk'u'x Kaj (Heart of the Heavens: God) believed when he created America, the earth, and all that exists on it.

As forgotten peoples, removed from the benefits of the resources created by our own kind, it is important to be conscious of the fact that we ourselves are responsible for our own development. For this reason let us not waste time in theoretical discussions and lifeless doctrines which have only caused the original peoples to become ever more divided. As an example of the disastrous effects of divisionism, for territorial reasons, our people are divided by the borders of Mexico, Belize, and Guatemala, causing us to live in three different states. Within Guatemala we are divided by departments and regions which obey economic premises and the politics of dominion. Finally, this region contains more than 16,000 churches and religious institutions. It is better to create a consensus based on results—the products of our actions and efforts—only taking care that our efforts are accompanied by vision, for action without vision is time wasted, while vision without action is an unachievable dream.

Matyox
Thank you

9. CONCLUSIONS

Susan Garzon

The Kaqchikel people have come in contact with many language groups during their long history, but rarely has the viability of their language been threatened. In pre-Conquest times contact with most groups from the Basin of Mexico was probably brokered by a small group of bilinguals or a bilingual elite and had little effect on the majority of Kaqchikel people or their language. Even the Toltecs, who reportedly invaded Kaqchikel territory and became the new rulers, were unable to undermine the hegemony of the Mayan language. Cut off from their own group and surrounded by a sea of indigenous speakers, including many potential marriage partners, they adopted the majority language and eventually lost their own language, leaving traces of Nahua in the form of loanwords in Kaqchikel.

The invasion by Spaniards in the early sixteenth century initiated a very different process, one that is still running its course almost five hundred years later. Like the Toltecs, the Spaniards wished to rule the Mayas. However, the Europeans remained outside of Mayan society, living in their own communities and establishing a barrier between Mayas and Spaniards which Mayas could only pass by discarding their Indian identity and joining the ranks of Ladinos.

The Spaniards succeeded in reorganizing Kaqchikel society, resettling the inhabitants in centralized towns, where Mayan culture reestablished itself, albeit in a modified form. The Kaqchikel language reasserted itself as the medium of communication, borrowing Spanish loanwords for new concepts in colonial life. Even in San Antonio Aguas Calientes, where the inhabitants had been brought in from other language areas, Kaqchikel became the common language.

For hundreds of years the two societies, Maya and Spanish, existed side by side in a relationship characterized by vast inequality, their economies intertwined in an economic order that systematically drained

Mayan towns of their resources. For most Kaqchikels, any rewards and satisfactions in life were to be found in their own communities, through living their lives in accordance with Mayan values. The Spanish language was the outsiders' language, the language of the exploiters, and it was unnecessary for daily activities. Communication was facilitated by bilingual brokers, often by members of the religious orders during the early Colonial Period and by Ladinos later on.

THE EARLY STAGE OF SHIFT: THE EXAMPLE
OF SAN MARCOS LA LAGUNA

The real challenge to Kaqchikel viability has come in recent years. Since the nineteenth century, many Mayan communities have faced a combination of political, economic, and social forces both compelling and facilitating integration into the national society. One result has been a change in language behavior: more Mayas have been learning Spanish. The recent history of San Marcos La Laguna gives us a glimpse of what the early stages of shift may have been like for other communities. Between 1974 and 1980 the town went from monolingualism in Kaqchikel to incipient bilingualism, with about 1 percent of adult males in San Marcos substantially bilingual. Fourteen years later, in 1994, the percentage of bilinguals had increased to about 5 percent. These bilingual men hold prestigious religious and civil positions in the community and are employed in nontraditional occupations.

For bilinguals in San Marcos, learning Spanish has not meant a weakening of traditional values or a loss of Mayan identity. Marqueños continue to place importance on verbal competence in Kaqchikel and value individuals who speak well according to prescribed canons of performance. For the bilingual men, a knowledge of Spanish is a useful supplementary skill, increasing their employment opportunities and furthering their status. The use of Spanish by high-status individuals within the community means that the language is now accorded a greater measure of prestige than it enjoyed previously; it can no longer be viewed simply as a language of the outsiders.

It is not certain that the first Spanish-speaking Mayas in a community are usually men with high status, although this is a likely scenario. As long as the number of bilinguals is very small, these individuals may simply serve as cultural brokers. However, an increasing number of bilinguals indicates a higher level of interaction between Ladinos and Indians. When a community reaches the stage of incipient bilingualism, this means that at least some individuals are willing and able to deal directly with Ladinos and have sufficient exposure to Spanish to gain proficiency in it. What is more, the community accepts this behavior as appropriate, at least for these members. Women may still be discouraged from entering into the kinds of close interaction with Ladinos that would enable them to gain mastery of Spanish, and there may be a general sense that people who use Spanish with other Kaqchikel speakers are acting self-important. To some extent, then, in the early stages of shift, social controls limit the amount of Spanish spoken within the community.

Nevertheless, the introduction of Spanish reflects a new opposition within the town: traditional Mayan values versus those of the Ladino world. As long as inhabitants remain monolingual in Kaqchikel and concern themselves with the internal workings of Mayan society, the colonial world view prevails. As Mayas begin to speak Spanish and take on other symbols of the Ladino world, the opposition between Mayan and Ladino worlds is incorporated into the culture of the Kaqchikel town. This is the beginning of a process that continues today in most Mayan towns, in which individuals must find ways to reconcile the competing values and behaviors associated with the two worlds.

WIDESPREAD BILINGUALISM AND ITS AFTERMATH

The inhabitants of San Antonio have been involved in a balancing act for many years. The town has been intimately tied into the colonial economy since contact, and by the late nineteenth century the inhabitants of San Antonio were speaking Spanish to some degree. During the long period of bilingualism that followed, townspeople continued to learn Kaqchikel as their first language, but the majority also acquired Spanish later. Although Antoneros interacted with outsiders, they maintained their traditional networks, continuing to place primary importance on their position within Mayan society. San Antonio's experience indicates that widespread bilingualism can be maintained in a Mayan community over a relatively long time span—in this case at least three or four generations.

In recent years the situation has changed, as the inhabitants have expanded their networks outside the town and as national institutions have become increasingly integrated into local life. As part of this process, the relationship between Kaqchikel and Spanish has changed. Individuals no longer learn Spanish as a second and supplementary language. Instead, Spanish is replacing Kaqchikel in the home, where it is taught to children as their first language. Worldwide, the decision by parents to speak the dominant language with their children has been identified as a crucial step in the loss of an indigenous language, and the Kaqchikel area is no exception.

Language shift is also underway in San Juan Comalapa, although it has not progressed as far as in San Antonio. Unlike San Antonio, Comalapa did not experience a long period of widespread bilingualism; monolingualism in Kaqchikel appears to have been the rule in the early part of this century. However, by the 1970s many Maya men and some women were bilingual.

Adults over the age of about fifty grew up at a time when Kaqchikel enjoyed status in the community. They learned the language at home and were first introduced to Spanish when they entered Guatemalan institutions. For some, school was the first encounter, although usually it was an unsuccessful one. A combination of obstacles resulted in students' failure to learn Spanish well or to acquire other basic skills. Some men succeeded in learning Spanish later, when they were conscripted into the army. For this age group, Spanish has been largely an outside language. As young adults in the 1960s and 1970s, the men might have used Spanish in certain public contexts or when discussing topics such as national politics. However, Kaqchikel remained the language of choice in many situations, including any that required the active participation of women.

Although by the 1970s Spanish had entered the verbal repertoire of many Mayas, it did not affect their ethnic identity; they continued to think of themselves as Comalapans and Indians, although they had little sense of unity with other Kaqchikels or Mayas. Farber (1978) found that attitudes toward Ladinos had also changed little, in spite of changing interactional patterns and inroads made by the Spanish language. Mayas in Comalapa, even bilingual ones, tended to view Ladinos as greedy, lazy, immoral, and corrupt (Farber 1978: 10). Those individuals who wished to reject their Indian identity had the option of leaving Comalapa and adopting a Ladino lifestyle, a decision accepted by other townspeople, although the change left the individuals in a somewhat marginal position relative to their former neighbors.

By the mid-1970s many Indian parents in Comalapa had begun speaking Spanish with their children. This decision highlights the contradictions that many Mayas lived with during this transitional period. Parents chose to use Spanish in the home because they recognized that their children would need Spanish to get along in the world. The parents took this step in spite of their own strong sense of Indian identity and allegiance to the town. Indeed, the shift to Spanish may have been seen as a measure necessary for the survival of the community. This action was not seen as detrimental to Kaqchikel; parents assumed their children would learn the language naturally by growing up in the town. Since the limited bilingualism that had existed in the past had been additive rather than replacive, this was a reasonable assumption, and, in fact, there are a number of young adults today who learned Kaqchikel as a second language. Thus, for the first generation of children raised in Spanish, the opportunity still existed to learn Kaqchikel, although some individuals never gained mastery of it. While most parents probably saw their shift to Spanish as a pragmatic reaction to changing expectations, the change reveals the extent to which the values and behaviors of the larger society had entered the community. For the first time the language of the outsiders, a group formerly despised, had become the language of hearth and home.

The Transitional Generation in Comalapa

The children who grew up in the 1970s are now adults in their twenties and thirties, and they constitute a transitional generation—bilinguals sandwiched between Kaqchikel-dominant parents and their own children, who are often Spanish-dominant or monolingual in Spanish. The experiences of this group, and their reactions to them, shed light on what it means in human terms for a community to lose its native language.

Many members of the transitional generation had families in which the fathers had some mastery of Spanish, while mothers did not. Consequently, women sometimes found that they were expected to raise their children in a language which they had not mastered and to which they had limited exposure. When the children reached school age, they faced some of the same obstacles their parents had: large classes, insensitive teachers, and a curriculum unsuited to the needs of Maya children in a Highland town. However, their chances of success were somewhat improved by two factors. First, they and a number of their classmates had already been introduced to Spanish by their parents. Those children with older siblings had the added advantage of listening to the Spanish the older children brought home from school. In addition, there was a shift in the attitude toward the schools; parents increasingly saw schooling as a necessary step in their children's preparation for the future.

Within the home, many families found themselves divided along linguistic lines. The father and school-age children spoke mostly Spanish, while the mother and older relatives spoke mostly Kaqchikel. This is a situation similar to that faced by some immigrant groups, although in this case it was the indigenous group facing loss of its language.

Parents who chose to speak Spanish with their children turned out to be accurate in their appraisal of future opportunities and needs. Many members of the shift generation have had extensive contacts with the Ladino world, working and studying in Guatemala City and other urban centers.

LANGUAGE SHIFT AND THE INTERNALIZATION
OF LADINO VALUES

One of the most culturally detrimental aspects of the integration of Mayan communities into Guatemalan society has been Mayas' internalization of Ladino attitudes toward Indians, as seen in the sense of shame that often prevents young Kaqchikel speakers from speaking the language publicly. While this change in values is tied most directly to the increasingly close contact of Mayas with Ladinos and their culture, the shift from use of Kaqchikel to Spanish as a mother tongue may itself have played a part in the process.

To some extent, when individuals master a language they learn the world view underlying the language. This can be a source of conflict or confusion when the two world views are opposed in the way they view the social realm. For example, the Kaqchikel and Spanish words used to refer to the Kaqchikel language have very different connotations.

Older Kaqchikel speakers refer to their language as *qachab'äl* or *qatzojob'äl* (our language or our speech). In so doing, they may bring to mind the richness of their language, including its many genres, ranging from casual conversation to formal, ritual speech. They may also bring to mind the skill of certain orators and the prestige accorded them.

In contrast to the Kaqchikel word *qachab'äl*, with its many positive connotations, the word used by many Spanish speakers to refer to Kaqchikel and other Mayan languages is *lengua*, literally 'tongue.' The use of *lengua*, along with *dialecto* (dialect), often suggests a type of speech which fails to meet the criteria of a true language or *idioma* like Spanish. Not only does the term *lengua* fail to recognize the distinctiveness of individual Mayan languages, but it does not even accord them the status of full languages. When Kaqchikel speakers use the word *lengua*, they may well bring to mind the negative associations which constitute the semantic context of the word for many Guatemalan Spanish speakers. Older individuals who learned Kaqchikel first probably internalized the positive associations related to their language and its ways of speaking before they had to deal with the negative associations of *lengua*. From this perspective, the intergenerational shift, which introduced Spanish as the first language of the home, also facilitated the entry of Ladino values, including those values that would cause Mayas to view their own culture with shame (Garzon 1995).

Because language is a potent symbol of Mayan identity, it is understandable that language choice has been a source of conflict for some Mayas. Young people growing up in the transitional generation were faced with conflicting messages about language. On one hand, Spanish was the language of power and success in the larger Ladino society into which they were becoming increasingly integrated. On the other hand, Ladino society continued to dominate and denigrate them as Indians, and the Spanish language symbolized Ladino values. Kaqchikel, for its part, was the language that embodied traditional community values and was used in a number of traditional contexts. To some extent, it was still the language of the home, used with grandparents and other older adults. However, it was a language that many had found little opportunity to learn.

IDENTITY CONFLICT

Young adults today are integrated into Ladino society to a much greater extent than previous generations and as a consequence have been affected more strongly by Ladino attitudes, including negative evaluations of Indians. While previous generations were well aware of these attitudes, they had less reason to internalize them, since Mayas and Ladinos essentially maintained separate belief systems and social structures.

Today Mayas and Ladinos interact in a number of settings, including classrooms, various social, religious, and political organizations, and the workplace. Although social relations between Mayas and Ladinos are becoming more egalitarian, Indians continue to face hostility and derision from members of the dominant group. It is not surprising that some Mayas prefer to leave behind their Indian identity and assimilate to Ladino culture. This is easier today than in earlier times, since young Mayas already have one traditional characteristic of Ladino identity—mastery of Spanish. The switch to Ladino identity may be most tempting for young men, whose clothing does not set them apart from Ladinos, as do the *corte* and *huipil* usually worn by Mayan women. For many young people, a break with their Mayan roots may be a rejection of the social stigma associated with being Indian or a reflection of their desire to distance themselves psychologically from the poverty and hardships their ancestors endured. For those who find jobs and spouses outside Comalapa, Indian identity may seem irrelevant in their new surroundings.

THE ROLE OF SCHOOLING IN LANGUAGE MAINTENANCE AND SHIFT

When multicultural societies adopt a strongly nationalistic ideology, they often identify minority ethnic groups as obstacles to national unity. In order to achieve cultural uniformity, they promote the idea that the nation will only progress when all its inhabitants embrace the values and behavior of the dominant group. One of the most effective means of disseminating this message is through the schools.

In earlier years many Mayan communities resisted the government's attempts to educate their children. Parents saw formal education as irrelevant if not detrimental to their children's development. The school system was not set up to further the goals of Mayan communities for their children; in fact, it was hostile to Mayan culture. Children learned little or nothing in terms of useful skills. What they learned instead was that they were a marginalized group with no legitimate history or culture of their own.

In recent years more Mayan families have begun to send their children to school, not simply out of legal necessity, but also in the expectation that the families will have a better chance of survival if their children learn the skills they will need outside their communities. Parents who choose to support their children's participation in school are also likely to teach them Spanish to the extent they can.

Comalapa underwent a transitional period in the 1970s when attitudes toward schooling started to change and increasing numbers of children began attending school for longer periods. The children arrived at school with varying skill levels in Spanish and Kaqchikel, and for a number of years the school was a setting in which Spanish-dominant children could learn Kaqchikel informally from their peers while Kaqchikel-dominant children learned Spanish in the classroom. In subsequent years, as Spanish use has spread through the younger population, the opportunity for a student to learn Kaqchikel from peers at school has greatly diminished. Today it is unlikely that a child would learn Kaqchikel at school, unless it was acquired from the formal Kaqchikel instruction which has recently been introduced into the curriculum of the primary schools.

In recent years the Ministry of Education has promoted bilingual education in Mayan areas. However, it has proven difficult to implement programs fully even when their goals are modest. Sometimes positions for bilingual teachers are filled by monolingual teachers, despite the fact that qualified bilingual teachers are looking for jobs. Discrimination may be a factor in the inability of Mayan teachers to secure these positions, or it may be that Mayas lack the resources and connections that have traditionally facilitated economic transactions in Guatemalan society.

Even when Kaqchikel-speaking teachers are hired, they may be sent to different language areas, where, as outsiders, they have difficulty becoming integrated into the community as Indians. In some cases Kaqchikel speakers may actually prefer to use Spanish with their students, as in the case of the bilingual teacher in San Marcos. Teachers who attended Spanish-medium schools themselves and internalized a nationalistic ideology may be uncomfortable with the kind of education which promotes maintenance of a subordinate (although not minority) culture.

The Kaqchikel literacy classes described by Brown were more successful in avoiding these obstacles to promotion of Mayan culture. The subject matter taught—the Kaqchikel language itself—was not filtered through a foreign lens, and the teachers were not only Mayas and members of the community, but trained linguists as well.

THE SPREAD OF LANGUAGE SHIFT

Within the Mayan area the shift to Spanish is progressing in waves. In municipalities like Comalapa it starts in the urban center and extends outward to the surrounding villages and hamlets. Currently, the children who suffer from a disjunction between the languages of home and school are those living in outlying areas, where many people are still Kaqchikel-dominant or monolingual in Kaqchikel. Recently, the transition to Spanish-speaking schools has been eased somewhat by preschool programs such as Live Better, which has allowed children in San Marcos to enter school with some low-level Spanish oral skills.

The shift to bilingualism has spread more quickly among men than women. Even in an urban area like Comalapa, many older women still have a very limited knowledge of Spanish, while their husbands know enough to get along. This means that the most traditional speakers, those most closely associated with the use of Kaqchikel, are older women and villagers, groups that do not usually enjoy high status. However, the revitalization movement may spread the use of Kaqchikel from the other direction. It is the educated, urban Mayas, including many men, who are most affected by the movement toward Mayan cultural revitalization, and they value Mayan languages as repositories of traditional culture and symbols of ethnic identity. As they return to their home communities to visit or live, they bring new attitudes with them, including a positive evaluation of Mayan culture.

One of the most striking characteristics of language shift is the speed with which it moves once momentum has been gained. Certainly Farber, carrying out research in Comalapa in the mid-1970s, had no idea that some fifteen years later there would be Indians monolingual in Spanish and women would no longer constitute a uniformly conservative influence on language use. However, there is variation in the rate at which communities experience the different stages of shift. While widespread bilingualism in San Antonio persisted for as long as seventy-five years before a real shift to Spanish began, in Comalapa bilingualism has been of more recent origin and is already succumbing to shift. The economic self-sufficiency of a town is probably a factor in its ability to maintain traditional social structures in the face of societal pressures to change. However, the size of the community and the strength of its social networks are also factors. In the Quinizilapa Valley it is the hamlets, with their dense, multiplex social networks, that are experiencing the fastest language shift.

OUTLOOK FOR THE FUTURE

As today's bilingual children grow up, they will have fewer opportunities and less necessity to speak Kaqchikel than their parents had. However, they may have fewer negative associations with the language. Older people remember the difficult time they had when they started school knowing little Spanish, and they fear that learning Kaqchikel may hinder their children's ability to learn Spanish. To confirm this belief, they need only listen to older individuals who are proficient in Kaqchikel but whose Spanish shows the effects of incomplete acquisition. Younger people have had a different experience. Because they started school with considerable knowledge of Spanish, they did not have the same frustrations over communication that their monolingual parents or grandparents did. In addition, many have regular contact with bilinguals who speak both Kaqchikel and fluent Spanish. Consequently, they may be less likely to see knowledge of Kaqchikel as a serious impediment to the acquisition of Spanish. They also have more consciousness of Kaqchikel as a legitimate language. Although some individuals still refer to it as a "dialect" or "tongue" rather than a real language, this attitude is likely to change now that children are studying the language formally in school and it is receiving institutional support on regional and national levels.

One of the greatest challenges to the maintenance of Mayan languages is the fact that many young people are drawn away from Mayan towns by educational and occupational opportunities in the capital and other Ladino cities. Those Mayas who leave their towns permanently may feel little need to assert their ethnic identity. However, as Wuqu' Ajpub' demonstrates, individuals may wish or need to return to their hometowns for extended periods. To some extent, the town acts as a safety net; family and friends provide support in economically unstable times. Beyond that, there are positive reasons for individuals to remain in their hometowns, especially in the larger centers like Comalapa, with its bustling energy. Those who stay are able to live in a place where the culture is theirs and where they can bring up their children as Mayas. In addition, some educated Comalapans choose to return because of a sense of responsibility to their town, a desire to share what they have learned and to work toward a better future for their people.

There are also young adults who live in both worlds, holding down jobs in the city during the week and commuting to their hometown on the weekend. In the larger towns, like Comalapa and San Antonio, many families have adapted to change by both maintaining a foothold in the traditional economy and exploiting the cash economy. Brown notes that the most successful individuals in San Antonio are those who manage to straddle both worlds. These individuals may continue to use Kaqchikel, in part because of its function as a symbol of community membership.

Mayas will continue to have instrumental reasons for learning Spanish, and indeed for some it has become a mother tongue. Their willingness to learn and maintain Kaqchikel will depend on the rewards—emotional, spiritual, and material—that derive from being Maya and speaking a Mayan language. It will also depend on their ability to create a Mayan identity within a society that has traditionally been hostile to Indians.

Scenario for Kaqchikel Maintenance

It is possible to create a scenario in which Kaqchikel and other Mayan languages continue to thrive. The scenario encompasses changes or the strengthening of recent trends at the levels of the society, the community, and the family. It includes the following elements.

1. Parents value Mayan culture and identify the language with that culture. They also view bilingualism in a positive light, seeing the acquisition of both Kaqchikel and Spanish as an important part of their children's education. As a result, these parents speak Kaqchikel with their children on a regular basis. They take an active role in education, supporting programs in the schools and community aimed at teaching and reinforcing the language.

2. Young people share their parents' evaluation of the language; they consider it important to participate in Mayan culture and use a Mayan language. Even if they live outside the home community during periods of their lives, they maintain contact with other Mayan speakers and instruct their children in a Mayan language. They support the continuing development and maintenance of Mayan literature.

3. Guatemalans of all backgrounds learn about Mayan culture and value it not only as a common heritage but as a source of knowledge and insights for living.

The recent movement toward pan-Mayan unity may be instrumental in achieving these goals. By promoting unity along with ethnic pride, Maya intellectuals are beginning to reverse a centuries-old pattern of isolation and factionalism among language groups and communities. By their participation in such crucial activities as drafting the Peace Accords, Maya leaders are demonstrating the benefits of unified action.

The more open Guatemalan society becomes, the more difficult it may be for Mayas to maintain their language, as any number of immigrant ethnic groups worldwide can attest. However, as Mayas continue to discover and embrace their own history, express their ethnicity in meaningful ways, and share their messages with others, many Mayas and non-Mayas will find ample reason to commit themselves to maintenance of Mayan languages.

NOTE

Part of this chapter was presented at the Twenty-fourth Annual Meeting of the Linguistic Association of the Southwest, Las Cruces, New Mexico, October 1995.

GLOSSARY

aldea—village, hamlet.

Annals of the Kaqchikels—document recounting Kaqchikel history, written in Kaqchikel shortly after the Spanish invasion.

barrio—neighborhood. In San Marcos it is used to refer to the three major residential divisions.

Básico—the first three years of secondary school.

cacique—leader.

Castellanización—a program instituted by the Ministry of Education in the mid-1960s to introduce monolingual Maya children to oral Spanish during a preschool year prior to the first grade of primary.

cofradía—local Catholic community organization whose activities include caring for a particular saint or holy image; generally associated with syncretistic or more conservative Catholic Church practices; a civic-religious brotherhood.

corte—Maya woman's skirt.

cosmovisión—world view, conception of the universe, cosmology.

cuerda—a unit used to measure land, in San Marcos roughly equivalent to 32 square *varas* or 625 square meters.

encomienda—a concession of land and inhabitants granted to a conquistador. The landholder is the *encomendero*.

finca—plantation.

gringo—foreigner, especially a white foreigner of North American or European descent.

huipil—Maya woman's traditional handwoven or hand-embroidered blouse.

indio—colonial racial category for Indians.

Instituto Indigenista Nacional—National Indigenist Institute.

Ladino—a Guatemalan non-Maya or mestizo, generally distinguished by such markers as use of the Spanish language and manufactured clothing, racial/historical descent, and identification with the dominant national society.

lengua—language (literally 'tongue'), used to refer to Indian speech in general, often used by non-Indians.

lingua franca—language used for communication among different language groups.

mestizo—colonial racial category for progeny of Europeans and Indians.

milpa—form of traditional small-scale agriculture; planted corn; plot of land used for planting corn, generally intercropped with beans, squash, and wild herbs.

muchachos—used to refer to boys, male adolescents, or young male adults. Used as a collectivity it can also refer to male peer groups, workers, students, gangs, and guerrillas.

municipio, municipalidad—municipality, an administrative division of a department, often consisting of a town center and outlying settlements, known as *aldeas* and *caseríos*. Each *municipio* is generally viewed as ethnically distinct and characterized by different customs, dress, speech, and religious celebrations. The *cabecera municipal* is the town center.

oficios domésticos—housekeeping tasks.

ojer tzij—traditional Kaqchikel speech genre consisting of legends, histories, counsels, prayers, and other ritual speech.

Popol Vuh—document recorded in K'iche' shortly after the invasion, telling the history of the K'iche'an peoples.

Preprimaria Bilingüe—preschool year in which initial literacy skills are first taught in the mother tongue and then transferred to reading and writing in Spanish.

promotor bilingüe—a noncertified Maya teacher of the Preprimaria Bilingüe.

PRONEBI—Programa Nacional de Educación Bilingüe (National Program of Bilingual Intercultural Education).

repartimiento—a system of forced labor, in which Indians were temporarily assigned to petitioning landowners by colonial officials.

ruk'u'x tzij—a San Marcos La Laguna Kaqchikel speech genre consisting of emotional, impassioned, or argumentative speech such as political and religious oratory, quarrels, word games, and speech used to provoke illness.

traje—traditional Mayan dress.

tzij—Kaqchikel for 'word,' 'speech,' 'language.'

tzojob'äl—term used by the inhabitants of San Marcos La Laguna to identify the Kaqchikel language variety spoken in their community; literally 'medium of speech.'

la violencia—a period of violence, considered by some to be a civil war, in which many Mayas were killed. In the Kaqchikel area it was most severe between about 1978 and 1983.

xa tzij—Kaqchikel speech genre consisting of common, ordinary, everyday speech and casual conversations.

xolon tzij—Kaqchikel word for code-switching; literally 'mixing words.'

zambo—colonial racial category for progeny of Indians and Africans.

BIBLIOGRAPHY

The following documents were consulted in the Archivo General de Centroamérica, Guatemala (AGCA). Documents cited by division (*asignatura*), bundle (*legajo*), document (*expediente*), and year:

A1.23 191 1511 139 1550
A1.23 191 1511 140 1550
A1.23 1512 479 1575
A1.29 1513 639 1584
A1.23 1514 68 1605
A1.23 1515 75 1620
A3.16 40 663 1672
A1.23 1523 36 1691
A3.2 B165 708 1770
A3.16 4741 239 21 1790
A3.16 4795 241 1798
A3.16 2803 521 40 1621
A3.1 4284 528 94 1793

Aguirre, Gerardo

1972   *La Cruz de Nimajuyú: Historia de la parroquia de San Pedro La Laguna.* Guatemala City: Iglesia Católica de Guatemala.

Aikio, Marjut

1992   Are Women Innovators in the Shift to a Second Language?: A Case Study of Reindeer Sámi Women and Men. *International Journal of the Sociology of Language* 94: 43–61.

The Annals of the Kaqchikels

1953   Translated by Adrian Recinos and Delia Goetz. Norman: University of Oklahoma Press.

Annis, Sheldon

1987   *God and Production in a Guatemalan Town.* Austin: University of Texas Press.

Bakker, Peter, and Maarten Mous, eds.

1994   *Mixed Languages.* Amsterdam: Institute for Functional Research into Language and Language Use.

Blanck, Evelyn, and Félix Colindres

1996   Renacimiento Maya. *Crónica* (Guatemala City), July 26: 19–24.

Blom, J. P., and J. Gumperz

1972   Social Meaning in Linguistic Structures: Code-switching in Norway. In *Directions in Sociolinguistics: The Ethnography of Communication,* ed. by J. Gumperz and D. Hymes, pp. 409–434. New York: Holt, Rinehart and Winston.

Bloomfield, Leonard

1933   *Language.* New York: Henry Holt and Company.

Brown, R. McKenna

1996a   The Maya Language Loyalty Movement. In *Maya Cultural Activism in Guatemala,* ed. by Edward Fischer and R. McKenna Brown, pp. 165–177. Austin: University of Texas Press.

1996b   San Antonio Aguas Calientes by Sheldon Annis: *God and Production Two Decades Later.* Paper presented at the Ninety-fifth Meetings of the American Anthropological Association, San Francisco, November 20.

Brown, R. McKenna, Edward Fischer, and Raxche' Demetrio Rodríguez Guaján

n.d.   Mayan Nationalization Movements. In *Indigenous Peoples' Politics: An Introduction,* vol. 2, ed. by Marc Sills and Glenn Morris. Denver: Fourth World Center of the Study of Indigenous Law and Politics, University of Colorado at Denver. In press.

Burgos Debray, Elisabeth, editor

1992   *I, Rigoberta Menchú.* Trans. Ann Wright. New York: Verso Press.

Campbell, Lyle

1977   *Quichean Linguistic Prehistory.* University of California Publications in Linguistics No. 81. Berkeley: University of California Press.

Campbell, Lyle, and Terrence Kaufman

1990   Lingüística mayance: Dónde nos encontramos ahora? In *Lecturas sobra la lingüística maya,* ed. by Nora England and Stephen Elliott, pp. 51–58. Guatemala City: CIRMA.

Campbell, Lyle, and Martha C. Muntzel

1989   The Structural Consequences of Language Death. In *Investigating Obsolescence: Studies in Language Contraction and Death,* ed. by Nancy Dorian, pp. 181–196. Cambridge: Cambridge University Press.

Cantoni, Gina, editor

1996   *Stabilizing Indigenous Languages.* Flagstaff: Northern Arizona University.

Carmack, Robert

1968   Toltec Influence in the Postclassic Culture History of Highland Guatemala. In *Archaeological Studies of Middle America*, pp. 42–92. Publication No. 26. New Orleans: Middle American Research Institute, Tulane University.

Chacach, Martín

1987   Los dialectos de Kaqchikel. Presented at Noveno Taller de Lingüística Maya, Antigua, Guatemala.

Cojtí Cuxil, Demetrio

1987   *La educación bilingüe: ¿Mecanismo para la uniformidad o para el pluralismo lingüístico?* Guatemala City: Universidad Rafael Landívar.

1990a   La influencia destructiva de la universidad, el sistema educativo, y las ciencias sociales en la identidad maya. Presented at Centro de Investigaciones Regionales de Mesoamerica (CIRMA), Antigua, Guatemala.

1990b   Lingüística e idiomas mayas en Guatemala. In *Lecturas sobre la lingüística maya*, ed. by Nora England and Stephen Elliott, pp. 1–25. Guatemala: CIRMA.

Cortés y Larraz, Pedro, Archbishop

1958   *Descripción geográfico-moral de la Diócesis de Goathemala.* Prologue by Adrian Recinos. Biblioteca "Goathemala," vol. 20, book 2. Guatemala: Sociedad de Geografía e Historia.

Denison, Norman

1977   Language Death or Language Suicide? *International Journal of the Sociology of Language* 12: 13–22.

Deutsch, Karl Wolfgang

1966   *Nationalism and Social Communication: An Inquiry into the Foundations of Nationality.* Cambridge, Mass.: MIT Press.

Dorian, Nancy C.

1981   *Language Death: The Life Cycle of a Scottish Gaelic Dialect.* Philadelphia: University of Pennsylvania Press.

Dorian, Nancy C., editor

1989   *Investigating Obsolescence: Studies in Language Contraction and Death.* Cambridge: Cambridge University Press.

Downing, John

1987   Comparative Perspectives on World Literacy. In *The Future of Literacy in a Changing World,* ed. by Daniel Wagner, pp. 25–47. New York: Pergamon Press.

Dressler, Wolfgang

1982   Acceleration, Retardation, and Reversal in Language Decay? In *Language Spread,* ed. by Robert Cooper, pp. 321–336. Bloomington: Indiana University Press.

Ebel, Roland

1988   When Indians Take Power: Conflict and Consensus in San Juan Ostuncalco. In *Harvest of Violence: The Maya Indians and the Guatemalan Crisis,* ed. by Robert Carmack, pp. 174–191. Norman: University of Oklahoma Press.

Edwards, John

1985   *Language, Society and Identity.* Oxford: Basil Blackwell.

England, Nora

1988   Language and Ethnic Definition among Guatemalan Mayans. Paper presented at the Eighty-seventh Annual Meetings of the American Anthropological Association, Phoenix, Arizona.

1992   *La autonomía de los idiomas mayas.* Guatemala City: Cholsamaj.

1996   The Role of Language Standardization in Revitalization. In *Maya Cultural Activism in Guatemala,* ed. by R. McKenna Brown and Edward Fischer, pp. 178–194. Austin: University of Texas Press.

Farber, Anne

1978   Language Choice and Problems of Identity in a Highland Mayan Town. Ph.D. dissertation. Columbia University.

Farriss, Nancy M.

1984   *Maya Society under Colonial Rule: The Collective Enterprise of Survival.* Princeton: Princeton University Press.

Fasold, Ralph

1984   *The Sociolinguistics of Society.* Oxford, England: Basil Blackwell.

Fischer, Edward

1992   Creating Political Space for Cultural Pluralism: The Guatemalan Case. Presented at the Ninety-first Annual Meetings of the American Anthropological Association, San Francisco.

1996   The Pan-Maya Movement in Global and Local Context. Ph.D. dissertation. Department of Anthropology, Tulane University.

Fischer, Edward, and R. McKenna Brown

1996a Introduction: Maya Cultural Activism in Guatemala. In *Maya Cultural Activism in Guatemala*, ed. by Edward Fischer and R. McKenna Brown, pp. 1–18. Austin: University of Texas Press.

Fischer, Edward, and R. McKenna Brown, editors

1996b *Maya Cultural Activism in Guatemala*. Austin: University of Texas Press.

Fishman, Joshua A.

1972 *Language in Sociocultural Change: Essays by Joshua A. Fishman*, ed. by Anwar S. Dil. Stanford: Stanford University Press.

1989 *Language and Ethnicity in Minority Sociolinguistic Perspective*. Clevedon, England: Multilingual Matters Ltd.

Flinspach, Susan

1989 An Evaluation of Basque Language Status Planning. Ph.D. dissertation. University of Iowa.

Fought, John

1985 Patterns of Sociolinguistic Inequality in Mesoamerica. In *Language of Inequality*, ed. by Nessa Wolfson and Joan Manes, pp. 21–40. Berlin: Mouton Publishers.

Fox, John

1978 *Quiché Conquest: Centralism and Regionalism in Highland Guatemalan State Development*. Albuquerque: University of New Mexico Press.

Freire, Paulo

1987 *Literacy: Reading the Word and the World*. South Hadley, Mass.: Bergin and Garvey Publishers.

Friedlander, Judith

1975 *Being Indian in Hueyapan: A Study of Forced Identity in Contemporary Mexico*. New York: St. Martin's Press.

Gal, Susan

1979 *Language Shift: Social Determinants of Linguistic Change in Bilingual Austria*. New York: Academic Press.

1984 Peasant Men Can't Get Wives: Language Change and Sex Roles in a Bilingual Community. In *Language in Use: Readings in Sociolinguistics*, ed. by John Baugh and Joel Sherzer, pp. 292–304. Englewood Cliffs, N.J.: Prentice Hall.

Gall, Francis

1976 *Diccionario geográfico de Guatemala*. Vol. 1. Guatemala City: Instituto Geográfico Nacional.

Galloway, Patricia

1995   *Choctaw Genesis: 1500–1700.* Lincoln: University of Nebraska Press.

Garzon, Susan

1985   Language Death in a Mayan Community in Southern Chiapas. M.A. thesis. University of Iowa.

1994   Language and Gender in a Kaqchikel Maya Community. In *Proceedings of the 1993 Mid-America Linguistics Conference,* ed. by Jule Gomez de Garcia and David Rood, pp. 47–56. Boulder: University of Colorado.

1995   Language Shift and Conflict of Values among Kaqchikel Mayas. Paper presented at the Twenty-fourth Annual Meeting of the Linguistic Association of the Southwest. Las Cruces, New Mexico, October 1995.

Gonzales Orellana, Carlos

1960   *Historia de la educación en Guatemala.* Colección Científica Pedagógica. Mexico City: Editorial B. Costa Annie.

González, Gaspar Pedro

1995   *A Mayan Life.* Trans. by Elaine Elliot. Rancho Palos Verdes, Calif.: Yax Te' Press. Translation of *La otra cara.*

Goody, J., and I. P. Watt

1962   The Consequences of Literacy. In *Comparative Studies in Society and History,* vol. 5, pp. 304–345. The Hague: Mouton and Company.

Gossen, Gary

1974   To Speak with a Heated Heart: Chamula Canons of Style and Good Performance. In *Explorations in the Ethnography of Speaking,* ed. by Richard Bauman and Joel Sherzer, pp. 389–413. Cambridge: Cambridge University Press.

Grillo, R. D.

1989   *Dominant Languages: Language and Hierarchy in Britain and France.* Cambridge: Cambridge University Press.

Gumperz, John

1976   *Social Network and Language Shift.* Working Paper 46. Berkeley: Language Behavior Research Laboratory.

1982   *Discourse Strategies.* Cambridge: Cambridge University Press.

Haarmann, Harald

1986   *Language in Ethnicity: A View of Basic Ecological Relations.* Berlin: Mouton de Gruyter.

Hardman de Bautista, Martha

1985   The Imperial Languages of the Andes. In *Language of Inequality,* ed. by Nessa Wolfson and Joan Manes, pp. 182–194. Berlin: Mouton.

Hawkins, John

1984 *Inverse Images: The Meaning of Culture, Ethnicity, and Family in Post-colonial Guatemala.* Albuquerque: University of New Mexico Press.

Heath, J. G.

1984 Language Contact and Language Change. *Annual Review of Anthropology* 13: 367–384.

Heath, Shirley Brice

1972 *Telling Tongues: Language Policy in Mexico, Colony to Nation.* New York: Teachers College Press.

Heath, Shirley Brice, and Richard Laprade

1982 Castilian Colonization and Indigenous Languages: The Cases of Quechua and Aymara. In *Language Spread,* ed. by Robert L. Cooper, pp. 118–147. Bloomington: Indiana University Press.

Hechter, Michael

1975 *Internal Colonialism: The Celtic Fringe in British National Development, 1536–1966.* Berkeley: University of California Press.

Hendrickson, Carol

1996a *Weaving Identities: Constructions of Dress and Self in a Highland Guatemala Town.* Austin: University of Texas Press.
1996b Women, Weaving, and Education in Maya Revitalization. In *Maya Cultural Activism in Guatemala,* ed. by Edward Fischer and R. McKenna Brown, pp. 156–164. Austin: University of Texas Press.

Hill, Jane

1983 Language Death in Uto-Aztecan. *International Journal of the Sociology of Language* 49: 258–276.
1989 The Social Functions of Relativization in Obsolescent and Non-obsolescent Languages. In *Investigating Obsolescence: Studies in Language Contraction and Death,* ed. by Nancy Dorian, pp. 149–164. Cambridge: Cambridge University Press.

Hill, Jane, and Kenneth Hill

1980a Metaphorical Switching in Modern Nahuatl: Change and Contradiction. In *Papers from the Sixteenth Regional Meeting of the Chicago Linguistic Society, April, 1980,* pp. 121–133. Chicago: University of Chicago.
1980b Mixed Grammar, Purist Grammar, and Language Attitudes in Modern Nahuatl. *Language in Society* 9: 321–348.
1981 Regularities in Vocabulary Replacement in Modern Nahuatl. *International Journal of American Linguistics* 47: 215–226.
1986 *Speaking Mexicano: The Dynamics of Syncretic Language in Central Mexico.* Tucson: University of Arizona Press.

Hinton, Leanne

1994   *Flutes of Fire: Essays on California Indian Languages*. Berkeley: Heyday Books.

Hogben, Lancelot

1965   *The Mother Tongue*. New York: Norton Press.

Huffines, Marion Lois

1980   Pennsylvania German: Maintenance and Shift. *International Journal of the Sociology of Language* 25: 43–57.

Human Organization

1988   Vol. 47, no. 4. Issue on Indian language renewal.

Jackson, Jean

1989   Language Identity of the Colombian Vaupés Indians. In *Explorations in the Ethnography of Speaking*, ed. by Richard Bauman and Joel Sherzer, pp. 50–64. 2nd ed. Cambridge: Cambridge University Press.

Jacobson, R.

1982   The Social Implications of Inter-sentential Code-switching. In *Spanish in the United States: Sociolinguistic Aspects*, ed. by J. Amastae and L. Elías Olivares. Cambridge: Cambridge University Press.

Kagan, Jerome, Robert Klein, Gordon Findley, Barbara Rogoff, and Elizabeth Nolan

1979   *A Cross-Cultural Study of Cognitive Development*. Monographs of the Society for Research in Child Development 44 (5, Serial No. 180).

Kaqchikel Cholchi' (Comunidad Lingüística Kaqchikel)

1995   *Rukemik K'ak'a Taq Tzij: Criterios para la creación de neologismos en Kaqchikel*. Guatemala City: Academia de las Lenguas Mayas de Guatemala.

Kaufman, Terrence

1973   Areal Linguistics in Middle America. In *Current Trends in Linguistics*, vol. 11, ed. by Thomas Sebeok, pp. 459–484. The Hague: Mouton.

1976   Archaeological and Linguistic Correlations in Mayaland and Associated Areas of Mesoamerica. *World Archaeology* 8(1):101–118.

King, Linda

1994   *Roots of Identity: Language and Literacy in Mexico*. Stanford: Stanford University Press.

Kirchoff, Paul

1952   Mesoamerica: Its Geographic Limits, Ethnic Composition, and Cultural Characteristics. In *Heritage of Conquest*, ed. by Sol Tax, pp. 17–30. Glencoe: Free Press.

Kroeber, Alfred

1939   *Cultural and Native Areas of Native North America.* Berkeley: University of California Press.

Kroskrity, Paul V.

1982   Language Contact and Linguistic Diffusion: The Arizona Tewa Speech Community. In *Bilingualism and Language Contact: Spanish, English, and Native American Languages,* ed. by Florence Barkin, Elizabeth Brandt, and Jacob Ornstein-Galicia, pp. 51–72. New York: Teachers College Press.

1993   *Language, History, and Identity: Ethnolinguistic Studies of the Arizona Tewa.* Tucson: University of Arizona Press.

Kulick, Don

1992   *Language Shift and Cultural Reproduction: Socialization, Self, and Syncretism in a Papua New Guinean Village.* Cambridge: Cambridge University Press.

Language

1992   Vol. 68, no. 1. Issue on endangered languages.

Lankshear, Colin

1989   *Literacy, Schooling and Revolution.* London: Falmer Press.

Lathbury, Virginia

1974   Textiles as the Expression of an Expanding World View. M.A. thesis. University of Pennsylvania.

Leap, William

1993   *American Indian English.* Salt Lake City: University of Utah Press.

López Raquec, Margarita

1989   *Acerca de los idiomas mayas de Guatemala.* Guatemala City: Ministerio de Cultura y Deportes.

Lovell, George

1985   *Conquest and Survival in Colonial Guatemala.* Kingston: McGill–Queen's University Press.

Lutz, Christopher

1976   Santiago de Guatemala, 1554–1773: The Socio-demographic History. Ph.D. dissertation. University of Wisconsin.

1994   *Santiago de Guatemala, 1541–1773: City, Caste, and the Colonial Experience.* Norman: University of Oklahoma Press.

MacLeod, Murdo

1973   *Spanish Central America: A Socioeconomic History, 1520–1720.* Berkeley: University of California Press.

Malinowski, Bronislaw

1961   *Argonauts of the Western Pacific*. New York: E. P. Dutton and Co. (original 1922).

Mannheim, Bruce

1991   *The Language of the Inka since the European Invasion*. Austin: University of Texas Press.

Martin, Laura

1991   Las implicaciones lingüísticas en la muerte del idioma Mochó. Paper presented at the Taller de Lingüística Maya, Sololá, Guatemala.

Maxwell, Judith M.

1996   Prescriptive Grammar and Kaqchikel Revitalization. In *Maya Cultural Activism in Guatemala*, ed. by Edward Fischer and R. McKenna Brown, pp. 195–207. Austin: University of Texas Press.

McBryde, Felix

1945   *Cultural and Historical Geography of Southwest Guatemala*. Institute of Social Anthropology Publication No. 4. Washington, D.C.: Smithsonian Institution.

Medicine, Bea

1987   The Role of American Indian Women in Cultural Continuity and Transition. In *Women and Language in Transition*, ed. by Joyce Penfield, pp. 159–166. Albany: State University of New York Press.

Mejía de Rodas, Idalma

1985   Comalapa. In *Comalapa: Native Dress and Its Significance*, ed. by Linda Asturias de Barrios, pp. 10–23. Guatemala City: Ixchel Museum Publications.

Miles, S. W.

1965   Summary of Pre-Conquest Ethnology of the Guatemalan-Chiapas Highlands and Pacific Slopes. In *Handbook of Middle American Indians*, vol. 2, pp. 276–287. Austin: University of Texas Press.

Miller, Wick R.

1971   The Death of Language or Serendipity among the Shoshoni. *Anthropological Linguistics* 13: 114–120.

1978   *Multilingualism in Its Social Context in Aboriginal North America*. Proceedings of the Annual Meeting of the Berkeley Linguistics Society. Berkeley: Berkeley Linguistics Society.

Milroy, Lesley

1987   *Language and Social Networks*. 2nd ed. Oxford: Basil Blackwell.

Morales, Mario Roberto

1996   Se venden petates de muerto. *Crónica,* July 19: 50.

Navarro, José María

1874   *Memorias de San Miguel Dueñas.* Guatemala: Imprenta de Luna.

Nebrija, Antonio de

1992   *Gramática de la lengua castellana.* Madrid: Ediciones de Cultura His-
        pánica, Instituto de Cooperación Iberoamericana.

Nichols, Patricia

1983   Linguistic Options and Choices for Black Women in the Rural South.
        In *Language, Gender and Society,* ed. by B. Thorne, C. Kramarae, and
        N. Henley, pp. 54–68. Rowley, Mass.: Newbury House Publishers.

Orellana, Sandra

1975   La introducción del sistema de la cofradía en el Lago de Atitlán. *América
        Indígena* 35(4): 845–856.

1984   *The Tzutujil Mayas: Continuity and Change, 1250–1630.* Norman:
        University of Oklahoma Press.

Otzoy, Irma

1988   Identity and Higher Education among Mayan Women. M.A. thesis. Uni-
        versity of Iowa.

1996   Maya Clothing and Identity. In *Maya Cultural Activism in Guatemala,*
        ed. by Edward Fischer and R. McKenna Brown, pp. 141–155. Austin:
        University of Texas Press.

**Oxlajuuj Keej Maya' Ajtz'iib' (Ixkem, Ajpub', Lolmay, Nik'te', Pakal, Saqijix,
Waykan)**

1993   *Maya' Chii': Los idiomas mayas de Guatemala.* Guatemala City:
        Cholsamaj.

Paul, Benjamin

1968   San Pedro La Laguna. In *Los pueblos del Lago de Atitlán,* pp. 93–158.
        Seminario de Integración Social Guatemalteca, 23. Guatemala City: Ti-
        pografía Nacional.

Penfield-Jasper, Susan

1982   Mohave English and Tribal Identity. In *Essays in Native American En-
        glish,* ed. H. Guillermo Bartelt, Susan Penfield-Jasper, and Bates Hoffer,
        pp. 23–32. San Antonio: Trinity University Press.

Piaget, Jean

1995   *Sociological Studies.* Ed. by Leslie Smith. Trans. by Terrance Brown.
        New York: Routledge.

Poitevin, Rodolfo

n.d.   *República de Guatemala: Departamento de Sacatepéquez, Población calculada, año 1972–1980.* Guatemala: Ministerio de Salud Pública. Cited in Annis 1987.

Polo Sifontes, Francis

1977   *Los Cakchikeles en la conquista de Guatemala.* Guatemala City: Editorial José de Pineda Ibarra.

Raxche' Demetrio Rodríguez Guaján

1996   Maya Culture and the Politics of Development. In *Maya Cultural Activism in Guatemala,* ed. by Edward Fischer and R. McKenna Brown, pp. 74–88. Austin: University of Texas Press.

Reuse, Willem Joseph de

1994   *Siberian Yupik Eskimo: The Language and Its Contacts with Chukchi.* Salt Lake City: University of Utah Press.

Reyhner, Jon, and Edward Tennant

1995   Maintaining and Renewing Native Languages. *Bilingual Research Journal* 19(2):279–304.

Richards, Julia Becker

1983   Dialect Distance in the Lake Atitlán Basin of Guatemala. M.A. thesis. Department of Linguistics, University of Wisconsin, Madison.

1987a Language, Education, and Cultural Identity in a Maya Community of Guatemala. Ph.D. dissertation. Department of Educational Policy Studies, University of Wisconsin, Madison.

1987b Learning Spanish and Classroom Dynamics: School Failure in a Guatemalan Maya Community. In *Success or Failure? Learning and the Language Minority Student,* ed. by Henry Trueba, pp. 109–130. Cambridge, Mass.: Newbury House Publishers.

1989   Mayan Language Planning for Bilingual Education in Guatemala. *International Journal of the Sociology of Language* 77: 93–115.

Richards, Julia Becker, and Michael Richards

1975   *San Marcos La Laguna: An Ethnography.* Guatemala: Instituto de Centro América y Panamá.

1987   Factores de inteligibilidad mutua en la cuenca del Lago de Atitlán, Guatemala. *Winak: Boletín Intercultural* 2(4): 204–222.

1988   A Profile of the Languages and Communities of the National Bilingual Education Program of Guatemala. Guatemala City: Guatemalan Ministry of Education.

1993   Lenguas mayas y procesos lingüísticos en Guatemala, 1524–1700. In *Historia de Guatemala,* ed. by Jorge Luján, vol. 2, pp. 345–360. Guatemala City: Asociación de Amigos del País.

1996   Maya Education: A Historical and Contemporary Analysis of Mayan

Language Education Policy. In *Maya Cultural Activism in Guatemala*, ed. by Edward Fischer and R. McKenna Brown, pp. 208–222. Austin: University of Texas Press.

Richards, Michael

1985   Cosmopolitan World View and Counterinsurgency in Guatemala. *Anthropological Quarterly* 58: 90–106.

1987   Seasonal Migration and Physiological Risk in a Guatemalan Maya Community. Ph.D. dissertation. Department of Anthropology, University of Wisconsin–Madison.

Richards, Michael, and Narciso Cojtí

1992   Final Report of Mapeo Sociolingüístico, Unidad de Lingüística Aplicada, Programa Nacional de Educación Bilingüe. Report prepared for USAID/Guatemala/Basic Education Strengthening Project.

Rohter, Larry

1996   Maya Renaissance in Guatemala Turns Political. *New York Times*, August 12, 1996, international edition: A1+.

Rubin, Joan

1985   The Special Relation of Guaraní and Spanish in Paraguay. In *Language of Inequality*, ed. by Nessa Wolfson and Joan Manes, pp. 111–120. Berlin: Mouton Publishers.

Sam Colop, Enrique

1983   Hacia una propuesta de ley de educación. Thesis. Universidad Rafael Landívar de Guatemala.

1996   The Discourse of Concealment and 1992. In *Maya Cultural Activism in Guatemala*, ed. by Edward Fischer and R. McKenna Brown, pp. 107–113. Austin: University of Texas Press.

Schele, Linda, and Nikolai Grube

1996   The Workshop for Maya on Hieroglyphic Writing. In *Maya Cultural Activism in Guatemala*, ed. by Edward Fischer and R. McKenna Brown, pp. 131–140. Austin: University of Texas Press.

Schermerhorn, R. A.

1978   *Comparative Ethnic Relations*. New York: Random House.

Service, Elman

1971   *Spanish-Guaraní Relations in Early Colonial Peru*. Westport, Conn.: Greenwood Press.

Sherzer, Joel

1973   Areal Linguistics in North America. In *Current Trends in Linguistics*, vol. 10, pp. 749–795. The Hague: Mouton.

Simón, Arnulfo (Wuqu' Ajpub')

1994   Personal interviews. September 1–December 15. University of Wisconsin, Green Bay.

Sims, Christine

1996   *Native Language Communities: A Descriptive Study of Two Community Efforts to Preserve Their Native Languages.* Washington, D.C.: George Washington University.

Smith, A. L.

1955   *Archaeological Reconnaissance in Central Guatemala.* Carnegie Institute Pub. 608. Washington, D.C.: Carnegie Institute.

Smith, Carol, and Jeff Boyer

1987   Central America since 1979: Part 1. *Annual Review of Anthropology,* vol. 16, ed. by B. Siegel, A. Beals, and S. Tyler, pp. 197–221. Palo Alto, Calif.: Annual Reviews, Inc.

Sorensen, Arthur

1967   Multilingualism in the Northwest Amazon. *American Anthropologist* 69: 670–684.

Spicer, Edward

1971   Persistent Cultural Systems. *Science* 174: 795–800.

Srivastava, R. N.

1989   Perspectives on Language Shift in Multilingual Settings. *International Journal of the Sociology of Language* 75: 9–26.

Stoll, David

1990   *Is Latin America Turning Protestant? The Politics of Evangelical Growth.* Berkeley: University of California Press.

Street, Brian

1987   Literacy and Social Change: The Significance of Social Context in the Development of Literacy Programs. In *The Future of Literacy in a Changing World,* ed. by David Wagner, pp. 48–64. Oxford: Pergamon Press.

Sturm, Circe

1996   Old Writing and New Messages: The Role of Hieroglyphic Literacy in Maya Cultural Activism. In *Maya Cultural Activism in Guatemala,* ed. by Edward Fischer and R. McKenna Brown, pp. 114–130. Austin: University of Texas Press.

Suárez, Jorge

1982 *Mesoamerican Indian Languages.* Cambridge: Cambridge University Press.

Tawney, R. H.

1966 *Land and Labor in China.* Boston: Houghton Mifflin (original 1933).

Tax, Sol

1937 The Municipios of the Midwestern Highlands of Guatemala. *American Anthropologist* 39: 423–444.

1953 *Penny Capitalism: A Guatemalan Indian Economy.* Smithsonian Institute of Social Anthropology Publication No. 16. Washington, D.C.: U.S. Government Printing Office.

Taylor, Allan R.

1981 Indian Lingua Francas. In *Language in the USA,* ed. by Charles Ferguson and Shirley Brice Heath, pp. 175–195. Cambridge: Cambridge University Press.

1989 Problems in Obsolescence Research: The Gros Ventres of Montana. In *Investigating Obsolescence: Studies in Language Contraction and Death,* ed. by Nancy Dorian, pp. 167–180. Cambridge: Cambridge University Press.

Tedlock, Barbara

1992 *Time and the Highland Maya.* Rev. ed. (orig. 1982). Albuquerque: University of New Mexico Press.

Tedlock, Dennis

1985 *Popol Vuh: The Definitive Edition of the Mayan Book of the Dawn of Life and the Glories of Gods and Kings.* New York: Simon and Schuster.

Thomason, Sarah Grey, and Terrence Kaufman

1988 *Language Contact, Creolization, and Genetic Linguistics.* Berkeley: University of California Press.

Timm, Lenora A.

1980 Bilingualism, Diglossia and Language Shift in Brittany. *International Journal of the Sociology of Language* 25: 29–41.

Trudgill, P., and G. A. Tzavaras

1977 Why Albanian-Greeks Are Not Albanians: Language Shift in Attica and Biotia. In *Language, Ethnicity and Intergroup Relations,* ed. by Howard Giles, pp. 171–184. London: Academic Press.

UNESCO

1953   *Uses of Vernacular Languages in Education.* Monographs on Fundamental Education 8. Paris: UNESCO.

Wagley, Charles

1949   *The Social and Religious Life of a Guatemalan Village.* Memoir Series No. 71. Menasha, Wis.: American Anthropological Association.

Wagner, Daniel, ed.

1987   *The Future of Literacy in a Changing World.* New York: Pergamon Press.

Warren, Kay

1978   *The Symbolism of Subordination: Indian Identity in a Guatemalan Town.* Austin: University of Texas Press.

1996   Reading History as Resistance: Maya Public Intellectuals in Guatemala. In *Maya Cultural Activism in Guatemala,* ed. by Edward Fischer and R. McKenna Brown, pp. 89–106. Austin: University of Texas Press.

Watanabe, John

1992   *Maya Saints and Souls in a Changing World.* Austin: University of Texas Press.

Waterhouse, Viola

1949   Learning a Second Language First. *International Journal of American Linguistics* 15: 106–109.

Weinreich, Uriel

1968   *Languages in Contact: Findings and Problems.* The Hague: Mouton.

Williamson, Robert, and John Van Eerde

1980   "Subcultural" Factors in the Survival of Secondary Languages: A Cross-National Sample. *International Journal of the Sociology of Language* 25: 59–83.

Wilson, Richard

1995   *Maya Resurgence in Guatemala: Q'eqchi' Experiences.* Norman: University of Oklahoma Press.

Wolf, Eric

1957   Closed Corporate Peasant Communities in Mesoamerica and Central Java. *Southwestern Journal of Anthropology* 13(1): 1–18.

Woodward, Ralph

1985   *Central America: A Nation Divided.* New York and Oxford: Oxford University Press.

Woolard, Kathryn A.

1985   Catalonia: The Dilemma of Language Rights. In *Language of Inequality*, ed. by Nessa Wolfson and Joan Manes, pp. 91–110. Berlin: Mouton Publishers.

1989   *Double Talk: Bilingualism and the Politics of Ethnicity in Catalonia.* Stanford: Stanford University Press.

Wurtzburg, Susan, and Lyle Campbell

1995   North American Indian Sign Language: Evidence of Its Existence before European Contact. *International Journal of American Linguistics* 61(2): 153–167.

Zapeta, Estuardo

1996   Waqxaqi' B'atz'. *Crónica*, July 26: 16.

INDEX

production of Protestants and
Catholics compared, 123; in Qui-
nizilapa Valley, 107, 111; in San
Andrés Cevallos, 113, 115; in San
Antonio Aguas Calientes, 113; in
San Juan Comalapa, 132, 135; in
Santiago Zamora, 116; and school
punishment, 175; and subsistence
agriculture, 28
Cortés y Larraz, Pedro, 117; 131
Cortes, 110, 111, 129, 195
Cortés, Hernán, 49
Costa Rica, 58, 168
Cotton plantations, 70, 71, 107
Coyoy, Alfredo Tay, 167
Co-educational Normal School,
Rafael Aqueche, 179
Creek Confederacy, 23
Cree language, 23, 24
Creole languages, 24
Creoles, 52, 55, 59, 60n.1
Cuchumatán Mountains, 9, 47
Cuchumatán region, 54
Cultural borrowing, 10
Cultural diversity, 2, 18, 172, 174,
175–178
Cultural identity, 80–81, 90. *See also*
Ethnic identity
Curruchich, Germán, 167
Cuzco, Peru, 16, 25

Dardón, Juan Pérez, 131
Debt labor, 71
Debt peonage, 60, 81
Delaware, 23
Delaware language, 23, 24
Delhil, 18
Demographics, 29
Denison, Norman, 40
Departments, map of, xv
Descultruados, 44
Deutsch, Karl Wolfgang, 124
Dialect shifts, 41
DIGEBI (General Office of Bilingual/
Bicultural Education), 166, 167
Diversificado, 179
Domains of use, 35, 36, 148–149

Dominant groups: and bilingualism,
15–17, 42; and cultural diversity,
18; and cultural intrusions, 47;
full participation in, 19; and
indigenous languages, 16; integration into, 2; language policies of,
6; and language shift, 25, 26, 29–
30; and mass media, 6; monolingualism of, 17; and multilingualism, 11, 15; sociocultural patterns
of, 27; value systems of, 195
Dominant languages: and children,
39, 40, 191; and domains of use,
35; and economics, 26, 27; and
education, 30, 32; and intergenerational break, 37; and language
shift, 15, 33; and marriage, 29;
men's use of, 41; and nationalism,
17; prestige of, 33–34; and social
networks, 35; as subordinate
language in other area, 18
Dominican order, 56, 103
Dorian, Nancy, 20, 31, 39–40
Dressler, Wolfgang, 21

Early childhood intervention programs, 69, 96
Early Classic Period, 47
Earthquakes, 5, 106, 130, 134, 157
Eastern Pueblo groups, 22
East Sutherland, 31, 39
Economics: and bilingualism, 96;
cash economy, 5, 29, 106–107,
123; of Colonial Period, 52–53;
and education, 178; and indigenous communities, 42–43; and
integration, 5; and language shift,
7, 26–29; and Mayan movement,
157; in modern period, 59; and
multilingualism, 11; of Quinizilapa Valley, 103, 104, 106–108,
122–123; of San Antonio Aguas
Calientes, 114, 190, 198; of San
Juan Comalapa, 132–133, 134,
135, 140, 198; of San Marcos La
Laguna, 69–70, 73, 98; and social
network changes, 34; and Spanish

Sololá Department, 62, 73
Sorenson, Arthur, 14, 15
South Carolina, 41
Southeastern Tzeltal language, 35
Spain and Spaniards: Alvarado's campaigns in, 52; and bilingualism, 12, 15; and Bourbon reforms, 58–59; colonial language policies of, 55–57; and language shift, 30; in modern period, 58; and Quechua, 25; and Quinizilapa Valley, 103; and racial mixing, 57. *See also* Colonial Period
Spanish Conquest: and bilingualism, 11–12; and education, 177; and ethnic identity, 188; of Guatemala, 4, 48–52; and Inkas, 25; and Kaqchikels, 49; and language death, 25; and Moctezuma, 49; and San Andrés Cevallos, 114–115; and San Juan Comalapa, 131; and Spanish language, 9; and Spanish loanwords, 84
Spanish Creoles, 15, 16
Spanish language: balance in use of, 1, 6; and bilingual education, 75, 76; and cash economy, 123; Castilian Spanish, 36, 55, 57; and Castilianization, 74; in Chiapas, 30; and children, 94, 96, 121, 127, 142–143, 148–149, 152, 191, 193, 197; and code-switching, 86–87, 99–100; and education, 7, 32, 100, 138, 148–149, 162, 173–178, 186, 191; and ethnic identity, 3, 151, 192; as first language, 38; and government officials, 91–92; and Jesuits, 12; and language contact relations, 8; and language shift, 29; literacy in, 160, 161, 164; loanwords from, 9, 84–86, 99, 156, 158, 188; and mass media, 6; and Mayan language survival, 2; need for, 60; and occupations, 149; in Paraguay, 16; and parents, 39, 118, 143–145, 152, 159, 173–174, 191–192, 195; in Quinizilapa

Valley, 124, 127; and *reducciones*, 54; and religious education, 56; in San Antonio Aguas Calientes, 113, 117, 190–191; in San Juan Comalapa, 131–132, 134, 135, 140, 141; in San Marcos La Laguna, 7, 84–86, 90–98, 99, 189; in Santiago Zamora, 126; and shift generation, 7; and teachers, 92; and Teko language, 13; in United States, 186; and urbanization, 28; in Vaupés region, 15; and women, 93–94, 97, 100, 141, 150, 192
Spice Islands, 52
St. Lawrence Island, Alaska, 25
Status: and bilingualism, 12, 42; and code switching, 89; and Kaqchikel language, 197, 198; and language's purpose, 83; of Mayan languages, 176; and race, 57; and Spanish language use, 87, 189
Street, Brian, 163
Suárez, Jorge, 46
Subordinate groups, 17–19, 25–34, 42
Subordinate languages: and community interaction, 20; and domains of use, 35; and education, 30–31; and intergenerational break, 37; and language shift, 26, 30; literary tradition of, 18; and multilingualism, 11; position of, 17–19; and prestige of dominant language, 33–34; as second language, 38–40; and social networks, 35; and unaccented speech, 37; and urbanization, 28
Subsistence, 28–29, 72, 132
Sustainable development, 184–185
Swedish explorers, 23–24
Switzerland, 18

Tabasco-Veracruz region, 47
Taiap language, 33
Taos, 22
Tawney, R. H., 98
Taylor, Allan, 22–23